PURS UNEXPLAINED

PURSUING THE UNEXPLAINED

PUZZLING MYSTERIES OF THE NATURAL WORLD

IVAN T. SANDERSON

ISBN-13: 978-1542508834
ISBN-10: 1542508835

PRINTING HISTORY
Prentice edition published 1972
Saucerian Press edition published 1982
New Saucerian Press edition published 2017

*I take the greatest
pleasure in dedicating this book,
and with considerable
ebullience,
to
Thelma Yohe
for
having done so much
for our Society: known as
SITU, or "The
Society for the Investigation
of the Unexplained."*

ACKNOWLEDGMENTS

MATERIAL REPRINTED OR reproduced from other sources includes the following:

The article on Charles Hatfield, reprinted by arrangement with Lyle Stuart, Inc.

"Ancient Electric Battery" by H. C. Goble, reprinted by special permission from *Fate* magazine, © Clark Publishing Company, 1958.

"The Baffling Burning Death" by Allan W. Eckert, reprinted from *True* magazine, copyright 1946, Fawcett Publications, Inc., and with Mr. Eckert's kind permission.

The World of the Paranormal by Walter J. McGraw, © 1969, for material on Rolf Alexander.

"The One True Batman" by Ivan T. Sanderson and Ernest Bartels, reprinted by special permission from *Fate* magazine, © Clark Publishing Company, 1966.

"Three Dimensions of Space Are Confirmed," with permission of *New Scientist,* London.

Figure 35, from *Kulturer fore Istiden,* by Ivan Troëng, Uppsala: Nybloms, 1964.

Figure 36, reproduced from *The Book of the Dead,* by E. A. Wallis Budge, London: Routledge & Kegan Paul Ltd.; New York: Barnes & Noble, Inc.

Plate I, from Chet Peterson, through the kindness of Captain Stanley Lee.

Plate III, reproduced from "A Gliding Reptile from the Triassic of New Jersey," by Edwin H. Colbert, *Novitates* (No. 2246, 19 May 1966), courtesy of the American Museum of Natural History, New York.

Plate IV, from Wide World Photos, Inc.; V from the Keystone Press Agency.

Plate VIII, from Gerard and Joan Bentryn.

Plate X, from the British Museum (Natural History).

Plate XII, from Roy Pinney.

Plates XIII and XIV, from Barney Nashold.

Plate XIV(b), from Manny Staub.

Plates XVI and XVII, from the University Museum of the University of Pennsylvania.

Plate XVIII, from the Edmund Scientific Company, 555 Edscorp Building, Barrington, N.J. 08007.

Plate XX, from the *St. Petersburg Times & Evening Independent,* St. Petersburg, Florida.

I also wish to acknowledge the help and assistance that I have received from:

Many members of the Society for the Investigation of the Unexplained, of which I am administrative director.

My personal associates: Miss Marion L. Fawcett, Michael R. Freedman, and my wife.

Certain individuals, in particular, Edwin H. Colbert, Charles H. Hapgood, Adolph L. Heuer, Jr., Emanuel M. Staub, Jack A. Ullrich, and Arthur M. Young.

CONTENTS

PROLOGUE

THE WORLD WE live on and the cosmos we live in constitute a much more interesting place than most of us appreciate. Of cabbages and, at least until recently, kings, we have had quite enough, so we often tend to overlook a number of things. City folk don't have much opportunity for the contemplation of anything worthwhile anymore, and the vast majority of country folk are still too busy working to indulge in anything but the lightest entertainment available and then flop into bed. We don't have wandering minstrels or monied intellectuals anymore; they're either standardized rock groups or over-capitalized patrons of the arts. Yet, despite worldwide physical and mental pollution, existence, and so far, life, go on, though all of us except a few Pygmy tribesmen seem to be becoming ever less aware of its reality.

People today may be, like Caesar's Gaul—apart, that is, from *Gallia Narbonnensis,* which is invariably forgotten—divided into three parts. The boundaries between these are, moreover, somewhat better defined than were those of Gaul, and we still are left with a sort of ancient "narbonnensis." They are simply: Mystics, Scientists, and Us, while the left-over from earlier days are the philosophers; and even they have become fossilized in our universities and have lost all touch with reality. The mystics, whose

1

job it is to concern themselves with the spiritual world, appear today to range from religionists who have forgotten what religion means, to crackpots who can't read the stars or even their own palms; while the scientists are almost all either technologists or technicians, and also just as confined in their enterprise and likewise in imminent danger of becoming fossilized. You can break the rest of us up into as many million parts as you wish, for despite the efforts of such as Lenin, Stalin, Mao, *et alii,* we persist in being individuals. At the same time, we are all basically and astonishingly alike in that we have one thing in common. This is simply that we are the ones who are *told* what to do.

I have always resented this and, in fact, refused flatly to be told anything from the earliest age, unless it made sense or I was given sensible reasons for it. Looking back, I perceive that I was graced with very intelligent parents, both of them incipient natural scientists in that they were greatly interested in natural history. I was also extremely lucky in many of those who "told me" professionally—i.e., taught me at school—but I early spotted that the *good* teachers could all be classed loosely as philosophical scientists. Becoming considerably encouraged, I therefore decided to study the natural sciences myself, but having done so, I even went so far as to take up teaching at the university where I received my degrees. However, two terms were enough for me. You see, I had travelled all my life, at first with my parents—apart from a season on a Norwegian whale-chaser at the age of ten—and on reaching the legal age for signing things, which is fourteen for a male in Scotland, on my own.

Now, a teenager who spends his seventeenth birthday stuck on the top of the Great Pyramid of Cheops (because his guide got drunk during Ramadan), and is then permitted to wander around the world for eighteen months, collecting rats and working in oil fields, cannot fail to run into a lot of things—and also "things." Further, as I say, I happen to have been born a sort of Missourian, so that when I found myself in the so-called intellectual milieu of a seat of higher learning and amongst professional teachers,

2

and teachers of the natural sciences at that, I became most depressed, though not for the reasons you might expect. Faculty teas could be avoided, and my students were grand—I was what is called on the other side, a Demonstrator, i.e., the low man on the totem pole—but what irked me was my discovery that nothing which was *not* in the text-books that we had to use was either permitted or even believed. What is more, this was carried to what was to me extreme limits of preposterousness. What finally "did it" was when a junior professor implied in committee that I should be sort of eliminated because I had mentioned flying snakes. But then, he was not a zoologist!

In this case it was not so much his sad lack of knowledge that startled me, but the realization that all knowledge is grossly compartmentalized, quite apart from being departmentalized in educational establishments. I have to admit that knowing there are flying snakes in Indonesia need not be of any specific worth to a geologist—though they are supposed to take a course in palaeontology—but to censure a trained zoologist *with* field experience for saying that there are, put that kind of scientist on a par with religionists, in my eyes. And once having had my eyes thus opened, I started sort of talking around discreetly, starting in my own fields of zoology, physical anthropology, botany, and geology. I became increasingly horrified. It was not that I had thought, or had for that matter been taught, that we knew everything. To the contrary, it had constantly been drummed into me that we know practically nothing about anything. Rather, it was the discovery that, in addition to anything new being suspect (a sound scientific approach), everybody was indulging in *research* to the total exclusion of making any *search*. I went to the head of my department.

His name was and still is well known in scientific circles. Professor Foster-Cooper was later Director of the British Museum (Natural History) in South Kensington. He was a very wise man. He granted me an interview. When I walked in, he just nodded at a chair and then sat and stared at me. The situation was not tense, however, since he maintained a wry smile. His opening gambit was simply: "I wonder why it's taken you so long." A bit startling, but worse was to follow. He even had a plan ready for me, and it was damned near the one I had prepared for him. The only difference was that I had expected to lose my job, whereas he wanted to rehire me. So we saved a lot of time by my quitting and his having me sign an application for a grant to help finance my second full-fledged field expedition.

Since then—and that was thirty-six years ago—I have been diligently prosecuting *search* in pursuit of the unknown, which dictionaries give as the first meaning of the word *science,* as opposed to either rehashing what others have already done, or bottle-washing and button-pushing, as the poor technologists spend their lives doing. And you'd be surprised what I've turned up. This book is a modest example of some of my latterday discoveries.

But just one more thing. This is very curious. On the one hand, I found that I greatly annoyed most of the specialists by collecting so many new things, and more so by stating some new ideas on matters that I knew about from actual experience. (They haven't yet got over the first luminous reptile that I found in a cave in Trinidad!) On the other hand, and to my much greater amazement, I found out that their own writings were stuffed full of oddities and enigmas and paradoxes that they had solemnly put on record but had either failed to explain or even tried to explain. When confronted with conflicting evidence of such, moreover, these intellectual gentry showed a distinct tendency to histrionics if not hysteria, often behaving like depraved members of the lower classes—that's Us, you know. This is a pity: all those fine brains going to waste.

So come with me out of the classroom into the harsh world of reality. Try to remember all you have been told, but don't believe a word of it until you see for yourself. Life should be fun, even if you do live in a city or get up before dawn to milk a cow or start planting rice. Anyhow, you'll find it's awfully funny, and in both senses of that word—"funny-ha-ha" and "funny-peculiar."

CHAPTER ONE

AN ALASKAN
LONGNECK

O N THE 15th of April, 1969,
the M.V. *Mylark,* a 65-foot, twin-engined shrimper owned by one
Chet Peterson and skippered by Bill Russell, out of Kodiak,
Alaska, was dragging for shrimp off Raspberry Peninsula in the
Shelikof Strait. The *Mylark* was equipped with the finest sonar
detection device, a Norwegian invention by the trade name of
Simrad that is used throughout the world by commercial fishing
fleets to detect either schools of marine life or large individual
items below the vessels so equipped. This device emits sonic
bursts at high frequency directed downwards and builds up, at
almost instantaneous speed, a profile of whatever the ship passes
over.

The Simrad was left running as a standard procedure, and nothing much worth a call-out was expected in this area. Suddenly,
however, the machine started to register something other than
the dull, low, undulating surface of the sea bottom. The machine
works fast even when the vessel it is on is only drifting, so that
in a very short time a clear picture (see Plate I) emerged on
the five-inch paper strip that rolls continuously out of it. The
operator appears to have boggled and then taken a few minutes
to absorb what he had in his hand before informing the wheel-
house who relayed his astonishing report to the skipper. Then the
"fun" began.

Sea Monsters, once at least in part commonly called Great Sea Serpents, have been with us throughout history. From time to time throughout historical times, moreover, they have been taken rather seriously; notably during the Viking expansion of the Norse at the end of the first millennium A.D. However, the reports of them got so garbled and contradictory that the whole thing became a major joke; and when the principles of modern scientific enquiry were laid down in the 18th century, the matter was dismissed as nothing more than the maunderings of mystics or tall tales by mariners. But the reports persisted, while the standing of those reporting having seen such things became ever more impressive, even unto one Sir Arthur Rostron, Commodore of the Cunard Line. Nonetheless, zoologists brushed the matter aside, and the popular press diverted it to the so-called "silly season" when other news is alleged to be light. Then something happened.

Similar, huge, as yet unidentified animals had been reported also from a considerable number of large, cold-water, northern, freshwater lakes spread all across Canada, Scotland and Ireland, Scandinavia, Russia and Siberia for centuries. The most famous was, of course, the so-called "Loch Ness Monster," and this got just about the biggest horse-laugh of all until an aeronautical engineer named Tim Dinsdale obtained a film of one in that loch, trekking along at some ten knots and leaving a bow-wave but no prop-wash. This film was analyzed by the Joint Air Reconnaissance Intelligence Centre of the British Royal Airforce, and was pronounced by them to be—and categorically—an animal. They said twelve to sixteen feet of its middle back was sticking out of the water to a height of three feet and that, in cross section, it "would be NOT LESS than 6 feet wide and 5 feet high." It could not have been a boat as it had no sail and it left no prop-wash.[1] (For more details, see next chapter.)

Once this report had been issued, all speculation and argument as to both the possibility and the probability of large, as yet uncaught and unidentified animals existing in certain northern lakes naturally came to an end. Further, any arguments put forward purporting to disprove the existence of similar creatures

6

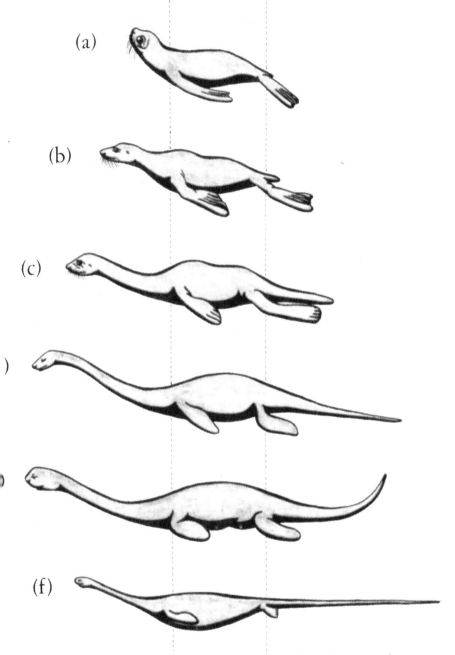

Fig. 1. Otariid Pinnepeds and descriptions of marine longnecks compared: (a) *young Northern Fur Seal or Sea Bear* (Otaria ursina); (b) *California Sea Lion* (Otaria gilles-piei); (c) *the Hoy Island, Orkneys, animal as seen in shallow water by Mr. J. Mackintosh Bell in 1919;* (d) *composite of all reports of longnecks;* (e) *the Raspberry Strait, Kodiak Island, echo-sounding profile;* (f) *composite of longnecks to 1890, according to Prof. Oudemans*

in the seas and oceans likewise collapsed finally and completely. As a result, the "great debate" between believers and non-believers ended; but in its stead, there started up an almost equally acrimonious one between various groups of believers. This rather naturally, and quite correctly, centered around the question, "What kind of animals are they?"

A really extraordinary number of most widely divergent suggestions were put forward. Many of these at first sounded quite mad, such as giant birds, salamanders, snails, worms, and so forth. However, on proper analysis, and provided one followed both common sense and plain logic on the one hand and sound zoological principles on the other, it had to be admitted that *none* of these was altogether balmy. In fact, almost anything can be in the world of nature, and it is in some ways fruitless to speculate until something concrete comes to hand. Nevertheless, as has been so rightly said, it is almost worthless to go look for anything unless you have at least some idea what you are looking for. So, the speculators should be at least respected.

Among these, half a dozen people stand out. The first was a wonderful old Hollander, director of the Royal Zoological and Botanical Society at the Hague, by the name of Professor A. C. Oudemans, who in 1892 published a 592-page book entitled *The Great Sea Serpent*.[2] In this he dealt with no fewer than 187 cases of reported Sea Monsters, and he came to the conclusion that such things existed, and that they were most probably very large seals (more of the sea-lion type), with long necks, small heads, and long tails. He even "constructed" a composite outline of such an animal, compounded from all the reports he had examined over the years; and here it is—see Fig. 1 (f). The second name that should take its place in this field is that of the late German palaeontologist (and rocket expert, one must add!) Willy Ley,[3] who was really the first to come right out and agree with not only Oudemans but that extraordinary Britisher, Commander Rupert T. Gould,[4] that such things *do* exist.

I now have to leave Loch Ness and the freshwater monsters aside for a moment and come to grips with the marine creatures;

and here, the most important name is that of Dr. Bernard Heuvelmans of Belgium, who spent ten years studying hundreds of reports of such animals, and from all countries and seas, and from all ages, which he finally published in 1968 in a monumental popular book entitled *In the Wake of the Sea Serpent.*[5] After Oudemans, those enthusiasts who devoted their research primarily to the marine monsters became increasingly convinced that they were not dealing with only one type of huge, as yet unidentified, animal species. Finally Heuvelmans decided to split up the reports into seven distinct categories, and he gave the animals to which each of these reports appeared to him to refer, very distinctive names. Throughout all this, one type—the Draki of the Norse —has most outstandingly persisted. As seen on the prows of some of their large longships (which, incidentally, they even called Draki) this creature is, for all the world, old Professor Oudeman's giant seal; albeit with prominent eye-lashes and other hairy excrescences somewhat exaggerated (note: only mammals have eyelashes). And this, so help us, is almost exactly what the Simrad on the M.V. *Mylark* came up with—see Fig. 1(e).

I said above that some fun began when this paper strip was shown to the press, but I am afraid that it soon ceased to be "fun." It became rather distressing. Matters like this seldom if ever have clear sailing and simply because people don't really want to be forced to accept anything new or outside established belief, and more especially when it has been the concensus of all so-called "expert" opinion for so long that such an item can *not* exist. You can't go around withdrawing all textbooks just because some idiot turns up with a genuine sea-monster corpse, and tens of thousands of $25,000-a-year PhDs can't suddenly announce to their classes that they were all wrong about something—or anything. The whole damned system would collapse. And perhaps because of such considerations, this priceless item ran into some heavy weather. This is a rather subtle but nonetheless somewhat gruesome story. I will tell it as a reporter.

The first intimation I had of this incident came to me in a letter [6] from an old friend of mine in Alaska, a retired officer of the U.S. Coast Guard, a pilot and shipowner, and a born Alaskan with considerable holdings on the south coast of that state and on certain offshore islands. Captain Stanley Lee is a much respected man in Kodiak. With his letter came some preliminary press clippings from the *Kodiak Mirror,* dated the 30th of April, 1969.[7] This was a fairly straightforward news story, but glutted with the usual facetious nonsense that editors insist that their reporters smear over any story they might turn in, which could be construed as having anything to do with anything like a "Sea Monster." Knowing Captain Stan, I asked for further and proper details; and in rather short order I received not only all that I could wish in this respect but also the original Simrad strip! (See Plate I.)

Now, I had in the meantime got to work investigating this device and had landed up with its manufacturer's American subsidiary, which is registered as Supervisors, Inc., of Kew Gardens, New York. Simrad is a Norwegian invention and one of, if not *the* most successful and widely used of all echo-sounders, throughout the world and especially by commercial fishing fleets. The model installed on the M.V. *Mylark* was what the company designates an EH2A. We initiated communication with this company both by phone and letter, and when we received the original "strip" we forwarded it to them for analysis. In turn, they kindly supplied us with massive printed material, both technical and popular, that described the working of their machines.[8] Up till this point, we had no cause to suppose that this would differ in any way from literally hundreds of other straightforward enquiries that we have made of a similar nature when trying to get at the facts of a case in which advanced techniques are involved. But something very strange went wrong this time.

Frankly, I don't know just what did go wrong, though I have a shrewd suspicion, and I have been unable to find out or even obtain any answer to my repeated enquiries on this score. So all I can do is simply report what happened. This is all a great pity as this case might constitute a very important contribution to knowledge, and if only it could have been handled sympathetically, might have gone far towards terminating one of the great debates of all time and saved innumerable headaches, heartaches, and useless recriminations. Doubtless there was a misunderstanding somewhere: at least this was my personal opinion, but I am afraid that I have to put it on record that this was not that of others. I will try to explain the significance of this remark after I have given you the facts.

After ascertaining who would be willing to receive the original of the "strip" for analysis in the appropriate technical department of the manufacturer's regional outfit, we forwarded the item to that department. In due course, they very kindly sent us such an analysis. This read in part as follows:

You certainly got hold of a very exciting echogram there, but I am afraid that I will have to disappoint you as to the credibility of what you see on it. It has a couple of "defects" which make its genuineness questionable.

Judging from the type of recording paper used and the overall quality of the recording, I would think that the "Mylark" has a SIMRAD EH2A Echo Sounder on board. This recorder has paper speeds of 10, 5, and 2.5 mm per minute. Using the most optimistic of these figures, 10mm/min., the "Mylark" would have used five (5) minutes to pass over the object. If the object is 200 feet long, as claimed, this means that the vessel drifted over it at a speed of approximately 0.5 miles per hour. Not at all impossible, but unlikely. If the vessel's speed was one (1) mile per hour, the object is more than 400 feet long, and if it ran at normal cruising speed for a fishing vessel, (10 mph), the object represents a distance of more than 4,000 feet. The vertical scale is 65 fathoms (390 feet) across the full width of the paper. Therefore, the vertical dimensions of the body could make sense: approximately 15 feet across the widest part and 3 to 4 feet across the neck.

To be able to give an exact statement on the length of the object, I would have to know: 1. The speed of the vessel, and 2. the paper speed used when the vessel passed over it, but it is hardly worth going after it *because I am pretty*

11

sure that the recorder had some help from a member of the
crew with some artistic abilities [*italics mine*].

If you study the bottom profile and the noise pattern
under the bottom line, you will see that the recording is
made up from vertical lines; this is because the recording pen
travels in straight lines across the paper. Then study the
marks that form the object and you will see that hardly any
of them are vertical.

I have drawn lines through them on a copy of the echogram
to illustrate what I mean. This particular SIMRAD model
has two pens, one that "prints" the information gathered by
the machine, and another one for the operator to use when he
wants to make notes on the recording paper. This second one
leaves a fairly characteristic imprint on the paper and I have
enclosed a sample where this pen was used as originally
intended. Compare the lines of the notes on the sample with
the lines in our object and I think you will see some similarities,
the little notch at the start of the line and the light shadow
in the middle of each line. So as I said before, I believe
the echo sounder has had some help in this case.[9]

The statement that the echogram must have been tampered
with because some of the lines therein do not appear to be vertical, or are *not* vertical, is not convincing; in fact, a study of other
echograms sent us by Supervisors, Inc., under a strong magnifying
glass reveals any number of non-vertical lines and a number of
tracings made up almost exclusively of "tents"! [10] Also, examination of the Alaskan echogram under a magnifying lens indicates that not only are most of the lines vertical, but that they
appear to be continuations of the vertical lines of the noise pattern. Many lines in the main body of the echogram are *not* vertical.
And the lines, particularly in the neck and tail, are minute and
could not have been made with the second needle which leaves a
very crude and recognizable mark. In their own literature, Simrad states that "At slow speed [of the vessel] the lines shorten
and curve. . . . The reason is that the number of echoes from a
single fish varies at different speeds."

Using the marked navigation chart supplied by Captain Lee,

(see Fig. 2) the original tracing, Simrad's analysis of the tracing, and the information on echo sounders sent by the Simrad people, the following picture emerges:

The maximum depth of water in the Raspberry Strait is 69 fathoms (414 feet), but this decreases rather abruptly to 30–40 fathoms and then to virtual shoal water with only 4.25 fathoms *at the point where the* Mylark *turned.* In these circumstances,

Fig. 2. Maps of Raspberry Strait and Kodiak Island

     – – →   = *Passage and course of the M.V.* Mylark
     ×   = *Point at which Simrad profile was obtained*

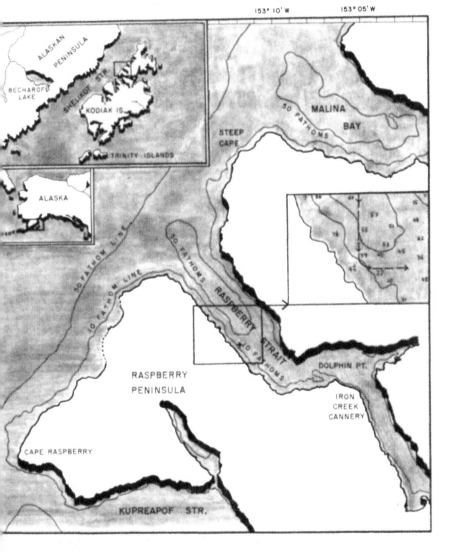

chaps dragging for shrimp on the bottom would have been using the following settings for their echo sounder: Depth selector set at A_1 for a range of 0–65 fathoms; a short pulse (96 "pings" per minute rather than 48 or 24) to show maximum detail; fast pen speed (this simply produces a larger mark); and the "white line" on. This last is a special feature of modern echo sounders, producing a white line just above the sea bottom and thus permitting the operator to distinguish between rocks on the bottom and schools of fish or what-have-you so close to the bottom that their echoes would otherwise blend with the bottom echoes.

If the white line at the top of the tracing is in fact a "white line," the boat at that point was in very shallow water and the beast was damned close to the bottom of the boat, the maximum depth of the white line being about 12 fathoms. These measurements are based on Simrad's estimate of the vertical width of the beast (5 mm equals 15 feet; ergo 10 mm equals 30 feet or 5 fathoms, hence our scale down the left). The dark line at the bottom of the tracing is probably a subsidiary echo from the bottom which is volcanic ash, mud, and hard-packed sand, underlain by volcanic shale.[11]

Unfortunately, one cannot use these figures to determine the creature's length—and apparently its length is the only thing really in dispute. To determine this, one needs to know the speed of the vessel and the paper speed—which latter can be 2.5, 5, or 10 mm per minute. The skipper of the *Mylark* reports that *generally* they were making 2 to 3 knots (2.30 to 3.45 mph) pulling a shrimp trawl behind but that *they were swinging at the time to avoid shallow water ahead.* In these circumstances the boat may have been virtually at a standstill when this echogram was made. They do not know at what rate the paper was moving. This is not as "suspicious" as it sounds, for the simple reason that the dials on these echo sounders do not indicate this information directly; e.g., on Model EH2E, paper speed is clearly labelled "mm/min," but it nowhere says how many! There are simply two markers to indicate the position of the switch for one or the other. The depth selector reads "A, B, C, A_1, A_2 . . ." all the way to C_4. Other models, judging from photographs, are equally helpful; and operators no doubt become used to using "B_2 and the paper speed to the left" as they learn which settings are most valuable in their particular kind of work.

The estimate by the *Mylark*'s crew was that the creature was between 180 and 210 feet long. It is possible to work out theoretical lengths based on the length of the image (50 mm), the standard paper speeds available, and "arbitrary" speeds of the vessel.

The major points to appear from all this, and which should be borne most clearly in mind, are the following: While the calculations that the Simrad people made of the length of whatever appeared on the strip are perfectly accurate, for the various speeds of the vessel and the three possible speeds for the tape, as they chose them, and as per their letter, they did not know, when making this assessment, just what the speed of the vessel was or that it might have been virtually at rest *vis-à-vis* the bottom. There is now every evidence that it was moving, if at all, at very slow speed.

When it comes to the business of the two pens, and the original strip having been tampered with by the operator using the secondary pen, their statements are complete rubbish. They even supplied us with an equivalent strip showing what the use of this second, manually operated pen looks like, and nothing of this nature appears on the original. Further, as an attorney specializing in technical court cases in the medical and other fields wherein strips and tapes of all kinds are constantly presented in evidence, pointed out, none of the little dots on the original have been tampered with, and they could not have been for two reasons. First, the perpetrator would have to have been a near genius and have worked under a low-powered microscope to (a) eliminate the dots that were on the strip, and then (b) work in lines of other ones. Second, this would have necessitated "re-pitching" all the lines of dots; and third, it would have had to be done simul-

15

taneously with the exit of the strip from the machine. (Also, one should add, nobody can tell us how to get *any* dots *out* of this treated paper!) Thus, to our satisfaction at least—and we have had fourteen experts in just such sonar-recording devices as this, from both naval and civilian life, the above mentioned attorneys, geographers and oceanologists, and biologists and others, to back us up—this strip was *not* tampered with.

If it was, it is up to those who say that it was, to show how it was done. The seaman watching the machine wasn't an expert engraver, didn't even know how the machine actually worked, and most certainly did not know how to alter its product. How did he come by the complex chemical and mechanical equipment to do such a thing, and if he did have any such equipment, how come and why was it aboard a small commercial fishing vessel in Alaska? Come, now!

Further, if Simrad's estimate that the mid-body (from top to bottom, that is) was 15 feet, then its length on the strip would be, proportionately, 150 feet; and it's no good saying that the faster the ship passed over the object the closer together would be the lines of pips, so shortening the length; or alternately, that the slower it went, the longer the thing would get. The object shown is exactly in accord with what might be expected, anatomically speaking, of such a beast; and the picture of it *could not have been tampered with.*

Even the chaps at Supervisors, Inc., don't say flatly *that the original image was constructed;* they suggest, and very cautiously, be it noted, that the echogram was "tampered" with, or had "some help"—you can't tamper with something unless you have something there to begin with!

Thus, I am afraid that I have to say simply, that until and unless somebody comes up with a lot more accurate and provable facts to the contrary and much better ones than the manufacturers of Simrad offered, we have here the first concrete proof of the existence of a marine longneck.

CHAPTER TWO

THE GREAT ORM

Though endless news stories and feature articles in newspapers, countless articles in leading magazines, and more than a dozen books have been published on what is called the Loch Ness Monster, the vast majority of our citizens still appear never to have even heard of the business. Only a minute percentage who have, really know what it is all about; and even fewer realize that there are similar "monsters" reported as living in lakes scattered all across Canada, Scandinavia, Russia and Siberia, and even a few in the United States. There have been literally thousands of reports of creatures of a size and shape that in no way conform to those of any known animal in any of these lakes. Moreover, these reports go back to the dawn of written history in the Old World and to the most ancient known verbal traditions of our Amerindians in the New; but reports, though facts in themselves, constitute only circumstantial evidence. There are now also quite a few still photographs emanating from both western Europe and, it is rumoured, from Russia; while several are allegedly being held in Canada by the photographers because they are frightened of being ridiculed if they release them.

Still photos are as suspect as hearsay today, since just about anything can be faked, but when it comes to a film strip (see Fig.

Fig. 3. Diagrammatic comparison of procedure of Loch Ness animal and motorboat as filmed by Mr. Tim Dinsdale: (a) *represents the "thing"*; (b) *the motorboat*. Note the propwash left by the latter.

3), especially if it is taken by an amateur and is immediately handed over to reliable experts who don't know what is in the can and have never even heard of a lake monster, we are dealing with something quite else. And this is just what we now are dealing with, since an aeronautical engineer by the name of Tim Dinsdale obtained such a film of a something crossing Loch Ness at ten mph (as later estimated by counting frames and camera speed), then turning sharp left under the opposite cliff. At that point, moreover, a white bus, that was later traced and measured, happened to pass along a road above, so that there was a double check on size. But why do I say this film strip is decisive?

The answer is really more than simple; it is basic, and anybody who doesn't immediately recognize this fact once the significance of the *whole* film has been pointed out to him by means of a diagram, and he has then viewed the film again, ought, in my opinion, to be "certified." You see: Tim Dinsdale left his camera on its tripod at the top of the cliff where he had obtained the shot, jumped into his car and roared down to a hamlet below the cliff, where he had a friend who had a motorboat. He asked the fellow to go to a point immediately below where his camera was left, and then, on a handkerchief signal to turn left about a hundred feet from the far shore. Dinsdale hot-rodded it back up onto the cliff and focussed on the boat.

The manoeuvre was performed exactly as requested, and Tim got a brief strip of just about the same length as his first. The two were, of course, on the same roll of film, which was immediately sealed in the presence of witnesses and rushed to a professional agency for development. Let me point out the single, basic feature that came to light that is the clincher: a "V"-shaped bow-wave was created by both the Thing and the boat, but there wasn't any propellor-wash in the former. So then, in the absence of an engine, what drove the thing along at ten mph, since it obviously hadn't got any sails? The only possible answer is that it *must* be an animal.

When it came to estimating the size of the Thing, monster hunters were for once lucky—and they seem to be the unluckiest people in the world. Every time they see one of their beasties in ideal conditions and close up, cameras are elsewhere or focussed elsewhere. When the scanners get a latch-on, it's either too foggy or too dark for photography; yet when they employ infra-red, nothing appears! It can't go on forever, but until this time, although they had got several film strips of a something or of a wake, there had not been any visible points of reference by which size could be judged, like the far shore in Tim's film, the bus that passed by, and a seagull that sailed across the frames half-way between Tim and the Thing. Further, Tim Dinsdale, with the assistance of David James, who for eight years has organized and maintained a round-the-clock watch all around the Loch for many months, got his film analyzed and assessed by one of the few organizations in the world who are real experts on the interpretation of aerial photographs, namely the Joint Air Reconnaissance Intelligence Centre of the British Royal Airforce.

For some reason I still cannot fathom, I happen to possess Copy No. 1 of this lengthy analysis issued officially by that organization [12] and I would sorely like to publish it in full right here, but all I have space for in this record is the following:—They stated that the part of the object showing *above* the water was "in the order of 12 ft. to 16 ft. wide and 5 ft. high," about 3 feet of this being above the waterline. They could not, of course, determine the length under water. The JARIC report also notes that the figure of 10 mph is the lowest speed at which it could have been moving, and points out that it is mechanically impossible for a vessel of that waterline length to travel at anything like that speed unless it has a planing hull—in which case it couldn't dive as the Thing did!

Once such a statement had been made and was taken in conjunction with the simple fact stated above, there could no longer be any argument as to whether there are large, as yet uncaught or unidentified animals in certain deep, coldwater lakes that ring the northern hemisphere in what is called the Northern Boreal Belt. Yet, believe it or not, many people have continued to so argue [13] and quite violently on occasion, while the one group who should have immediately understood its import—the zoologists—have become the most violent of all. Happily, however, a few among this fraternity have come to place scientific enquiry before their prejudices and their so precious reputations, and have tackled the problem in a truly scientific manner. [14]

When any new thing pops up in nature, scientists normally, and rightly, go into a period of argument, discussion, doubt, and worry, while the technologists start trying to devise means of testing their various theories. This being a zoological affair, the first problem is the age-old starting-point of the "What?," meaning in this case, What kind of animal could it be? Let us get into the fray.

There are well over a million kinds of animals known and described today. Millions more remain to be discovered—the bug-hunters have suggested that they have not yet discovered more than a *tenth* of the insects that exist—nor are all those as yet undiscovered by any means necessarily little insects, worms, and so forth. The second bulkiest land animal, called Cotton's Ceratothere, the Sudanese race of what is popularly called the White Rhinoceros, was not discovered until 1916, and several mammals larger than cats have turned up in the past decade. As for new kinds of fish and other aquatic creatures, they just seem to keep popping up forever.

All this host, which is quite apart, of course, from the microscopic single-celled creatures, can be clearly and cleanly divided into twenty-six distinct groups called phyla. These phyla are not all of the same size numerically by any means, ranging as they do in the number of known kinds from a dozen or so to hundreds of thousands, as in the insects. This list may be both interesting and somewhat enlightening, so I include it in the accompanying chart. Don't be alarmed by the mostly impossible "Latin" names; just ignore them, but please appreciate the fact that they are necessary because several of those for which there are no English names are of the utmost importance to this enquiry.

CLASSIFICATION OF ANIMAL LIFE

A. *ANIMALS WITH SKELETONS INSIDE*
1. *Chordates:* Mammals, Birds, Reptiles, Amphibians, Bony-Fishes, Selachians (Sharks, Rays), Protochordates (Lancelets and Sea-squirts)
2. *Hemichordates:* Acorn-Worms
3   *Chaetognaths:* Arrow-Worms
B. *ANIMALS WITH SKELETONS OUTSIDE*
4. *Arthropods:* Insects, Arachnids (Spiders, Scorpions, etc.), Horse-shoe Crabs, Whale "Lice," Crustaceans (Crabs, Lobsters, Shrimps, and many others), Centipedes, Millipedes, and three other little groups
C. *WORM-SHAPED ANIMALS*
5. *Annelids:* Segmented worms like Earth and Lug Worms
6. *Acanthocephalans:* Parasitic worms with hooks on heads
7. *Phoronids:* Marine; living in fibrous tubes
8. *Echiuroids:* Marine; impossible to describe
9. *Siphunculoids:* Marine; called Peanut-Worms
10. *Pogonophores:* Bearded Worms
11. *Priapulids:* Marine; impossible to describe
12. *Platyhelminthes:* Flat Worms, like Planaria you cut up at school
13. *Nemerteans:* Ribbon Worms
14. *Nematomorphs:* Horsehair Worms
15. *Nematodes:* Round Worms, mostly parasitic

D. RADIALLY CONSTRUCTED ANIMALS

16. *Echinoderms:*   Sea Lilies, Sea Cucumbers, Starfish, Sea Urchins, Brittle Stars

E. ANIMALS THAT MAKE SHELLS

17. *Molluscs:*   Commonly called "shellfish." There are six lots: the Monoplacoids which are very primitive, the Amphineura which have hinged shells, Gastropods with coiled shells like snails, Scaphopoda or tooth shells, Pelecypods with two shells like oysters, and Cephalopods (octopuses and squids) which have *internal* skeletons

18. *Brachiopods:*   Lamp Shells, which have two shells, but one on the back and the other underneath

F. ANIMALS WITH GELATINOUS BODIES

19. *Ctenophores:*   Ribbon-shaped Jellyfish

20. *Coelenterates:*   also called Zoophytes: Jellyfish and Corals

G. ODD LOTS

21. *Bryozoans:*   Moss Animals

22. *Rotifers:*   Mostly microscopic. Nobody really knows what to do with these. They are also called Wheel Animalcules

23. *Gastrotrichs:*   no other name

24. *Kinorhynchs:*   (ditto)

25. *Entoprocts:*   (ditto)

H. SEMI-ANIMALS

26. *Sponges:*   These are really colonies or sort of "civilizations" with division of labor

The first thing we have to consider when we come to Lake Monsters is that they are aquatic, but this doesn't help at all because all of the major twenty-six groups of animals are either wholly aquatic or have numerous aquatic representatives. Then, in view of the fact that they are called Monsters on account of their size rather than simply being monstrous in form, one would have hoped to be able to knock out most of the groups because all their known members are small; but this also is impossible because many of the groups contain comparatively or truly enormous members. For instance, among the invertebrates or backboneless animals, we have a one-ton jellyfish, a shellfish up to fifty feet long' (the giant squid), crabs with a twelve-foot arm-span, and worms thirty feet long. Notice this last. Moreover, there is no mechanical reason why any animal buoyed up by the counter-gravity of water cannot grow to *any* size.

All this, therefore, can mean only that there are no basic criteria for identifying aquatic "monsters" of any kind, while descriptions of them as given by people who say they have observed them have to be classified by a very fully trained and experienced morphologist—i.e., a specialist in the external form of animals—preferably with very wide field experience. Unfortunately, few monster hunters have these qualifications, even zoologists, so that said observers are wide open to the most popular line of criticism directed at their reports—to wit, "They don't know how to interpret what they see." This, perhaps more than anything else, has held up the search for these creatures; and when the other common accusations such as drunkenness, hallucination, hoaxing, and publicity-seeking are added to this, it is small wonder that the vast majority of those who *do* see these things do not report them. This makes identification all the more difficult. Then, there is still another complication, and one that not even monster hunters seem to appreciate.

This is that, just as with the abominable snowman, flying saucers, and even such things as whales and rats, the average person appears to think that there is only *one* kind of each. Even the most educated people go around talking about *"The* Whale" and *"The* Abominable Snowman" just as if there was only one poor creature wandering around without parents or progeny. By the same token, just about everybody is convinced that there were things called dinosaurs. There is no such thing as *"The Dinosaur"*; there are literally thousands of extinct reptiles (and some amphibians for that matter) that are popularly called "dinosaurs," but even the term itself is inaccurate as it means only "terrible reptiles." There is no Class of *Dinosauria*. Moreover, only comparatively few of the creatures called dinosaurs were monsters. Some were only two feet long!

Fig. 4. *Ceratosaurus:* (a) *as reconstructed by O. C. Marsh. However, it is doubtful that an animal of these proportions could maintain this pose. As Newman has now demonstrated, it probably stood like a bird* (b) *with the backbone forming an " S ."* (c) *Ceratosaurus resting, as suggested by Newman for Tyrannosaurus. If this form had nuchal and sagittal crests, it would look astonishingly like the traditional "dragon" of the Saint George fable.*

The same must be said for the sea and lake monsters because, if the reports are to be believed, they show not just very considerable but what can only be called drastic differences in general appearance. This applies much more to the sea monsters, however, than to those reported from lakes. The latter, as a matter of fact, appear to fall into two rather distinct classes—a tropical, which almost always is alleged to display reptilian characteristics such as scales and nose-horns [15] (see Fig. 4a) and which, all in all, looks awfully like one of the extinct groups of reptiles called theropods, and a northern one which forms the basis of this discussion. It must be stressed, nevertheless, that this latter type has been reported also from the equivalent climatic belt in the southern hemisphere—i.e., in Tasmania and southern South America.[16]

Despite all this, we can slice down the spectrum to manageable limits when discussing northern lake monsters. They are aquatic and large as animals go; in fact, in view of the fact that the common housefly is the average size of all animal life on this planet, they are monsters indeed! On the other hand, they all seem to conform to a considerable extent to one outward bodily shape. What is this?

To save verbiage, I present herewith a sort of compendium of the seemingly most reliable reports arranged according to the various types of animals suggested (see: Figs. 5, 6, 7, 8, 9, and 10). In Figures 5 and 6 you will note that I have deliberately *not*

Fig. 5. *Composites of descriptions given by eye-witnesses of freshwater longnecks: (a) the commonest form when allegedly seen close-up. Several people have reported a pair of flippers, forward, but nobody has ever seen a back pair. (b) The traditional form, seen long-distance, with varying number of humps. The only valid suggestion as to what these could be is inflatable hydrostatic organs, any number of which can be elevated at will by the animal.*

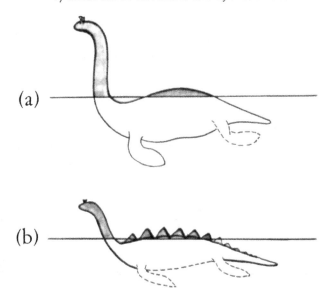

(a)

(b)

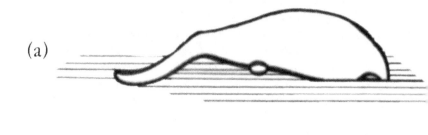

(a)

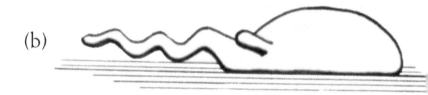

(b)

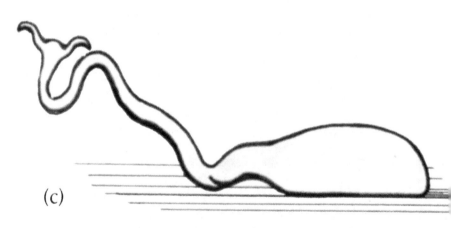

(c)

Fig. 6. *The slug-like or other invertebrate form of longneck:* (a) *sketch of an animate object photographed by a Mr. Hugh Gray in Loch Ness in 1933;* (b) *the creature reported by a Mr. and Mrs. Spicer to have crossed a road and plunged into Loch Ness, on the 22nd July, 1933;* (c) *an Echiuroid* (Bonellia), *18 inches long with a three-foot extensible proboscis. The minute males live as parasites inside the females.*

included an eye. This is because I have yet to obtain a single report of one being seen. (Among sea monsters, this is often the most prominent feature to catch the attention of the viewer.) The other surprise is the shape of the tail (in Fig. 4) which is most unexpected. Bear in mind that this is a compendium, not a sketch of any particular thing observed, nor even of a group in any one lake, or of a type.

Armed with this overall compendium, zoologists and what are so scathingly called amateurs, some time ago started to speculate as to which class of known animals, living or extinct, such a creature might belong. This was where they may have made an initial mistake because we are still nowhere near knowing just how many *different* kinds of aquatic monsters there might be or how widely separated they might be on the tree of life. Just because two animals look alike does not mean that they need be even vaguely related. Take a whale-shark and a whale of similar dimensions. A more extreme case of morphological similarity, but widely divergent genetic origin, is that of a ribbon-fish and a giant ctenophore.

Nonetheless, the boys got to work with vigour, arguing about the northern lake monsters which have now come to be called "Longnecks." Perhaps naturally they all at first plonked for some kind of vertebrate animal and, in view of their long necks, fishes were eliminated. Then, simply because nobody could conceive of a bird of the size required or being able to stay below water for so long, this group was also set aside. Actually, I personally feel that it ought to be kept in the field, at least when we are dealing with sea monsters, because of the penguins and a horrible "thing" we have come to call "Old Three-Toes," but that is another story.[17] Next, they eliminated the amphibians, but on the grounds that while some extinct ones were enormous, they cannot live in such cold waters. This reasoning is suspect too, since there is a salamander in Alaska![18] The protochordates do seem most unlikely candidates and on all counts. This left only mammals and reptiles, and I propose to dispose of these rather rapidly.

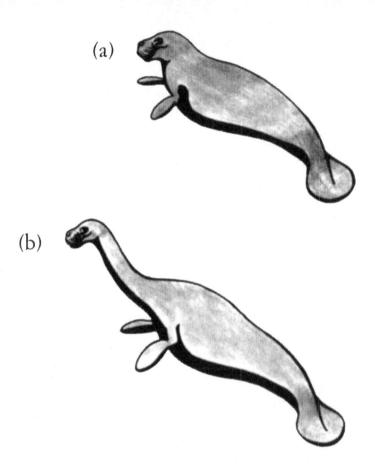

(a)

(b)

Fig. 7. *The Sirenian Suggestion, first put forward by Dr. Roy Mackal of Chicago: (a) a manatee; (b) Dr. Mackal's conception*

Among the former, there are two most promising and a few other more dubious candidates, such as giant otters and swimming deer, which are not worth further consideration. The two best suggestions are: (1) a giant, very long-necked seal of the sea-lion type, and (2) some kind of long-necked sirenian, a tiny group of mammals represented today only by our manatees and the dugong of the Indian Ocean (see Fig. 7), and, until recently —if it is truly extinct [19]—by a much larger creature known as Steller's sea cow that lived on some islands off the east coast of

Fig. 8. *A large Plesiosaur from the early Cretaceous. These reptiles led the lives of sea turtles and could not possibly have moved in a straight line as fast as the creature filmed by Tim Dinsdale—speed estimated at 10 knots.*

Siberia until wiped out by the sealers in the 18th century. Among the reptiles, the obvious choice was the plesiosaurians (Fig. 8), of which a fairly wide variety of size and form are known intimately from their fossilized skeletons derived from the rocks of the Secondary or Mesozoic Period, prior to about 70 million B.C., and it would certainly seem that it is into this category that the freshwater longnecks could be most nearly placed. However, we do not know if plesiosaurs could live in freshwater or tolerate the perpetually low temperatures of these lakes. They may well have been live-bearers so that eggs would not be found, and they could have been warm-blooded: which two points would make them much more worthy of consideration.

Reverting to the mammals for a moment, let it be said that we do not know of any fossil sirenian with a long neck, and all the living ones have whale-like or paddle-shaped tails borne horizontally, a feature that has never been mentioned in any description of a lake monster. The sea lions, on the other hand, do have rather long necks and stubby, albeit very tiny, tails. Thus, by sort of pulling out a giant sea lion one would get a pretty fair copy of the Loch Ness monster. What is more, sea lions like plesiosaurs have four flipper-shaped appendages. However, the former can travel only by an up-and-down undulatory movement, while a reptile, due to the construction of its vertebrae, can only go from

29

side to side. This is a vitally important point, since no long-neck has ever been reported as weaving from side-to-side like a water snake, but many have been reported as humping along. (See again, Fig. 1.)

The business thus finally boiled down to a choice between a long-necked mammal and a long-necked reptile, and everybody was fairly happy since the proposition seemed at least manageable. But then must needs come along a perfectly splendid chap by the name of Ted Holiday to completely upset the proverbial cart and to somewhat annoy the amateur monster hunters and greatly confuse the public; though strangely, and for once, his suggestion gave those zoologists who have taken this whole matter seriously only a slight jolt. It was actually more of a friendly nudge to their professional outlook as a reminder that they too must not develop closed minds. Ted's suggestion at first sounded quite absurd; but don't jump to any conclusions until you have read what follows and have read his book.* So what was this bombshell?

Ted Holiday told me once that it was the report of a couple named Spicer [20] who said that they had nearly run into a Loch Ness longneck as it crossed the new lakeshore road, at 4 P.M., in 1933, that started him along his line of speculation. The brute humped across the road, going downwards through the bracken, and sploshed into the loch. The Spicers were more horrified than terrified by its appearance and kept harping on the fact that it looked to them more like a gigantic slug or snail without a shell than anything else. There had been some people who had previously mumbled vaguely about the notion that these things might be *in*vertebrates, but nobody, and least of all the zoologists, paid any attention. It remained for Ted to gather up all possible suggestions that might support this crazy-sounding theory. It was not long, moreover, before other monster hunters began to listen seriously to these "ravings"; and principally because they found it increasingly difficult to refute them entirely on either zoological

---

* *The Great Orm,* W. W. Norton & Co., 1968 (Avon Books, 1970).

or purely logical grounds. In fact, grounds for rejecting them proved either nonexistent or even slimmer than those for excluding birds, amphibians, and fish.

First, while there are twenty-five phyla of animals to choose from, after the vertebrates have been taken out of the list (temporarily, that is), no less than eighteen of these *could* present candidates. Of course with a very few exceptions, all the living examples of these groups are very small, but there are exceptions: *vide,* the giant squids among the molluscs and the fantastic ctenophores mentioned above. Then there is another thing that we must not overlook: that we have *very* few recognizable fossils of soft-bodied invertebrates that do not have exoskeletons like insects, crabs, and lobsters and so forth; shells like molluscs, brachiopods, and echinoderms; or which do not build things like the corals, or tubes like some worms. We simply don't know *what* skeletonless or shell-less animals lived in the past; and we probably have very little idea of what large ones are living today, since their bodies sink on death and disintegrate very rapidly.

So Ted and some others started probing around among these twenty-five groups of invertebrate animals, looking for the most likely candidates. Practically everybody's first choice was the molluscs because of the shape of some slugs which have comparatively long necks and the really enormous size of the giant squids; but most of all because there are some absolutely delightful little beasts called pteropods that look for all the world like tiny manatees, and which swim about the surface of the sea with a pair of little paddles at the front end. However, no known mollusc combines all these characters, while the length of the neck of the monsters constitutes quite a stumbling block, although snails and slugs do have extrusible "horns" which actually bear their eyes aloft. A lot of people besides Ted became extremely enthusiastic over the idea of giant aquatic slugs, more especially because some sea slugs, so-called (meaning either shell-less marine molluscs or those with reduced shells inside their bodies), can indeed look alarmingly like tiny longnecks when viewed from certain angles.

I myself was never over-enthusiastic about this suggestion, but as I have always adopted the Anglo-Saxon as opposed to the Napoleonic code—namely, regarding things and other animals as well as humans as being innocent until proven otherwise—I not only went along with it but spent a lot of time looking at both land and saltwater slugs and photographs of same. My final conclusion was "out," and mostly because, while sea slugs do sometimes progress by up-and-down undulatory motions of their lateral flanges or appendages, their whole bodies seldom do so; while I have yet to see any mollusc with a long thin neck and a noticeable head on the end of it.

As a matter of fact, both Ted and I came to this point at about the same time, but for somewhat different reasons. Ted went off on a worm jag, and mostly because one of his hobbies has always been ancient Celtic cultural anthropology and history, and he had stumbled across a mysterious monster called "The Great Orm," which has either been totally overlooked, swept under the historical rug, or classed as a purely mythical beast.[21] Though the etymology of the word *orm* is not the same as *worm*,[22] the beast depicted looks just like an enormous worm, and, for various reasons, definitely not like a snake. The creature was said to have come out of rivers or lakes and to have committed general mayhem in areas where it took up residence, being so large, fast, and savage that primitive communities were powerless in face of it. It took a mounted knight in armour with a lance to get at it —e.g., Saint George!

In fact, Ted Holiday went on to pursue the orm into the dragon myths and became increasingly disturbed on the one hand and encouraged on the other, because he found ever more dragons that had all the appurtenances of orms, even unto some Chinese types, while some of those in subtropical and tropical areas appeared to blend with the dinosaurian type of semiaquatic monsters therein. The pursuit became so exciting that, if I may say so of an old personal friend, he almost went overboard on the matter. However, before we had to drag him back, a process that we had started with regard to the tropical ."dragons" in any case, something else caught his attention. And this is where we joined forces again.

Before I go into this I would like to explain my somewhat negative attitude to "worms" as well as to molluscs as candidates for the longneck class of lake monsters. First, there is no more such a thing as *a* worm, in a manner of speaking, than there is *a* dinosaur. There is no class called simply *Vermes*. There are worm-shaped members of the arthropods, the echinoderms, the molluscs, and the so-called jellyfish. Then there are no less than eleven other phyla that are more commonly called worms; one of which, the annelids, includes the earthworms and the saltwater lugworms. Nor is this all to be said on the subject of "worms," for we have two phyla of what I designate completely hopeless animals called the peanut-worms (*Sipunculoidea*) and the echiuroids (*Echiuroidea*). There are some 250 of the first kind and 60 of the latter known, and both lots live in the sea. As a candidate for the longneck class, the former are "out" but the latter, of which the largest species measures some sixteen inches in overall length, most definitely qualifies but, of course, *only if* these monsters prove to be invertebrates. I present a modest example of one of these rather unpleasant-looking things with a particularly long "neck" which divides at the tip into sort of flabby "horns." It looks very much like a miniature of the thing the Spicers and Mr. Gray said they saw (see Fig. 5; compare also Plate II).

Fig. 9. *A "Great Orm" as shown in a Neolithic Age pictograph, found at Balmacaan, near Loch Ness in Scotland.*

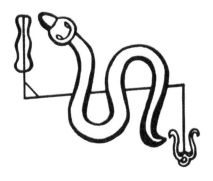

While we have a parasitic worm (a form of tapeworm) over thirty feet long, and there are earthworms up to twelve feet long and two inches in diameter when contracted,[23] and some awfully long lugworms, none of these are bulky or have humps or appendages, while the way they are constructed and the composition of their outer coverings would not seem to lend itself to truly giant size. Yet the great orm (see Fig. 9) is definitely and most clearly wormlike, even to having rings or constrictions all along its body, no eyes and an ability to curve both sidewise and upwards. Which brings us to still another business that must be dredged up at this point.

The amphibians, which are vertebrates, are divided into three groups—the frogs and toads, the salamanders, and some worm-like, legless creatures called the caecilians. Almost all of these last start their life in water and most of them go back into it regularly. Many amphibians are subterranean dwellers as well; particularly many salamanders and all the caecilians. Now, some positively enormous amphibians of extinct groups are known from fossils, and there is one living salamander which is quite a healthy size, the Giant of Japan. Some of the salamanders, like our so-called Congo eels, have only one pair of tiny legs up behind their heads, and the caecilians are legless and annulated like worms. Then, there is the semi-mythical *Tatzelwurm* [24] of Scandinavia and the European Alps.

No example of this creature has ever been caught, or if it has, it has never reached a museum, but it is regarded as not uncommon in some country districts in Sweden where it is said sometimes to be found under piles of potatoes in damp cellars. It is said to grow to about twelve feet in length and to be as thick as a large man's calf, to have a great array of very sharp teeth, and to be exceedingly aggressive and vicious. The caecilians also have a great array of sharp teeth and are true predators.

The caecilians or legless amphibians are very odd creatures and inhabit only very moist soils or swamps but, and this is important, two kinds are wholly aquatic. Today, they are confined to the moist tropical areas, though they extend north to Central Mexico and south to the Rio La Plata in the New World. The largest is over four feet in length, but some of the longest are the slimmest, while the shortest are the fattest. There are several most peculiar points about their anatomy that are of particular interest to this discussion. First, some have lost their eyes entirely, while others have them covered with skin but, in place of visibility, they have a pair of small extrusible tentacles or "horns" that lie in a groove between the eye-sockets and the nostrils. Second, while their bodies are slick and slimy like frogs and salamanders, there are rings of small scales just beneath the surface of the skin, something that is not found in other living amphibians but which is among a group of extinct creatures called the *Stegocephalia*. Moreover, the body is truly annulated and some caecilians can "bunch" up their skins in a most remarkable manner. They cannot contract as a whole like earthworms, as they have a vertebrated backbone, but they can stretch long sections of their skin, so bunching up the portions in between. One species I collected in West Africa was almost impossible to hold in a closed fist, as it thus "wormed" its way out between your fingers, however firmly held. If you had a vast aquatic caecilian lying at the surface of a calm lake, and it put on such an act, you'd have all the bumps or humps for which anybody could ask.

Just because all caecilians are today confined to the tropics and subtropics, does not mean that they could not once have lived in cooler climates, because some species today are found up to ten thousand feet above sea level where it is perpetually cool and in areas such as Buenos Aires where the ground temperature varies from intense heat to really very cold. No fossil caecilians are known, so we cannot tell anything of their past distribution; nor can we know of the maximum size to which they might grow. Actually, there is really no limit to size among any group of multi-celled animals, by which I mean no limiting factors, as is shown by the giant jellyfish and squids. That there could be enormous ones is, moreover, rendered more possible by the fact that many of the internal anatomical features of these strange creatures also point to their origin from, and somewhat close relationship to,

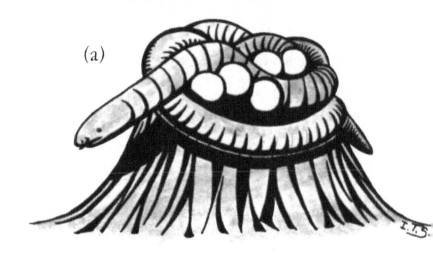

(a)

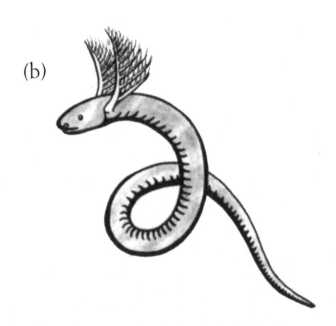

(b)

Fig. 10. *It has long been suggested that the Loch Ness animals could be giant amphibians—either salamanders or two-legged ones, like Congo Eels. However, the legless caecilians have been overlooked but would seem to fit more closely the descriptions of one form of "Lake Monster." (a) an adult caecilian* (Idiocranium) *nursing eggs on a mud-mound in a gallery in a swamp; (b) the aquatic larva of same with plume-like external gills.*

these extinct Stegocephalia, some of which were as big as rhinoceroses.

One of the most astonishing things about the caecilians is that they have two rows of teeth in the upper jaw, and this was reported by two Austrian professional mountain climbers' guides of a tatzelwurm that they said they saw peering out from between two fallen, moss-covered logs in the high pine forests.[25] We have very little but vague stories of the tatzelwurm to go on but everything that I have ever heard of them fits the caecilians and *only* the caecilians. Almost all of these animals have an aquatic larval stage with beautiful pairs of external, fernlike gills (see Fig. 10b). These larvae are, of course, smaller than the adults, but there is a curious thing called neoteny found among the amphibians. This is the condition arising when the larvae of some kinds go on growing, and sometimes to a much larger size than the adults, and they may then never metamorphose into an adult at all. Might it be, then, that the great orms are gigantic neotenous forms of some huge kind of tatzelwurm, the adult form of which is "extinct" but which have left their larvae to carry on?

Should anything so bizarre be the case, it might explain why the orms have so constantly been described as coming out onto the land and then taking up residences in caves. Maybe, like the axolodtl, which is the neotenous form of a large salamander, they occasionally get the "urge" (purely physiological) to revert for a generation to their ancestral adult form which probably lived in peat bogs and swamps into which it could burrow. And, be it noted, it is in just those areas where such are available that stories of great orms coming out of the water persist. There has always been a tradition of such behaviour rife all over Ireland, and during the past two decades there have been dozens of alleged eyewitness accounts of their doing so, received from all over that country. Several people, including Ted Holiday, have investigated these reports and interviewed the people who have said they had actually seen this performance, and from these reports one most notable observation may be gleaned.

I remarked above that the caecilians have slimy, mucous-covered skins like salamanders, and when you hold them and they perform their trick of forcing their way out of your closed fist, they leave masses of this mucous inside as they sort of pump their skins forward and then bunch them up. Several of the reports from Ireland make a point of the fact that the great orms, when passing from one small lake to another, flatten down the weeds and even the heather and *leave huge slime tracks.*[26] No wonder so many of the pro-invertebrate school of monster hunters plunked for their animals being slugs or other forms of molluscs!

Rather than being any kind of worm, I therefore incline to the idea that the great orm was/is a sort of gigantic caecilian or tatzelwurm. But, let it be most clearly understood that I do not even suggest putting forward any kind of amphibian as a candidate for the *longnecks*. Actually, as of now, I still adhere to my original assessment of these animals, made some thirty years ago and without having seen Professor Oudemans' monumental classic [27] on the matter, as being enormous, long-necked, sea-lion-like seals or pinnipedes.

To sum up, I will be so bold as to place it on record that, as of now, I believe there could be *two quite separate kinds* of animals involved in the lake monster bit. The first would seem most likely to be a giant, long-necked, long-tailed sea lion and related to the marine longnecks that, in Canada and the northern United States at least, have repeatedly been reported going up rivers and far into the center of the continent. The second has all the attributes of the amphibians known as caecilians, both in external form, behaviour, habits, *and* in its ecological distribution. If twelve feet, two-inch-thick earthworms can force their way through the soil of montane forests way up in the clouds as they do in Colombia, could not a much more powerful (due to having a backbone) twenty-four-foot, eight-inch thick, or even a forty-foot, three-feet in diameter orm do so through a peat bog? And if some living amphibians are any criterion, a forty-foot adult might well have an eighty-foot neotenous aquatic larva.

CHAPTER THREE

THE OLITIAU AND
THE AHOOL

THERE HAS BEEN a very curious business going on in the Orient since time immemorial, spoken of widely but spottily by a number of peoples native to several countries and most notably Vietnam and Java. The Indians and Singhalese mention it, but mostly in a mythological context, and it wasn't until the turn of the century that Europeans even heard of it. Only two scientists, both of them Hollanders, seem ever to have investigated the matter, and as far as I know, only one of these has ever published anything on the business. He is Dr. Ernest Bartels, now retired to the Netherlands.

I think I stumbled across an equivalent if not like item in West Africa,[28] and similar things have been reported from Samoa to the east, and from Madagascar and southern Tanzania to the west. The subject for tonight is "Giant Bats."

Before I go any further, however, I would like to clear one possible confusion out of the way, and try to put it in its proper place, so that I may refer back to it later without danger of misinterpretation and, at the same time, make as sure as possible that you will not latch onto this on your own and start building all kinds of happy theories relative to it that would then have to be taken apart later on. So, I say here and now, and categorically, that I am *not* implying in any way that the things I shall describe are,

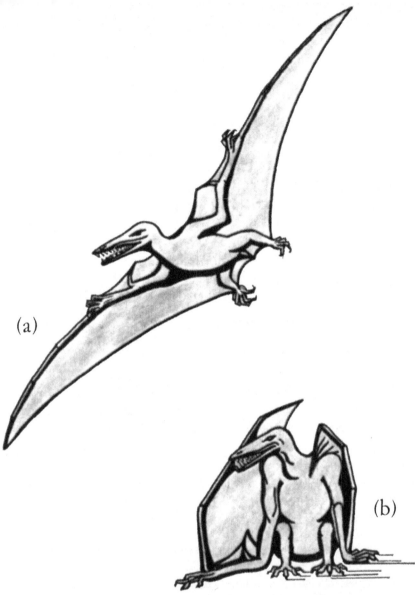

Fig. 11. *A Pteranodont-type pterodactyl—these reptiles were apparently "sail-planes" and could launch from the ground, using only slight updraughts due to heat evaporation from ground surface. (a) Airborne, the animals were manifestly graceful and mechanically highly efficient. (b) Grounded, they would seem to have sat more like birds. However, it must be noted that they actually had seven working joints in their forearms; the third being a greatly extended manus, and the remaining three enormously enlarged and developed bones of the "little" or fifth finger.*

could be, or even might be living pterodactyls—those vast flying reptiles known from fossils and which are so exciting to both young and old (see Fig. 11). To the contrary, I *do* think they are giant bats, and I will give my reasons for so thinking as I go along.

That these things exist you must take from me. I saw one, and with a European and two Africans as witnesses. I can offer no more by way of evidence. The first intimation I had of these things was when I encountered one literally face to face. Funny, but so many of the really great things that happen to one are not only unexpected, but make only a slight impression upon one at the time, and are then usually either forgotten or dismissed from one's mind. If the incident occurred again tomorrow, I'd spend the rest of my life until I got to the bottom of the business, but back in 1932 when it happened, I appear to have just sort of shrugged it off, and this despite the fact that I was where I was specifically to search for and to collect new animals. (Similarly, I once saw a really beautiful hand-carved set of wine and shot glasses made from tropical woods in a run-down gift shop in Florida, being offered for a few cents apiece. I bought one of each and remember saying to myself "I'll get some more when I get back to New York." Neither I nor anybody else I know of has ever seen anything like them since!)

My first encounter with one of the things of which I speak here took place in the Assumbo Mountains of the Cameroon in West Africa one evening when my companion, Gerald Russell, and two of our African helpers were wading down a mountain stream to search for tortoises and to shoot bats when it got dark enough for them to start flying. I was about a hundred feet ahead of Gerald, and the Africans were creeping along under the bushes on the banks in order to drive the small wildlife into the river. When the bats began to arrive, flying up and down the river catching insects, we blazed away. Curiously, my first bag was a fruit-eating bat of most grotesque appearance called a hammer-headed bat, which has a wingspan of over two feet. I was perched on a large boulder above the torrent.

41

The plan was that our head preparator, Bensun Onun Edet, who was downstream from me, would retrieve the bats that fell into the water. One began to sink, however, so I put down my gun and jumped down into the water. But I landed on a tortoise that skidded out from under me, resulting in my going "arse-over-tip" into a fairly deep pool. Just as I regained shallow water and was floundering about among the slippery boulders, Gerald suddenly yelled "Look out!" Whipping around toward him, I was confronted by an apparition, such as I had never imagined existed, about fifteen feet away and just above the level of my eyes. It was coming straight at me awfully fast, so I ducked down into the water.

Gerald Russell came to stay with me last fall (1970) and we had a chance to discuss this incident. We both kept very detailed diaries while we were in Africa, and happily mine was saved from the bombing in London. I had recently consulted this for details of this incident, as time can play havoc with one's memory. Gerald, however, confirmed what I thought that I remembered; and both our versions were confirmed by our diaries. We had measured the river at that point, and it was forty feet wide, plus or minus a couple of feet. The wings of this creature spread across at least a third of this span and, as seen by Gerald looking downstream and I looking upstream, and judging by the fact that it was dead center, there appeared to both of us to be the same width of sky between its wing-tips and the trees that lined the banks of the river to either side. Our diaries say "at least a twelve-foot wingspan."

Though this apparition was entirely unexpected, it must be borne in mind that I had spent many years "hunting" in the tropics and was pretty well geared to the unexpected. Also, as a professional animal collector, nothing short of a dinosaur popping up would faze me too much—and, incidentally, I think we had actually had just such a thing pop up a couple of months before down in the high forest, but that's another story.[29] However, the size of this creature really shook me, because there are no birds with such a wingspan in Africa. In fact, the only bird with a comparable one is the great condor of the Andes. Worse was the fact that I got a very good and close look at its face and, to put it facetiously, "That weren't no boid." Its lower jaw hung down and, as the last light of the sun was directly shining onto its face, I could have counted the huge white teeth if I had had the time. They were a good two inches long, all about the same length, and all equally separated by spaces of the same width.

Now this is the one feature of this "apparition" that I will admit would seem to be more reptilian than mammalian. However, some bats have rather small canines, so that their jaws as seen from the front, do seem to present a strangely regular semicircle of about equally-sized teeth. This animal that flew at me had a muzzle more like that of a monkey than of a dog or of any kind of reptile, in that it was not drawn out to a point. The whole animal was coal black in color, including the wings, which were quite opaque. It did not appear to be hairy, but then neither do most bats until you examine them in your hand. The few strokes of its flight that I saw before I "went to ground," as it were, were very leisurely for the speed that it was going, and they were of the "flapping" motion of a fruit bat rather than the clawing of the lesser bats, which actually "swim" through the air.

Recovering my gun, I swung around and called to Gerald to watch out for it to come back, and a short time later it did so; but in those few minutes the last rays of the sun had moved up, and there was deep shadow over the river. We both blazed away with both barrels, but the great creature just sailed right over us, uninterrupted and making a "ssssh-sssshing" sound, so fast was it going. In fact, its speed of flight was much greater than we had estimated, and this may have been the reason we missed it, though Gerald is deadly at snap shots, and it was almost on top of us. I have often wondered if we *did* hit it, but that our shot, which was for collecting small animals, just failed to penetrate its hide. Alternatively, we may simply have blasted holes through its vast wing-membranes. We made haste back to our camp about a mile upstream.

Now, our African helpers were either from forest tribes some two hundred miles to the south, or from the savannahs a hundred miles to the north. None of them were scared by this thing, but

43

all were deeply interested and sincerely disappointed that we had not shot it down, because they were by then as keen on our work as we were. When we got back to camp we found several local hunters waiting for us with some specimens of various small animals laid out for sale. Our gang started jabbering about what we had seen, and our interpreter passed this on to these locals. They became greatly excited and asked us where we had seen this thing. When we pointed down the river, they yelled, *"Olitiau,"* then grabbed up their dane-guns and spears and dashed off for the village some miles upstream, leaving all their hard-earned prizes behind. This is not normal procedure in Africa, even in an emergency. Moreover, the next day the chief and his whole village council turned up, something even less usual.

Old Chief Ekumaw was somewhat shy and very grave, but with typical African good manners he at first avoided the main issue, asking us rather if we *must* stay in that particular location. When we said that we had to do so for our work, he became even graver and went so far as to offer us all the carriers necessary, free of charge, to move us up into the mountains, back to the village, or anywhere else we wanted to go. When I sought the reason for this, all he would say, over and over, was *"Olitiau, Olitiau."* Then he and his council departed for the twelve-mile walk back to the village.

We got very little further information on this business, since our people could not talk the local language, and our interpreter, who was a Court Messenger (a sort of minor government official), could say only that it was "very bad beef for true, Sir." I think he tried, but no amount of questioning could elicit anything further such as to why it was so "bad" an "animal," where it lived, or anything else. So, in the maddening way that all of us have, as I said at the beginning of this chapter, we just dropped the matter. I had convinced myself that we had seen the granddaddy of all bats, and am still so convinced. So is Gerald Russell. But most others, and some professional zoologists among them, have felt otherwise, and have said so in print.[30] These people lean to the opinion that this thing

44

was more likely a living relic pterodactyl, as is also their view about cases reported from East Africa and Madagascar. However, I don't think any of them had ever heard of its Oriental equivalent.

This came to my attention only a few years ago when my colleague, Dr. Bernard Heuvelmans of Belgium, forwarded to me a manuscript by a Dr. Ernest Bartels whom he had recently met, asking me if I could help in getting it published. It is a priceless document in which are given not only secondhand accounts but some firsthand information by Dr. Bartels himself. And Dr. Bartels is not to be sneezed at. His father was a very prominent, well-known, and subsequently honored ornithologist, by the name of Dr. M. E. G. Bartels, who was responsible for the discovery of a number of entirely new species of birds in Java, and (what is much more important) he was the first to publish detailed records of their habits and ethology.*

The younger Bartels—now himself an older man—was born and brought up in western Java and was raised trilingually; his "native" tongue being Hollands and his second, Sundanese,* the language of the peoples indigenous to the west end of the island of Java. From the age of five he was taken daily into the primaeval forest that surrounded the plantation that his father managed, and always in company with one of his father's staff. These men had been with the elder Bartels for many years and were, on the one hand, experienced hunters and trappers, and on the other, trained preparators who skinned, stuffed, and labelled the elder Bartels' collections of birds and other animals. Thus the youngster—now Doctor Ernest—was from the earliest age indoctrinated with the wildlife of the region in which he was raised, and he always had the guidance of intelligent and educated men of the country who knew exactly what western science was looking for.

This was a unique marriage of minds between European and Oriental, and one that has, alas, now become extinct due to the sad aftermath and effects of World War II. I suppose that it is difficult

---

* And please do not confuse Ethology with Ethnology; or Sundanese with Sudanese.

for westerners to believe this, but the Indonesians are among the most highly civilized and most intelligent human beings on earth. That the colonial system intervened and that they and the Hollanders sort of "got off on the wrong foot" is sad; but it happened, and there is nothing we can do about it. The *Orang Blunda*—as the Hollanders were called in "kitchen-Malay"—will for generations be loathed and disrespected by the Indonesians. However, a few of each did once get on together and truly understood each other—like Ernest Bartels and his Indonesian friends.

Dr. Bartels' account of this matter [31] contains a great deal of background information and many more details than I have the space to offer here. The essential point that he makes is that, while there is a fairly widespread tradition of the Ahool in western Java, which survives principally in the form of a myth with all the fantastic accoutrements of such lore, the creature itself was (and apparently still is) quite real and well known to the locals in several areas. This distribution may be seen on the accompanying map (Fig. 12). Dr. Bartels himself encountered the creature and so is able to both confirm and correlate the reports that he obtained

Fig. 12. *Map of Java and western Java to show the area in which Dr. Bartels investigated the Ahool*

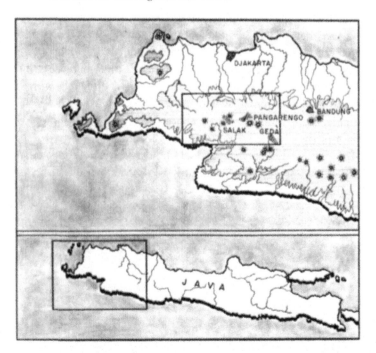

from reliable local people who had spent their lives in their own jungles as professional hunters or collectors of the fronds of the rattan or climbing palm that has considerable economic value in Indonesia. Other Europeans had stumbled across similar reports, but none of them had been born and raised in the country and among the Sundanese. Ernest Bartels was; and he not only spoke their language, but he could also *think* in it.

After completing his education in Europe, Ernest Bartels took employment on another estate in western Java on the slopes of the Salak Mountains. Once established there, he began a systematic program of investigation into the local wildlife, with particular emphasis on two forms of birds called swifts—the giant and the spine-tailed—which were alleged to nest behind waterfalls. To this end, he sought out the most experienced rattan-cutters, since this palm favors cliffs beside waterfalls of which there were literally hundreds within reasonable distance of his place of residence.

In due course Ernest Bartels met a most respected old gentleman by the name of PaHaltam who said that he knew where such birds resided. He led Dr. Bartels to a waterfall with the delightful name of "The Waterfall of the Gong," where the birds were duly found and observed. But, when they returned down the valley to their camp on the evening of the first day, the following occurred (and I quote Dr. Bartels'[32] original manuscript, with his kind permission).

Old PaHaltam handed me a steaming cup of local coffee and then asked me in a most matter-of-fact way if I had heard the Ahool. I nearly dropped the coffee cup. There was a prolonged silence because all of us just stared, open-mouthed at old PaHaltam. Finally he coughed and stared at us.

"The Ahool," he repeated, "It flew right over you, Gamparan [a polite form of address that may be translated as Sir]. Did you hear it too, Sando? [My father's assistant who was with me.]"

"Most certainly, Gan; it called three times as it flew by, following the river upstream."

"How did it call?" I asked.

"Ah-OOOoool," PaHaltam imitated, raising his head slightly.

"PaHaltam," I asked, "did you ever see an Ahool yourself?"

"Sumuhun dawah," he replied; meaning, more or less, "Yes, with your permission."

"Please proceed," I rejoined, using a form of respect in his own language. And this was the substance of his story.

"When I had three children, I camped somewhere along this same river bank to gather rattan. As usual, I was alone. I worked till dusk. Then I would cook my meal and after eating it, stretch out until about midnight, because the fire had to be tended once more. The waking coincided with my wanting to urinate. One night when I woke up I found that there was company. I saw a dark form the size of a child of about one year old faintly outlined by the light of the glowing embers. I half rose, shoved smouldering logs on the heap, and presently there were little flames. Now I saw what sat there . . . an Ahool. It had gray hair, its head looked like a monkey's. The strangest thing was that its feet were *malik katukang* [turned backward], showing the heels in front. It was a male. I saw its sex organ plainly. Do not believe the silly stories of all Ahools being female!" (PaHaltam said this passionately.) "I saw a male one, no mistaking, with both my eyes!" [See Fig. 14.]

"What did you do?" I asked.

"I did not stir. I only stared. But the visitor grew uneasy. It shuffled clumsily backward"—PaHaltam made a slightly wobbling movement with his behind—"and suddenly spread its wings, which had claws, as I had seen, and it disappeared from sight, uttering its call, Ah-OOooool!"

I was very impressed and anxious to learn more so then I asked the first question that came to my lips. "What does the Ahool feed on, PaHaltam?"

"Big fish" came the astonishing reply immediately. "And specially the *Soro.*" This is a fair-sized river fish known to

science as *Labeobarbatus soro* which inhabits some of the
rivers of this region, a point which PaHaltam went on to
point out. Then he continued:

"Gamparan, let me explain. The Ahool has forearms that
are flat, with claws on top of them. It grabs fish from underneath the stones of the river-bed. For that reason it lives
along rivers which, like this one, have plenty of fish, and
big fish."

This I did not quite understand or believe at that time,
but I pressed on with my questioning while the wise old
gentleman was willing to talk on the subject.

"Where does it hide or sleep during the day?" I asked.

"In caves, mostly underneath or behind waterfalls," he
answered without hesitation.

This gave me pause to think, so that I had time for
only one further question before PaHaltam decided, as is the
way of the ancient, that he had had enough of the subject.
"You mean, PaHaltam, that the Ahools do not frequent river
valleys where there are only small fish in the waters?"

"That is correct, Gamparan. I never heard of an Ahool
east of this river." And the discussion was closed.

It was only a little later that I brought up the subject
with my father's chief "preparator," by name, Pakih. He had
apparently known of my increasing scientific interest in this
matter for a long time but, with the wisdom of his people,
he had not volunteered information until it was specifically
solicited. He had been with us for over ten years. He was
quite prepared to discuss the matter, but made it absolutely
clear to me that he had not personally seen an Ahool but
that a cousin of his had done so, and had reported to him
immediately afterwards. Said cousin was a professional hunte
The incident had, he told me, occurred as follows:

"The River Tjilétuh divides the basin roughly in two; the
east side is cultivated, the west side is virgin forest. [This
basin lies on Java's south coast and is surrounded by a great
horseshoe of steep mountain walls. Two waterfalls tumble int
this.] Last year [this was 1925] there raged a frightful rain
and lightning storm. That afternoon my cousin wanted to

49

visit a friend living beyond the wooded west side. He stayed
at home to let the storm tide over. About an hour after the
rains stopped, the water of Tjilétuh had fallen sufficiently to
venture a crossing. Being in a hurry, my cousin borrowed a
horse and, since he was a hunter, took his gun along. By
means of a raft hooked onto a steel cable, he made the crossing
in safety and was soon riding under a canopy of great
thorny bamboos.

"He had travelled about half a mile when he saw an animal
land on the road not more than fifty feet ahead. It sat upright,
with folded wings. The pony stopped abruptly. It quivered
and whinnied and snorted. My cousin was so frightened that
he could not move for the first moments, while the creature
kept staring at him. It refrained from any sort of action.
When my cousin had recovered from his bewilderment, he
reached for his gun. This movement induced the creature *to
shift backward* [animals *never* back up, they turn]. It then
spread its great wings and flew away, ejaculating: 'Ah-OOoooool!'
and disappeared around the curve of the road. My cousin
sent a round of buckshot after it, but it must have gone
wild. He had had enough; he turned his mount and galloped
homeward. He said that it was the size of a child about one
year old. The face was like a man's and that was what made
him so frightened. The feet were stubby. He said the eyes
were black and large."

Next I stumbled upon an old and very wise professional
hunter at a small place called Tjeuri [pronounced "churry"
to rhyme with "hurry"]. His story went as follows:

"Some years ago we went on a hunt for banteng [a form
of wild buffalo] which had retired into an almost inaccessible
thicket of wild cane. We set our dogs on them, but we could
not move around fast enough and we never saw more than
the tips of their horns. During all this the sky turned blue-
black and then came *that* storm. We gave up hunting and
hurried back to the Tjilaki river, but we found it a tearing
flood with whole trees hurtling past and the boulders thundering
along the river bed below. We were soaked to the skin, and
it was too wet to make a fire for the night, and there
were many tiger thereabouts. It was not good.

"Then somebody remembered that there was a Leles
Tree [a kind of giant fig] that spanned the gorge somewhat
downstream. We headed for this and after some rough going,
found it spanning the torrent with its roots still engaged in
one bank but now only a spear's height above the waters.
Luckily, since the tree was still alive, strong branches had
grown upward from its fallen trunk and these made good
handholds for us. We started to cross in single file, I being
the second in line, and the dogs being hauled over on short
leashes. Suddenly the lead man stopped and pointed.

" 'Ahool,' he shouted. I come up and peered over his
shoulder. And there, only a few yards ahead of us stood a
creature with a body about the size of a one-year-old child;
bulu hiris [dark gray] in color; with a head like that of a
macaque monkey or a gibbon. It was on our tree-trunk bridge,
and at first it did not budge but just stared at us. The men
behind were yelling over the uproar of the river; and then
one of the dogs yelped. The Ahool rose a little on its feet,
leaned over, hopped off the tree trunk, opened its wings,
and flew off *ngajapak* [meaning cumbersomely] downstream.
Some spearlengths off, it called out only once, 'AH-OOooool.'
I never saw another one, but I heard them some other times."

I asked how it flew.

"*Tjara kalong*" came the immediate answer; and this
meant "like a flying fox," which is our name for the large
fruit bats that inhabit the Orient. This was to me, as a
zoologist, the most significant statement that the man had
made. Things were beginning to fall into place—in my mind,
at least.

A respondent to an article I published on this subject in
1962,[33] whose communication impressed me very much was
a Mr. G. J. van Maarsseven now resident of the Hague.
He related that many years ago he had met a Sundanese in
the forest near Tjisondari (in our same area) who was badly
wounded on both arms. When asked what had happened, the
man's companions said, "*Dikadek aul*" which means, literally,
"Hacked by an Ahool." The use of this word, *dikadek*, is
extremely odd and significant. There are adequate and available
words for "cut," "chop," "slash," and so on; but this means

"hack" and *only* hack; and that means with a flat thing.
Note that the Ahool's forearms are said to be "flat."

So what can, or should, one make of all of this? Frankly, I personally feel that it is clear evidence of the continued existence of an animal that has not as yet been caught, but which is not in any way beyond the pale of possibility. We have birds with twelve foot wingspans; we have the fossil skeletons of reptiles (those pterodactyls, see Fig. 10) with wingspans of up to twenty-five feet; [34] we have fruit bats with bodies bigger than crows and wingspans of five feet; so what is so impossible about the suggestion that there are bats with wingspans of twelve feet? But there is one point that should be of real interest to zoologists. This is as follows:

Bats are divided, and very clearly, into two groups: The *Mega* (great) *Chiroptera* (bats), and the *Micro* (small) bats. The former are fruit-eaters; the latter eat insects, fish, and small animals. The former, when at rest and/or sleeping, wrap their wings about themselves; the latter, while hanging upside down to rest or sleep,

Fig. 13. *Microbats:* (a) *a typical insectivorous microbat asleep, suspended from a twig.* (b) *The same "inverted," or "upverted." Should this animal be able to thus "stand erect" on a branch, its head would hang down, so that the face would be seen as shown.*

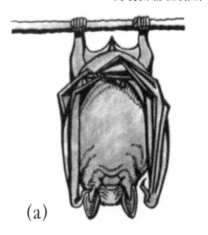

(a)   (b)

Fig. 14. *Artist's conception of the ahool. If this creature is a giant microbat and a fish-eater, it would have to look like this. Its face might well be likened to that of a monkey, and its feet would point backwards.*

close their wings as shown in Fig. 13(a). The biggest known bats are mega, or fruit-eaters, but just to muddle the issue, the largest micro—a horrible-looking denizen of the South American tropics named *Vampyrus spectrum,* with a wingspan of over two feet—is a fruit-eater! [35] Nonetheless, no micro wraps its wings around itself when suspended. Next, we come to this.

The hind feet of all bats, both mega and micro, point backwards, and they are the only mammals that display such a feature. Many microbats can run about on all fours like mice but their back feet still point backwards. Some of these bats can stand almost upright. No megabat ever does this. Now, if a microbat on all fours tilted back another 45 degrees, it *would* be standing upright; but its feet would still be pointing backwards.

The way in which the Ahool is said to stand, and the way in which it is said to fold its wings, would seem most clearly to indicate that it is a giant micro. Further, that its face should always be described as being sort of pushed in like that of some monkeys is also in conformity with the general run of micros, and especially the fish-eaters. And there *are* fish-eaters, such as the *Noctilionidae* of tropical America which scoop small fish and shrimp out of the surface waters of rivers and lagoons.[36] In fact, everything that the Javanese hunters told Dr. Bartels about the Ahool conforms exactly to what might be expected of an enormous fish-eating micro bat. One does not have to go into further details, like the claws on the wings. Only the young of a strange bird called the Hoatzin or Stinking Pheasant of the Guianas has any such thing.

If this Ahool exists—and I personally accept the accounts given by Dr. Bartels and, through him, those of his Sundanese Indonesian friends—it is my opinion that both it and the Olitiau of West Africa are giant *Microchiroptera.*

CHAPTER FOUR

ICARUS AND DRACO

W**HEN WE WERE** disc⟨
the great orm we very nearly became involved in the irk
matter of dragons, but managed to avoid the issue by the
manoeuvre of stepping smartly to one side. At the time wher
manoeuvred I did not know that I would be confronted witl
old bugbear again so soon. In fact, this piece of "dishonesty,"
nature so inherent in all of us—namely sweeping *things*
"things" under rugs—has come back to haunt me; and in a
with the general practice of haunts, it has popped up in the
unexpected quarter. I started out upon the road laid down fo
chapter with a somewhat glad heart, but a couple of months' rc
research upon what I had supposed to be a cut and dried "tl
albeit one enveloped in mystery, marvel, and paradox, has l⟨
me with a rather heavy heart. But, nonetheless, let me begin ⟨
beginning.

In the fall of 1960, three high school students who had
hobby the search for fossils, discovered some bones extruding
a lump of rock in an old quarry in Bergen County, New J
just across the Hudson River from New York.[37] The piece ol
in which they found this fossil was known to them to be of w
called Triassic age—which is to say, as now dated, some 180 t⟨

Fig. 15. *The skeleton of* Icarosaurus, *as revealed in the rock, enlarged from the photograph, Plate V*

millions of years old, and in which only the upper or latest levels contain the remains of the earliest dinosaurian-type reptiles.

This splendid trio of young men—Messrs. Alfred Siefker, Joseph Geiler, and Michael Bandrowski—were what are called "pretty bright kids," which is what I prefer to call "extremely intelligent young men." Despite the fact that only small portions of this fossil were visible, while the whole stratum was stuffed with other fossils, they immediately felt that they had something unique. So they took it over to the American Museum of Natural History in New York for identification. Dr. Edwin H. Colbert, then head of the Department of Palaeontology of that institution, and the man who probably knows more about fossil vertebrates than anybody else, took one look at this specimen and confirmed the boys' initial belief. From even what little of it could be seen at that time, Dr. Colbert was immediately able to state that the thing was indeed unique and constituted a discovery that could lead to the necessity for very considerable revision of our thinking upon many aspects of the remote history of the reptiles.[38]

As a result, the finders concurred in the suggestion that as much of the rest of the skeleton as might lie within the rock be brought to light by the most advanced techniques available in the museum's laboratories. This laborious work was undertaken by Mr. Gilbert Stucker, who spent many months working on it, so bringing many of the bones to light. This he did by using a jet-abrasive device under high power magnification. These bones were so delicate that this job could never have been done by the old methods, employing chisels. The results were stunning.

The original fossil is displayed in Plate III, but to understand what you are looking at, please take a look at Fig. 15, taken from a technical drawing made by Mr. Michael Insinna of the American Museum of Natural History, and precisely outlining and identifying all the bones as disposed. You should then take a look at Fig. 16 in which the skeleton is straightened out, and as many missing bones as possible on either side are drawn in by reversal; while "missing ones," the conformation and disposition of which would

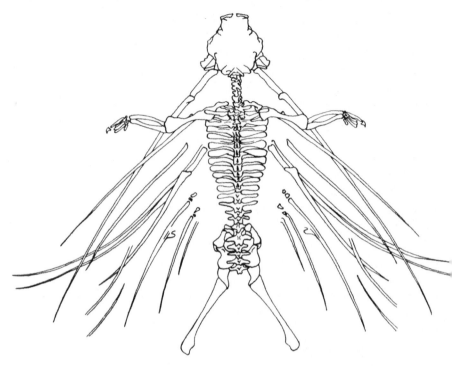

Fig. 16. *The same, with the spinal column straightened, and all bones present on both sides "mirrored"*

seem to be highly probable, are also displayed. Of the lower extremities of the hind legs we know nothing; but from the upper leg bones, it has been inferred that the legs were twice as long as the arms. This is a very important point to bear in mind. Next, in Fig. 17, we see all these bones assembled in their proper positions. Finally, we come to what is customarily called an artist's conception of this thing, fleshed-out (Fig. 18). In this case, we are lucky enough to have something well known to guide us, at least along general lines, as is herewith depicted in Fig. 19. This is the living flying lizard, or *Draco*. And here comes the "thing" out from under the rug.

Without going into technical details (which may be consulted in Dr. Colbert's paper [39]), I must ask you just to take me at my word upon the following matters. The *class* of backboned animals called reptiles are of considerably ancient origin, probably some 300 millions of years, though the earliest known fossils that can definitely be said to be reptiles, as distinct from their amphibian ancestors, are somewhat younger, geologically speaking. Reptiles may be divided into sixteen major groupings or *orders* if one takes into account both extinct and living forms. Of these, four have living representatives—the *Rynchocephalia,* represented today only by the little tuatara of New Zealand; the *Chelonia,* or tortoises and

Fig. 17. *Anterior portion of the skeleton of* Icarosaurus; *expanded, and rough outline of "flesh" added*

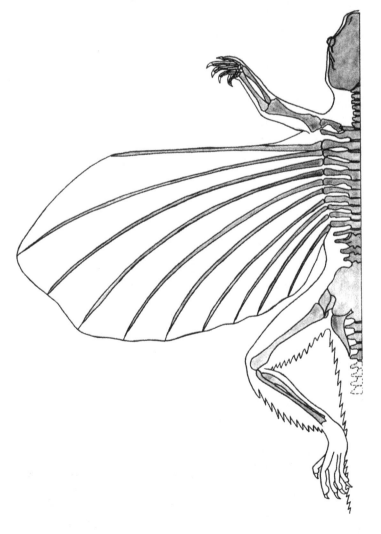

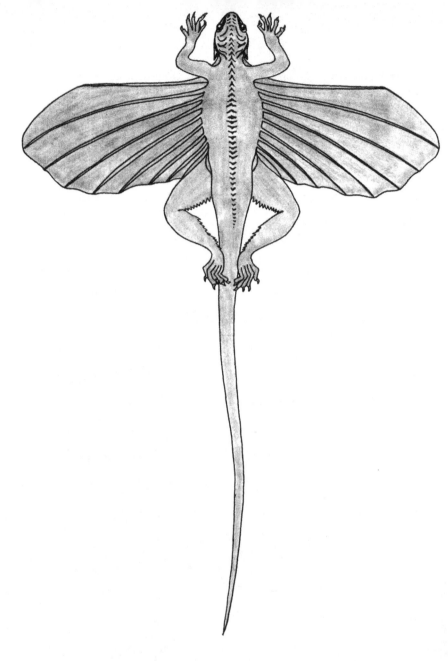

Fig. 18. *Icarosaurus*, "Fleshed Out." *This represents the nearest approximation possible (working from the reconstructed skeleton, as we know it) of this remarkable animal. Note that the wings are so large that, when folded, they must have been collapsed either above or below the hind legs. It is the considered opinion of Dr. Edwin H. Colbert (in a private communication) that they were so folded under the legs.*

Fig. 19. *Flying lizard* (Draco). *Outline of the living animal of the Oriental region*

turtles; the *Crocodilia;* and the *Squamata,* or snakes and lizards. Bearing in mind that there never was an *order* of reptiles entitled *Dinosauria,* we may simply say that all such creatures, so called properly, are extinct as far as we know; and, along with them, all the others of the total of twelve remaining orders.

Now, the little tuatara is a remnant of one of the earliest developed forms of reptiles, and the chelonians also go back to long before the evolution of the first creatures that might be called "dinosaurs." The crocodilians too have a most venerable ancestry; but the snakes and lizards have always been considered to be much later developments. Only comparatively recently have palaeontologists come into possession of *true* lizards of any kind from really early times, and now comes this thing from New Jersey.

This has been named *Icarosaurus,*[40] after the Cretan chap who legend states made a pair of wax wings but got too close to the sun so that they melted, and he fell into the Icarian Sea and was washed ashore on the Island of—even more appropriately—Icaria. The trouble with this fossil is that, instead of being a primitive sort of generalized reptile, showing only primitive lacertilian tendencies, it is a most highly evolved and almost ridiculously specialized creature, and thus obviously the end product of a very long line of development. It was, in fact, a glider, and of a most special type.

However, before proceeding to the more esoteric aspects of this case, I should clear the historical air by mentioning that while this specimen is itself unique, it does not stand absolutely alone: some bones, which, from their description (the specimens have been lost) by the famous collector Edward Drinker Cope, seem to be similar, though larger, were found in an equivalent Triassic formation at a place called Gwynned in Pennsylvania in 1866.[41] Also, another true lizard or lacertilian had turned up a few years before the discovery of this *Icarosaurus,* and also in a Triassic formation, but in southern England.[42] This was given the name *Kuehneosaurus.*

It is somewhat startling to realize that while all the so-called dinosaurs and millions of other types of reptiles great and small that got themselves evolved became extinct, "ordinary" lizards apparently got going even earlier and have persisted until today. It smacks of the marvellous to me that one of these lizards should further have been such an advanced creature as to have developed gliding flight. And there I would have rested my case had it not been for a fellow who named the living gliding lizards of the Orient, *Draco.*

As you may have gathered by now, I am a sort of semantic buff. I have always had a compulsive desire to ascertain the origin and meaning of words, and I have a very nice collection of dictionaries to which I fly at the drop of an *umlaut.* Thus, contemplating the attribution of the scientific name *Draco* to the flying lizards, I so flew (or perhaps glided) to these sources of all knowledge, and therein immediately ran head-on into a most extraordinary sort of bestiary. I still can't quite believe it; but there it all is, in print, and in two dozen languages—apart from Webster! That some of the statements made in these standard tomes should have been lying therein, unquestioned, for hundreds of years is quite beyond my comprehension. Let's start with *Draco.*

It transpires, at least according to the best sources, that this word was originally Greek but allegedly derived from the Sanskrit *Darc,* meaning "to see" (due to its fiery eyes).[43] I must admit that I take a somewhat dim view of this Sanskrit and those who trace modern words back to it. How does the sound *darsth* (i.e., *darç*) get converted to *drakk?* But be that as it may, we find the Greeks coming up with drakon from this root *drakk* (or *derk*) as in *derkomai,* meaning "to see." Next, of course, the Romans come along and put it down as *draco.* But then two things appear to have happened. The first is highly significant, the second almost incomprehensible. Let me endeavour to dispose of them in this order.

It appears that when the Romans ran into the Dacians, a warlike bunch of people who inhabited the lowlands from what is now Hungary east to Bessarabia, they found contingents of Parthians fighting with these, their enemies. These were wild mounted nomads from the far eastern plains who carried banners bearing great orms, with gaping jaws, heads made of silver, and bodies constructed of silk bags which ballooned when air entered their mouths as the horsemen galloped.[44] The Romans immediately identified them as their dracones; and when Trajan conquered the Dacians and romanized them—hence the present Romanians—he bestowed this dragon emblem upon a group of legions. So the Parthian "Dragons" reached western Europe as a standard, giving rise to the *dragons* of the French and the *dragoons* of the British armies. It also became the royal war standard of the British kings. Later the French bore guns with a dragon's head and mouth around their muzzles.[45]

The interesting point about this bunch of dragons is that they were both wingless and legless, and thus altogether of northern rather than southern or Mediterranean provenance. They were neither the drakon of the Greeks nor the traditional dragons of the Chinese, while they exactly fit the great orms of the far north. It should be noted, tangentially here, that the same creature popped up again later in the form of the Draki of the Norse, which was often used as the figurehead on the prow of their larger war ships called by that name. In this the Norse seem to have combined their longnecks of the sea with the great orm of the land.

None of this, however, had anything to do with the little winged things of the eastern Mediterranean; and this brings us to the other outcome of the adoption of said Greek concept by the Romans. If you will look up *Draco* in a Latin-English dictionary, you will find that the word is masculine and that it means: "A species of serpent or snake; a dragon (those of the tame sort, especially the Epidaurian, were kept as pets by luxurious Romans)." [46] Now what on earth is all this about? Moreover, certain larger dictionaries, such as the Oxford, further state: "Mythical monster, like crocodile or snake with wings and claws, and often breathing fire." [47] Since when were there snakes with wings or claws or aerial crocodiles? Mythical they may have been, but what then *did* these "luxurious" (*sic*)—one assumes they mean "luxury-loving"—Romans keep as pets? And just what did this Epidaurus place have that nobody else had? There is a further mix-up here in that there were two Epidauruses in late Roman times; one on the Dalmatian coast and the other on the Arcian Gulf, between the Peloponnese and the main body of the Hellenic peninsula on the Aegean side. The word means literally "The place upon a place that is the color of gold." Both Epidauruses were indeed built on areas of yellowish colored rocks.

Now, while there are some small lizards and snakes in both areas, there are not and almost certainly never have been flying examples of either at either place. However, comes then a very strange coincidence. The Greek Epidaurus was the headquarters of one Aesculapius, the "father" of medicine, and his symbol has come down to us as a staff around which are twined two snakes. But what is much more significant is that said entwined snakes have a number of pairs of little, fingerlike appendages evenly distributed down their bodies. What is this? It smacks of a great orm.

Next, we have the Daedalus-Icarus so-called myth from about the same parts.[48] The general impression left by this tale, and duly recorded by the pragmatic Romans, was that the father made a pair of very large but light-weight wings and flapped off into the sky like a bird, but that his son's wings melted and he fell into the sea. The bit about said wings being made of wax is obviously nonsense, even for a myth, so that we may infer that whatever they were made of was "waxed." This is a reasonable assumption if we would go along with Strabo and certain very early Veddic Indian chroniclers and look upon this whole account as being that of a Cretan who developed a *glider.* There are all kinds of hints about gliders in ancient literature, and there are some dashed rum aspects to the whole business of gliding. Let me quote from an ex-military glider pilot, Mr. Jack A. Ullrich:

> The most efficient glider configurations are seen among
> birds, which have very high aspect-ratio—by this I mean
> wing-span versus width of wing. Powered aircraft do not have
> high-aspect ratios—with the notable exception of the U-2
> of Gary Powers fame. Unpowered gliders—i.e., sail planes—do
> have a very high ratio, and the best performance was exhibited
> by a flying wing design of the brothers Horten in Germany

during the 1940s. Their glide ratio was 1:45, greater than an albatross, and I do not believe this has been exceeded.

Everybody has always assumed that to glide one has to start off from a high point and launch out over a low point, as in our own early gliders that we shoved off hills or, as all these flying squirrels, opossums, and these so-called flying lizards do, from trees. However, quite a number of years ago we learned that we could get gliders aloft by towing them or catapulting them along a runway into a wind. Now, a rather agile chap has pointed out that the larger pterodactyls (see Fig. 12), that had an even greater wing-area ratio than any albatross or any of Jack Ullrich's German experimental sailplanes, would not have had to launch themselves from anything.[49] Rather, all they had to do was spread their enormous wings, head into any breeze there might be, or if there was even the slightest updraft from a sun-heated surface, give a little jump and then go soaring off. The whole process is dependent upon the ratio of wing area to body weight, and in this the short-tailed pterodactyls such as this pteranodon far surpassed any other known animal, living or extinct. To get a man thus airborne would require positively enormous wings and these of very light weight. The best materials with which to construct such are fabrics, and the best way to preserve these in rain and shine is to *wax* them. (Shellac and plastics were unknown in those days.)

This brings us back to our *Icarosaurus* and the little *Dracos* of today. These so-called "flying" lizards are the most enchanting little creatures, found from Burma to Indonesia and in a limited area in southern India and in Ceylon. I spent many delightful hours watching them in the deep gorges of the northern mountains of Sumatra on my first trip to the tropics. These little narrow valleys were choked with rather widely-spaced giant forest trees between which was a sort of fairy garden of beautiful flowering shrubs and palms of all sizes. The sun drenched these paradises every day, and all day, until the great black thunder clouds gathered over the mountains and the lightning started flickering at some three beats to the minute as it does every night before the rains come in that country.

These gorges are full of life, notably of the most gorgeously colored butterflies, so imagine my surprise and delight when I first -saw what I imagined to be a butterfly, arc across the gorge as if propelled by a jet drive. It was bright green in color with vivid iridescent blue and black bands on its wings. These wings fluttered, but in a most odd manner and quite unlike those of a butterfly. Greatly puzzled, as I was comparatively very young then and not prepared for three-quarters of the wildlife that I would encounter in the East Indies, I stalked this creature, only to put to flight dozens more of an extraordinary variety of color patterns. They all landed on tree trunks and became instantly invisible by closing their wings, but eventually I got near enough to one to observe it closely. I then noted a most pertinent fact.

These little lizards close their "wings" so tightly that you really can not see them. After they land they proceed to run up the tree trunks in fits and starts, and very fast, but using their limbs in the typical left-front, right-back, right-front, left-back way of ordinary terrestrial lizards and other animals. Moreover, their front and back limbs are just about equal in length. (Bear this in mind.) These lovely little animals have also three head appendages, one a gular flap under their chins, the others on either hind edge of the lower jaws. They constantly bob their heads, after they have reversed themselves on the tree boles and have their heads pointing downwards. Then at the slightest sign of danger, or if they spot insect food at a distance, they launch out into the air, but this they do in a most curious way, and quite unlike what one might expect.

Instead of jumping off and then opening their "wings"—which are, of course, thin membranes supported by greatly lengthened ribs that point outwards, horizontally on both sides—they open them first and then rush down the trunk with their heads held upwards, and with the submandibular gular flange fully extended; which, of course, running fore and aft, acts as a vane, like the upright fin on the tail of an airplane. Gathering speed and aided by gravity, they then just let go of the tree trunk, but keep on "running" in the air for a brief period, even after they are airborne.

Now, this brings us squarely back to *Icarosaurus*. We must note, and I quote from Dr. Colbert's paper in *Novitates* [50], that this beastie had legs twice as long as the *Dracos*: the hind limb evidently being considerably longer than the forelimb, as indicated by the fact that the femur is about twice the length of the humerus. This means that the animal had more the proportions of a bird, and a perching bird at that. These are also the proportions of the terrestrial running dinosaurian reptiles and of certain lizards today, notably some iguanids of Central America known as *basilisks* (*Basiliscus, Coryophanes, et alii*), which, so help me, gets us involved in still another aggravation.

These living basilisk lizards are primarily terrestrial, but they do climb trees, though for the most part by hopping like birds; and they leap off them from really rather alarming heights when disturbed, and then go high-tailing it along the ground, gathering so much speed that they can actually *run over the surface* of quite wide streams. This is the most amazing thing to witness. When they run, they rise on their hind legs alone, curve their tails up into the air, raise their heads, spread what gular folds they have and just dash. They also have sort of vanes on the backs of their heads; these also aid them in steering at high speed.

From all this, it might be suggested that the little *Icarosaurus* was of like habits; and, as opposed to behaving like the present-day *Dracos* which run up or down tree-trunks, use all four legs, spread-eagle fashion. Let us, then, contemplate a high-speed terrestrial lizard like *Basiliscus* which might have developed two flaps of skin along the sides of its body. Such devices would soon become most handy in dashes across open stretches of water, and the more rigid they were, the bigger lift they would give such an hysterical dasher. What more obvious than that the outer (previously inner, having been curved under the belly) joint of the ribs should grow out to support these flaps? Might *Icarosaurus* have been such a super-dasher-abouter in swamps, rather than a tree climber, and *Draco* be a case of mere parallel evolution, using the same anatomical structures (the ribs) but for a quite different purpose? And this brings us to the matter of birds.

There are really three quite separate groups of what we call birds: the penguins, the ratites, and all the rest. The ratites, which includes the extinct moas, and the ostriches, emus, cassowaries, rheas and such, have long running legs and either small (the ostriches) or minute wing bones (the kiwis), none of which are capable of sustaining the birds in the air. However, the ostrich and the rhea get a very considerable "lift" from them, when going flat out into the wind. In fact, rheas sometimes are actually airborne for short distances. From the construction of the bones of the forelimbs of ratites, it has been inferred that they are descended from birds that once flew. I'm not so sure. Take a look at a creature called *Struthiomimus* (Fig. 20). Reduce its tail, which was obviously only a balancing organ; and then its little hands, and you end up with something altogether too much like an ostrich for comfort. In fact, could the forelimb construction of ratites, on the one hand, and of other birds, on the other, also be a case of parallel evolution?

Fig. 20. *Struthiomimus. A late Cretaceous, Ornithopod dinosaur. Note the way in which this animal balanced itself* (after *Gerhard Heilmann*).

The famous *Archaeornis* (see Fig. 21) would seem to show how ordinary birds developed. But while they had claws on the wings and their limbs were subequal in length, they were still "hoppers" and not climbers like the *Dracos*, as is shown by the construction of their back legs. Is it possible that they also developed from fast runners rather than from tree-jumpers? Suppose that both the ratites and the other birds—and let's leave the penguins out of this—*both* started as runners, using their forelimbs as planes, but that the former never got farther than that, while the others started flapping them and so managed to get up into the air and then stay aloft.

So, once again, we come back to the ratio of wingspan and area, to body size, form, and weight. Once you have such a dichotomy started, the virtually "armless'" kiwis form an end of the first development, and the heavy-bodied but small-winged ducks that of the other. In the middle, stand the soarers and gliders like the albatrosses, gulls, eagles, and such; while the swifts that spend almost their entire lives in the air have got something else again in that, although basically gliders, they have developed a form of

Fig. 21. *Archaeornis. Combined reconstruction* (after *Gerhard Heilmann*) *of the famous reptile-bird found in the Solenhofen slate deposits of Bavaria, Germany, in 1877.*

jet propulsion which, combined with what we regard as normal flapping flight, makes them the fastest of all birds. Some giant swifts passed an RAF plane flying over Iran at 200 mph.[51]

Reptiles took to the air in two ways. The pterodactyls planed and probably also actually flap-flew, while *Icarosaurus* and the *Dracos* took to gliding. And in doing these things, the former sort of "used up" their forelimbs, but the latter did not. This brings us back to the things I call third class dragons.

As of now I designate the standard, scaly creatures of the Far East, depicted with tentacles and four reptilian-type legs—with five toes for royalty, four for aristocrats, three for gentry, and two for the nouveau riche—as first class dragons. The legless, slimy great orms I regard as second class; while these winged things which appear to be originally West Eurasian, with headquarters in the Near East, I now consider to be definitely of third class status.

These third class dragons are all small compared to the others, but they are the traditional dragons of our western cultures, because they had wings as well as limbs. Later artists did, in truth, sometimes add wings to second class dragons, such as those with which Saints George, Patrick, Michael, and the Germanic heroes coped, but none of the contemporary representations of these ever had wings or limbs. They were, in fact, great orms. The little third class dragons, on the other hand, always had wings *as well as clawed limbs,* and some had little crowns on their heads! These were called basilisks and were said to live in wells and to produce the direst results upon anyone who looked upon them.[52]

Then there is this Aesculapius character in Greece with his serpents entwined on a staff, and the Cretan fellows trying to cross the Aegean with a glider; and finally, we come to this (seemingly ridiculous) statement in the dictionaries to the effect that "Luxurious Romans kept the tamer kind [of winged dragon] from Epidaurus, as pets." What on earth could have started this myth, or tradition, around the Aegean?

They don't have any large lizards there, and while crocodiles could have been imported from Egypt as babies and kept as pets, just as we used to keep baby Alligators from Florida, crocodiles don't have wings. Beside, they were perfectly well known to the Romans. Then again, these basilisks and other third class dragons were always said to have also had *two* pairs of clawed appendages. Nothing known fits such a bizarre description except the living *Dracos* of the Orient, and this *Icarosaurus*. But, who has ever suggested that there were gliding lizards in the eastern Mediterranean area? So what are we left with?

The word *drakon* in earlier Greek parlance meant basically any large snake, so that this weird reference to a "tame variety from Epidaurus kept by "luxurious Romans" might have been meant to imply no more than that they kept large non-poisonous snakes. Although really large snakes are not known ever to have been indigenous to the Hellenic area, we *do* have "Python," a mythical beast that haunted the caves of Parnassus and which was slain by Apollo (read Saint George!), that in every way conforms to the notion of a great orm, being a subterranean dweller and limbless.[53] Also we have Laocoön, who clearly shows that the large pythons of Africa or the Orient were imported; and—although you doubtless won't believe this—these snakes can make extremely amiable, reliable, and considerably intelligent pets.

However, there are two features of these third class dragons that argue against their being either great orms or very large snakes. These are, first, the emphasis on great vision and, second, their wings. The great orms, according to carvings, do not seem to have had any eyes at all—and the eyes of caecilians are either minute or under the skin (see Chapter 2)—while the pythons have small eyes and are notoriously bad of vision.

I do not have an answer to all this and I have been unable even to come up with a logical suggestion, unless perhaps that those marvellous seamen who carried on trade between Egypt and Mesopotamia and the Orient might have brought some gliding lizards or *Dracos*—along with apes and peacocks—as curiosities for sale to the "luxurious" in the Mediterranean. But this is very far-fetched, so I suppose we just have to sweep this irksome matter, once again, under some rug or blanket of obfuscation and obscurity.

CHAPTER FIVE

EGGS, AWFUL AND
SO ON

ALAS, WE ALL take eggs for granted, and thus miss one of the greater pleasures of life. Eggs have rightly been pointed out to be one of the two best efforts of the Almighty—the other being bananas. Given a quota of water, you can live exclusively on either of them, while both are devoid of pips, pits, bones, or other included nuisances, and both come in neat packets with outer, more or less impervious, coverings that can be easily and cleanly removed. So what is there to get so excited about *in re* "oeufs"?

I have mentioned before [54] the considerably shocking effect upon my complacency occasioned by discovering a dime in the yolk of a hen's egg served to me on a train going from New York to Woods Hole, Massachusetts, on my way to Nantucket. It was a genuine dime and had the profile of the late Franklin Delano Roosevelt embossed upon it. It was scabrous and surrounded by a nimbus of horrible gangrenous-looking stuff. The egg itself was, nonetheless, perfectly fresh. Point: ask any biologist, or even a medical doctor, how such an object can get into the fallopian tubes of a hen and thus into one of the eggs maturing therein. There is no connection between the alimentary canal of an animal and its reproductive apparatus. Nor is this the only unpleasantness that I have found in otherwise perfectly decent hens' eggs, and I am not the only person so to discover. The list of such "unauthorized" objects that I have accumulated is absolutely shocking, but since no biologist worth his salt would allow any such nonsense and no ordinary citizen should even so much as mention such obscenities, I will not list the details here.

Then there are the funny and outrageous eggs, of domestic birds *per se,* which is to say hens, give or take a few ducks, turkeys, and geese. Who has not broken into an egg with two yolks? Fair enough: "We get twins, don't we?" But when you ge-slosh an ordinary-looking egg into a pan with a view to poaching same, and *four* yolks come out, you may well be permitted to become vaguely enthusiastic. So what about the poor lady in Milano, Italy, who alleges that 37 yolks fell out? [55] Then again, the average hen is a modest bird, size-wise (despite those enormous Buff Orpingtons that they display in poultry shows); while its cloaca, which is the technical term for the orifice at its back end out of which eggs come, is agreeably expandable, one really does begin to wonder when a standard model (Rhode Island Red) gives rise (or descent) to an egg of the proportions shown in the accompanying photograph (see Plate IV). The caption attached to the original of this masterpiece read as follows: "THE EGGONY AND EGGSTACY. Proud mother hen inspects her young fry in Salem, Oregon, where she laid an egg eight inches in diameter and lived to cackle about it. Another hen was killed by a 6¾-inch egg." [56] This caption, we contend, is a masterpiece in its own right and could probably not have been penned by any except the New York *Daily News*.

But there is something wrong here, and on several counts. First, judging from the hen's head, this egg is by no means 8 inches in *diameter,* even measured through its long axis; so it would seem that its *circumference* is meant, and around the short axis at that. This would give a diameter of about 2.6 inches, which is still quite an egg for an ordinary hen to lay. That this would seem to be the true dimensions is somewhat confirmed by the accompanying photograph of a mynah bird (see Plate V) inspecting an ostrich egg which had a diameter of 4½ inches across its shorter axis.

Since my general theme here is awful eggs, I cannot help but interject another class of oological "atrocity" before proceeding with my special theme, which is the *size* of eggs. One such item that I stumbled across several years ago was an egg laid by a White Leghorn owned by a Mr. T. R. Reed of Kincardine, Ontario, Canada. This had on one side a perfectly circular clock or watch face with little, smudgy, but quite clear spots, regularly arranged around, as on a clock-face, and the hands showing two o'clock precisely.[57] (There was no evidence that it had been laid at that time.) A most peculiar feature of this was that the dial only *appeared* to be precisely circular when the egg was held exactly horizontally. In fact, the outline of the dial was a most complicated ovoid when traced off and flattened out, and which somehow overcame the optical effects of the complex curvatures of the egg-shell! This is by no means the only record of an egg with a depiction on it; but it shows signs of getting us into a somewhat different field, one that I propose to take up in detail only at another time, since it would seem to me to fall, rather, into the matter of "marked animals."

Suffice it to say on this score that I had never believed in this (or even the published photographs of such), until a perfectly splendid crossbred Dalmatian-English-Foxhound bitch was given to me by a neighbour and gave birth to a litter of five absolutely irresistible, fluffy, black and white pups. All these had basically white bodies but with black ears and some sparse but large black blotches. Precisely central on the foreheads of three of these puppies were most clearly defined capital letters "A," "B," and "C," while the other two had designs that could well have been letters in some other script for all I know. We kept A, B, and C (as we naturally called them) until they reached maturity. Then, in the space of two months, they were killed by being run over by a car, a diesel train, and a motorcycle respectively—and in precisely alphabetical order! I frankly don't like this kind of business.

But to revert to the size of eggs: very few people realize just how small our human cranium or brain-box is. It averages only about eight inches in length and is thus just about the same size, and of the same capacity, as a large ostrich egg *—as is demonstrated by the courtesy of Mr. Adolph Heuer (see Plate VI).

This is not an entirely frivolous exercise because it serves to bring to popular attention another really very startling fact about eggs. This is that, while a human brain contains several billion cells, all eggs are *single* cells. If a mere ostrich egg can have the same capacity as my friend Adolph Heuer's brain-box, we might really wonder about certain other comparisons—at least, by the time we get to the end of this parade of awful eggs.

Eggs are the basis of everything in the world of life. Actually, they are nothing more than the resting stage of single-celled animals, so that an encysted amoeba is really "an egg." All multicelled plants and animals start out as "eggs," in which are contained the "plans" for the creature that will emerge from said egg, typed into the DNA molecules of its genes. Most eggs are microscopic, and not just because the majority of animals are exceedingly small. For instance, the egg of an elephant is also microscopic. In every class of animals, some eggs may be encountered with large stores of nutrient for the development of their embryos before hatching. The size of the parent, however, does not seem to have much to do with the size of its egg. A dreary form of arthropod creature related to spiders, called a podogonid, which I happened to discover deep in a cave in Yucatan at a time when it was breeding, staggers about with an egg clasped under its body, between two special, spiked organs. The egg is nearly twice the size of the animal's own body. On the other hand, the record sturgeon fish measured over 28 feet; but it still started from a single egg (of Beluga caviar) only an eighth of an inch in diameter. But it is the hard-shelled eggs that have always intrigued people.

Our lower primate progenitors appear to have been well aware of such eggs as food; and lower still on the scale of our ancestry, we

---

* The average Modern Caucasoid Man has a brain capacity of 1450 cc; [58] the average ostrich egg, 1050 cc. However, Anatole France's brain-box had a capacity of only 1000 cc.

find quite a number of exclusive egg-eaters. Several birds, and notably the curious Secretary Bird of Africa, have a predilection for eggs, swallowing them whole, to be crushed by stones in their crops.

Reptile eggs are rather dull, but birds' eggs can be very pretty, and they long ago gave rise to the destructive hobby of egg-collecting and also to the science of oology. (The eggs of the mammals called the duckbilled platypus and the spiny-anteaters, or echidnas, are odd but dreary.) The avian branch of oology is an absorbing subject; and this quite apart from the lovely colors and color patterns of the eggs themselves. There is an enormous textbook on the hen's egg,[59] and the egg industry is equally enormous, having its own trade journal, the name of which has always delighted me—to wit, *Cackle and Crow.* The average citizen regards a bird's egg as being merely a yolk surrounded by "white" and encased in a shell. Actually, it has two dozen major parts and an enormous list of lesser ones, and quite apart from the complexities of its chemistry.

To return once again to our main theme, we have to put on record some observations on birds' eggs generally before we can get on to their more awful aspects. The shape of eggs constitutes another whole subject and one that drives solid-geometers crazy. Most eggs —apart from freaks—have a precise geometric form. Among birds, these are either the spherical, or the ovoid. The latter is a rather loose term, since the proportions of ovoids vary greatly. The reason given for the majority of eggs being ovoids is that, when blown about by wind or otherwise disturbed while in the nest (or simply laid on a flat rock surface), they roll around in a circle instead of going over the edge like Ping-Pong balls. The spherical eggs of owls, be it noted, are laid in the bottom of holes in trees and so forth, so that they are in no danger of rolling off.

I don't know how many of you may have had the good luck to find a hummingbird's nest. They are absolutely delightful in their tininess and their perfection of construction. I was once clearing some tall weeds and little saplings by one of my ponds and sud-

77

denly received a sharp bash behind my left ear. At first I thought a wasp had dive-bombed me, but then a hummingbird came and helicoptered right in front of my nose with obvious intent to renew her warning. As I flicked my eyes down in case she jab one with her needle-sharp bill, I found myself staring into her nest which was precisely centered between four large leaves at the top of a slender woody stem, and right below my nose. In it were four minute eggs neatly arranged north, south, east, and west. I could hardly believe my eyes, so small were they. However, one of the sun birds, which are in no way related to the hummingbirds but which fill the equivalent ecological niche in the Old World, has even smaller eggs than this ruby-throated hummingbird that I encountered. An Englishman interested in ornithology showed me a clutch of three of the eggs of a tiny species in West Africa. They were colored vivid blue and were smaller than the individual eggs of a common frog.

Now, reptiles lay eggs, and one might therefore reasonably presume that the largest reptiles laid the largest eggs of all time. Of course, we do not know even whether the majority of the larger dinosaurian reptiles laid eggs at all, or whether they were live-bearers, but the only dinosaurian eggs that we do have, and which we can type precisely because fully formed embryos were found in some, were of modest proportions, if not very small for the animals that emerged from them. These were the famous eggs found by the late Roy Chapman Andrews in the Gobi Desert [60] and were those of a donkey-sized reptile, related to the super-rhino-sized *Triceratops,* and named *Monoclonius.* Egg size is not necessarily related to adult body size as we pointed out in the case of caviar and the sturgeons. If a 28-foot fish can grow from an egg only $\frac{1}{8}$ of an inch in diameter, one can but allow that an 80-foot brontosaur could lay eggs not necessarily bigger than those of a chicken—or even of a hummingbird, I suppose. A grotesque thought indeed!

Naturally, eggs laid in water need not be as big as those deposited in air with hard shells because they do not need the large amounts of food storage for the growing embryo. In fact, one would suppose that hard-shelled eggs would increase in size as the food available for the emerged animal decreased, such as for vegetable feeders in deserts. This again is not the case. The largest eggs, compared to the size of the animals that lay them, appear to be those of such primitive birds as the kiwi of New Zealand, the eggs of both species of which are positively enormous, being about a third of the size of the parent; whereas the eggs of the giant moa (*Dinornis maximus*) of the same country—which when standing up ostrich-style reached 15 feet—were comparatively modest in proportion, being not much more than two ostrich eggs in capacity. Which brings us to the awful department.

The ratites or flightless birds do not, on the whole, have the biggest eggs in proportion to their size. Ratites are a strange lot. Some of them have tiny degenerated bone and muscular wing structures, others have none at all, but the ostriches have pretty fair ones. From the construction of these wings it is inferred that the ratites are descended from birds that once flew. Birds are, however, nothing but reptiles that developed feathers and some other special anatomical features. A missing link between the two groups are the famous *Archaeopteryx* and *Archaeornis* (see Fig. 21), found in the Solenhofen slate quarries in Germany. However, there are some late, cursorial (running) dinosaurian-type reptiles—notably a splendid beast named *Struthiomimus* (see Fig. 20)—that look for all the world like long-tailed ostriches. I am not suggesting that the ratites are descended from these, but I do go along with the suggestion that the birds have a dual or multiple origin. What is more, the construction of the eggs of the ratites sets them clearly apart from all other living birds.

The largest egg known is that of another equally splendid extinct creature known to science as *Aepyornis*. This is believed to be the origin of the story of the Ruc or "Roc" of fable, a legend emanating from Madagascar. Sinbad the Sailor tells of having encountered, or heard of, these huge birds, firsthand; but his account, as it surfaced in *The Thousand and One Nights,* became a bit exaggerated to say the least. The thing was said therein to fly and to be so big that it could carry off elephants! *Aepyornis,* otherwise

79

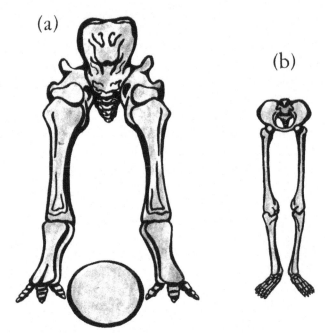

Fig. 22. *Pelvis and lower limbs of the extinct Madagascan giant flightless bird,* Aepyornis (a), *and those of a man* (b). *Note the size of the egg of the former; while that of the latter is microscopic.*

known as the elephant bird on account of its enormously massive leg bones (see Fig. 22), was flightless as we now know from complete fossil skeletons. It stood up to nine feet tall, ostrich-fashion, and it was undoubtedly still existing at the time of Marco Polo (who mentioned it also) [61] and of the early Arabian travellers. Its bones are quite plentiful in a semi- or sub-fossilized condition, and its vast eggs are almost common, still being found in swamps by probing with light canes, or coming out of sandbanks. These awful eggs have a volume of some two gallons and thus the equivalent of more than six ostrich eggs or a full gross of hens' eggs, and they weigh about 18 pounds. They range in size from 10%₁₆ to 15⅜ inches in length (see chart).

Now, these eggs greatly impressed the first European mariners to reach the island of Madagascar where they found them being used by the locals for storing water and other liquids, and they took them away in considerable numbers both to hold rum (distilled on other islands where there were no bottles or other containers available) and farther afield, as curios. And here come a couple of od- -dities and enigmas. In fact, both are truly awful.

The first goes as follows and is quoted directly from a very serious, pompous, and long-established British publication called *The Field*: [62]

> Sir, Recently, while fishing the famous Stowe Lakes near
> Buckingham, a well-known local angler, Mr. Dick Herring,
> made a remarkable "catch." He noticed a strange looking object
> floating half-submerged and partly covered with black mud
> and when he had successfully netted it he found he had
> "caught" a giant egg with a circumference of no less than 35
> inches. The shell was the colour of weathered stone and was
> in excellent condition. It had not been pierced. The verdict
> of an expert ornithologist is that it was laid by a member of
> the genus *Aepyornis,* the enormous flightless birds which
> inhabited the marshes of Madagascar but which have been
> extinct for 200 years. Giant egg shells have been found there
> from time to time, and from these probably arose the legends
> of the "roc" of the ancient Arabian voyagers. Naturalists have
> been rewarded by the discovery of bones of these birds,
> showing them to have reached a height of 10 feet. They were
> ostrich-like, but had no wings. The age of the Stowe egg has
> been estimated to be 500 years. It is likely that it was once in
> a collection that belonged to one of the Dukes of Buckingham.
> The mystery remains—how long has it been floating undiscovered
> in Stowe Lakes, and how did it come to be there?
>
> J. Gray
Quest,
Maids Moreton, Buckingham

This is really very alarming, and if you want to see for yourself just why, borrow a seamstress' tape measure and make a circle of thirty-five inches on a table top and then measure the diameter.

It comes out at 11.4 inches, and by calculation from the photograph of this egg, its long-axis diameter would be 14.58 inches. Of course, one must allow that it could have been mere ducal dejecta that somehow got away and remained floating, but as we say in Scotland and especially of anything reported from England, "I ha' me doots," and therefore I personally prefer to think that it was washed out of some swamps, such as are still prevalent along the upper reaches of the River Ouse, and that it could, therefore, be an example of another type of awful egg that we will now encounter. This comes from, of all places, southern Australia.

In the year 1930, the younger son of a ranching family living near a place called Nannup, some 250 miles south of Perth, Western Australia, was rounding up cattle down in the coastal sand dunes and left his horse tethered in order to look around for cattle tracks. This man's name was Vic Roberts, and he had with him a friend named Chris Morris. Vic spotted a vast egg just lying on top of the sand. It was very heavy. (It has not yet been stated whether it is fossilized, filled with something, petrified, or just plain heavy.) Nearby he found some bones and a very large skull with a beak.

Vic Roberts' mother was a school teacher and a lady of rather wide knowledge, and she was considerably excited by her son's find. She said it looked like the egg of an *Aepyornis.* She wrote to the West Australian Museum in Perth about this thing, but the curators there merely asked her to bring it in for them to look at. It was a long haul in those days, so she had her daughter take some photographs with a hen's egg for comparison and sent these in. Nothing happened, so she gave up and just sat on the thing until one Harry Butler, a well-known Australian naturalist who has done much collecting for Australian and foreign museums in his country, got wind of it in 1962. He visited the farm, was shown the egg, and set some wheels in motion. Finally, the object was given to the museum in Perth on permanent loan by Vic Roberts. It was put on display and became a worldwide five-day wonder, but then it just sat on its pedestal in the museum forever after.

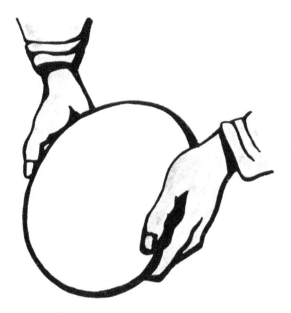

Fig. 23. *The "Awful Australian Egg"*

This is a fascinating enough story in itself, but it has a wildly fortean aspect that has been overlooked. Harry Butler tells in his article [63] of Vic Roberts having later found some more bones and another skull; while he himself was shown some flat rocks on which were the imprints of kangaroos' and other modern animal's tracks, as well as some enormous *four*-toed bird tracks. These form nearly a "cross" in that the middle toe, front, is in direct line with a backwardly-pointing one.

Now, most people will immediately say that you can't imprint tracks into solid stone, and they would be quite right. However, imprints in mud or other soft ground surfaces can be very rapidly "fossilized" themselves, if said surface is dried hard and then a layer of silt is deposited upon it which then too dries.[64] Mere chemical leaching and drying may turn many surface materials, and especially in lagoons and beaches, to stone in very short order. We once assisted the Mexican police in chiselling some truck tracks out of what was very tough and solid sandstone! [65] The Australia

83

tracks, however, look more like weather-worn petroglyphs made by man, as they included also some strange symbols.

Harry Butler goes on to speculate what bird could have laid this egg, giving several possibilities. First, that it was some huge species of emu, suspected from some bones and eggshell fragments found in Queensland (and some locations in South Australia) to have existed in Pleistocene times. Second, that it might be an *Aepyornis* egg that had been washed out of a sandbank in Madagascar and floated across the Indian Ocean. (The currents to make this possible *do* exist, and junk from the other side of the ocean *does* sometimes come ashore about this point.) Another suggestion was that it was a trophy that came off one of the whalers that used customarily to call in at Southwest Australia after leaving Madagascar. But his last suggestion is the most pertinent. He says: "New evidence may turn up that will clinch matters for one of these possibilities—*or that will indicate that an entirely new explanation is correct* [Italics mine]." [66]

In 1948 there was a tremendous uproar in Florida about a protracted series of enormous three-toed foot tracks that cropped up on beaches for several months, ending about forty miles up the Suwannee River. We investigated this case personally and it is described in detail in my book entitled *More "Things."* [67] It is a very long story, but may be summarized by saying that, when all was said and done, the *only* known kind of animal that could leave such tracks would be a giant penguin; and two dozen sane, sober citizens said they saw just such a creature along that coast that year, and all concurred in that it stood about fifteen feet tall and had enormous feet! The same year, the skeleton of a seven-foot penguin was found in New Zealand. Then, the presence of such creatures was brought to light through early descriptions of the Kerguelen Islands which lie in the middle of the south Indian Ocean. Penguins are southern hemisphere birds—though one species just gets north of the equator in the Galápagos Islands—and they are essentially sub-Antarctic creatures. They all go ashore together once a year to lay their eggs and to rear their young, and at special places only.

Giant penguin tracks have been recorded from all around the

*S*UPER-*E*GGS

Animal	Short-axis Diameter*			Long-axis Diameter*			Circumference*			Capacity
	in.	cm.	mm.	in.	cm.	mm.	in.	cm.	mm.	cc.
Record Chicken	2 9/16	7	66	3 3/8	9	86	8 1/2	21	207	151
Kiwi	2 3/4	7	70	5	13	127	8 5/8	22	219	179
Ostrich	4 1/2	11	114	6 1/2	17	165	14 1/8	36	359	777-1,005
Modern Human Brain										(average) 1,480
Largest Moa	7 3/4	20	197	10 1/4	26	261	24 5/16	62	617	3,948
Small Aepyornis	8 1/2	22	217	10 9/16	27	269	26 11/16	68	678	5,283
Australian	8 1/2	22	217	11 1/2	29	292	26 11/16	68	678	5,283
English Floater	11 1/8	28	283	14 9/16	37	370	35	89	891	10,187
Largest Aepyornis	12 9/16	32	320	15 3/8	39	391	39 1/2	101	1005	16,720

* To nearest 1/16" or round number.

Antarctic oceans and as far north as Queensland, and even Nantucket Island in the northern hemisphere. Penguins are great
wanderers and they might, in some cases, lose their way and get
north of the equator via the great cold Humboldt, Benguella, and
West Australian currents. Southwest Australia is right in their natural range. Did one get washed ashore there in a storm and have a
ready-to-lay egg in it, which was left intact when the body rotted
away or was taken apart by beachcombing animals, and then just
lay around on the surface of the sand? If there are such giant
penguins, this could have happened only a couple of years, or even
months, before Vic Roberts found the egg.

The easiest, simplest, and most comfortable way in which to
explain this awful egg is to attribute it to *Aepyornis* of Madagascar
—within the range and size of which (see chart) it falls—and
to infer that it was a trophy carried away by seamen. But not only is
this somewhat extreme, it is not as yet backed up by any concrete
evidence; evidence, moreover, that could quite well be obtained.
The shell construction and composition of ratite eggs is most distinctive; so are those of penguins. Then also, the eggs of these
creatures have, each, distinctive and very stable forms; so do those
of the penguins. The British and Australian eggs mentioned above
do not "look" like *Aepyornis* eggs. Thus, until these eggs are
analyzed as to structure and composition, there must remain a very
considerable doubt.

So perhaps we should not laugh at one scientist's remark made
to me after I returned from investigating the Florida three-toes'
foot tracks. This was meant facetiously and to chide me when I
had asked why this wanderer, obviously an aquatic marine creature, should have repeatedly come pounding out of the sea and
struggled up banks into freshwater lagoons, landside. His suggestion was simply: "Perhaps it wanted to lay an egg." In view of the
egg-laying habits of the penguins, and the matching of old three-
toes' fingerprints *only* with those of penguins, I have to admit
that this joking remark about egg-laying has, for me at least, taken
on quite another connotation.

86

CHAPTER SIX

PICKLED DANES
AND OTHERS

IT IS NOT an invariable rule
that when you die your body will return to dust—at least in the
shortest possible order. Quite the contrary, it seems that it can lie
around for an awfully long time if it is not speedily demolished by
other living things, which is the orderly and hygienic plan of
Nature to keep the surface of our planet free from an accumulation
of old bodies. However, when this orderly procedure fails, we
are confronted with some amazing phenomena. Whole animals,
complete with flesh and blood, and clothed in the fur that they
wore when alive, may be preserved for as long as a hundred thousand years; while bits of animals, quite unchanged in form or
chemical constitution, have lasted for over 100 million years. All
manner of animals, and even men, have in fact been pickled, dried,
preserved in deep freeze, set in plastic, or otherwise embalmed by
Nature, and often with much better results than those achieved by
our modern canning industry.

Residents of Jutland at the northern tip of Denmark are periodically roused to a considerable pitch of local excitement by the
discovery of what they invariably at first take to be evidence of a
gruesome murder on the open moors of their somewhat bleak
land. Corpses with every appearance of freshness, and often with
a rope pulled tightly around their throats, are discovered just below

the surface, usually in small peat-filled depressions, and the police, coroners, and other officials are hurriedly summoned. There have been several dozen cases during the last century, but the impact of these chance discoveries never fails to arouse mild popular hysteria, although the same conclusion is always reached—namely, that the murdered lady or gentleman has lain undisturbed in the ground for at least 2000 years.

All living things, except certain minute, single-celled creatures which reproduce by splitting in half and which are therefore in a manner of speaking immortal, eventually die, and forthwith their bodies disappear rather rapidly. In the ordinary course of events, corpses are *eaten,* regardless of whether they sink down into the sea, lakes, or rivers, are deposited on the land, or are buried beneath it. They do not just dissolve away or disintegrate chemically; they have to be taken apart, either in chunks by larger animals or literally piece by molecular piece by such tiny living things as bacteria. If all carrion-eaters, both great and small, are totally excluded from the corpse, however, it apparently remains intact unless it is destroyed by fire, macerated by mechanical action or, in exceptional circumstances, dissolved by special fluids such as the digestive juices of some plants. The very simplicity of this natural procedure often eludes us.

Nevertheless, rather special circumstances are obviously required to prevent the body of an animal from being eaten; and it is almost as miraculous as one might at first suppose that any corpse, however large, can survive for more than a few hours. The hard shells of certain scorpion-like creatures, called eurypterids, that lived in the seas over 300 million years ago are found today still embedded deep in most ancient rock strata, but they are still composed wholly of the same material, known as chitin, of which they were formed during their lives.

The preservation of old bones and of such things as shells and teeth is fairly understandable, for they can be extremely solid and indestructible. Anyone who has tried to break open a conch shell or smash a deer antler can attest to this fact. Ox skulls can lie about on a desert for years, and even things as seemingly impermanent as fish bones may crop up in a garden, months after they have been buried. But who would ever expect to find a whole dead fish in a pool of water, more than a year after it had been killed? I witnessed just this in Scotland when I was a youngster, and it made a lasting impression upon me.

A cousin and I used to be taken fishing among the highland tarns by an old game-keeper. As we landed the fish, we were instructed to disengage the hooks and throw them into little, coffee-coloured pools of stagnant water about the size of a bucket, which formed among the tufts of grass that covered the moors around the tarns. This was in order to keep them fresh until we went home. We caught so many fish that sometimes we did not bother to retrieve them all from these pools, and among fish so left to die—for they always did so in a few hours—there was, on one occasion, a stout eight-incher, with a bright red fly firmly hooked through its head because my leader broke and I couldn't get it out. Shortly afterwards, our summer vacation came to an end and my cousin and I returned south to school.

Then, quite by chance, the following season I happened to flounder into the same little pool and spotted something white floating up from the muddy bottom. Grabbing this, I found myself holding a silvery, white fish which was rigid and as firm as hard rubber, and from which a slightly rusted hook protruded, still retaining a number of damp, red feathers. There was no question about this; it was my trout of the previous year! I took it to the old gillie who told me that in some places the water was "verruh piezinous" and killed all living things; but then preserved them apparently forever! My fish seemed to be pickled right through and was perfect in every respect both outside and in; but it did not stink—even of fish! This present-day fossilization, or the first stages in such a process, is fairly common in peat bogs throughout the world.

Peat is a most extraordinary substance that is little understood by those who do not live in areas where it is found, and seldom, if ever, even by those who *do* live there. Peat occurs all over the world but most notably in a great belt around the Arctic Circle, from Greenland, Labrador, and Newfoundland, all across Canada to Alaska, thence right through Siberia and northern Russia to Scandinavia, the British Isles, and Iceland. There are numerous peat bogs in the United States and even in southern Europe, and there is a kind of peat in the tropics. A third kind occurs on oceanic islands, and in that of Mauritius the bones, feet, beaks, and feathers of the extinct dodo are still to be found.

Peat may be composed of a great variety of vegetable materials and may vary in color from pale yellow to jet black, while it may be as much as 90 percent water-logged, or almost devoid of moisture. It is formed in both marshes and bogs by the gradual decay and sinking of sedges, mosses and other water plants. It may reach over thirty feet in depth, and two million tons of dried fuel can be extracted from a square mile of it by digging down to a depth of only some fifteen feet! It is composed of (apart from water) almost three-quarters carbon and one quarter oxygen, the remainder being hydrogen and gritty ash. It is highly acid, and the water it contains can be so rich in certain chemicals that it will preserve animals just as does formalin or alcohol. The ancient human corpses found in Denmark, western Germany, and Holland which cause so much official consternation, are preserved in this manner; and so perfect is the pickling process that it is often hard to believe that they have been buried for more than a few days.

An extremely fine old Dane was brought to light at a place known as the Tollund Bog in central Jutland [68] (see Plate VII). This gentleman, for such he was, although somewhat shrunken and dark peat-brown in colour, was found lying on his side, quite nude except for a small cap on his head made of eight separate pieces of leather. He had also a leather belt about his waist, and a rope of plaited leather thongs pulled tightly around his neck. His features are perfectly preserved and display a face of considerable refinement and sensitivity, with chiselled lips, slightly wrinkled forehead, and a long, aristocratic nose. The oddest thing about him, however, was his last meal, which still remained undigested in his stomach. This consisted of porridge made from various grains that were cultivated during the Iron Age of Europe, in the first millennium B.C., mixed with parts of a number of plants that have never been cultivated, such as sheep's sorrel, white goosefoot, and a thing known in Europe as corn spurrey. This man, like the great majority of the other five hundred or so such pickled corpses that have now been found in that part of Europe, had obviously not fallen into the bog by mistake. This man was formally buried, although no funerary objects such as are normally found in graves dating from that period were present with his body.

However, by meshing together many separate threads of evidence concerning this discovery, scientists have now reconstructed a most remarkable picture of this old Dane's background. It appears that he lived and died some hundreds of years before the Christian era; that he normally fed on porridges of mixed seeds; and that he was sacrificed to his gods by his own people in the belief that his demise would promote the fertility of the soil. This may appear to be a remarkable human procedure in itself, but we must not let it blind us to the much more extraordinary part played by nature in this seeming "tragedy."

People have been dying by the billions all over the earth for hundreds of thousands of years, and their friends and relatives have been burying them in all manner of ways and all kinds of soils, but despite extreme technical efforts on the part of the ancient Egyptians and some others to preserve corporate bodies by mummification, man has never wholly succeeded in holding Nature's disposal units at bay. Yet, here we find Nature herself completely reversing her normal procedure and perfecting a process of preservation apparently in defiance of her own laws. Nor is this a unique case.

At the time that I used to be sent fishing for trout in Scotland, I had another wonderful experience. In London, whenever possible, I would sneak away from parental supervision and roam around the vast galleries of the British Museum. One day, with notebook in hand and my nose glued to a glass case containing an Egyptian mummy, I felt a tap on my shoulder and turned to see a kindly old gentleman peering at me. When he asked me what I was doing and I explained that I was trying to compile a list of the dynastic Egyptian kings, he took me into a back room and entertained me for the most exciting afternoon of my young life. Only when I left did I learn that I had been given a personally conducted tour of the most priceless collection of relics that ever came out of the past; and, by perhaps the greatest Egyptologist who ever lived —Dr. E. Wallis Budge.

What impressed me most that afternoon was an enormous stone coffin that Dr. Budge showed me. It was shaped like a bathtub in a very small modern apartment; but it had a heavy stone lid. This, Dr. Budge told me, was the oldest Egyptian burial ever found and had been excavated far out in the western desert, where it has been excessively dry for the past six thousand years. In this tub-like coffin, lying on his left side with his hands held as if in prayer and his knees pulled up under his chin, was a little golden-brown man, looking somewhat undernourished but otherwise quite normal. He had been lying thus for over 5000 years—in fact, since *before* the first king of the first dynasty of Egypt was born.

The first requirement for the preservation of an animal body is that it should be completely insulated from all living things as soon after death as possible. Protection from fire and mechanical destruction is really only of secondary importance. But, in view of the almost universal presence of voracious living things in the form of bacteria, even in the dead bodies themselves, we may well ask how this may be accomplished. The answer is simply to cut off the oxygen supply from the outset and then, either by this alone, or by further moves, similarly to prevent a supply of free nitrogen from accumulating. By doing these two things, the principal body-eating bacteria are suffocated or held at bay. Some acid waters in peat bogs accomplish this by completely enveloping and then permeating the body. Likewise, absolutely dry air may produce the same effect because, without moisture, the bacteria cannot live. In the case of the very ancient Egyptian mummy, the air happened to have been very hot as well as dry in the initial stages, though it must have become cold in due course, for the nights even in the hottest deserts are usually cool and often extremely cold. The air does not have to be hot, however, for there are excessively cold deserts at the poles where the air is equally germ-free. This is really the basis of refrigeration, and accounts for Nature's most outstanding morgues.

It is now well known that the Arctic regions are positively littered with the corpses of all manner of animals both great and small. The most outstanding are those of the great woolly elephants known as mammoths. Most of these permanently-refrigerated corpses are thousands of years old, and some have tens or even hundreds of thousands of years to their credit, and yet their flesh is in some cases so perfectly preserved that present-day wolves and other predaceous animals can eat it. They have been preserved for all this time in frozen earth, not, as most people believe, in ice. The reason for this is that they died and were originally preserved in air, *not water*. Had they remained in water for even a short time, their own contained moisture would have permitted bacterial action to start, which in turn would have produced enough heat to permit the growth of more bacteria—and so on, until the whole or a substantial part of the corpse had been demolished. In the Arctic, sometimes only the skins or outer layers of bodies are found, indicating that just this did occur. But to preserve a complete corpse, the body must die, biologically, and then remain in dry, germ-free air until it is chilled right through. The woolly mammoths and rhinoceroses, outsized bison, extinct forms of muskox, and other animals found in the Arctic are now buried to various depths in frozen soil; but there have been other specimens, admittedly not of such enormous antiquity, discovered in caves, both natural and man-made, that are still lying, or even standing, just as they died twenty centuries ago or more.

At a place named Pazyryk in the Altai Mountains of central eastern Siberia, a Russian anthropologist named Professor Grysanov set about excavating some ancient burial mounds on a small plain by the river Yan-Oulagan, in 1929.[69] The mounds did not look any different from the innumerable other prehistoric burial heaps that are strewn all over the plains of Siberia and Russia, but a great surprise was in store for the professor. Instead of being solid piles of earth, these mounds contained large vaults, which in turn housed remarkable wooden cages made like Indian fishtraps, rectangular in shape, and with platforms within. Upon these platforms were placed the bodies of men, women, and children. The vaults were piled with Stone-Age artefacts, ornaments, primitive costume jewelry, textile and leather clothing, weapons, and other items which were manifestly the possessions of the deceased. It appeared as if the women and children were the families and servants of the principal man laid out on the platform, and there was evidence that they had been sacrificed at the time of his death.

Similar cages with air-chilled mummies had been found two years before in crypts near a place called Chibe on the Oursoul River not far away, but they contained only human remains. These mound-vaults in Yan-Oulagan disclosed something new—namely a number of small, shaggy ponies of a breed no longer known anywhere in the world today, that had been killed, frozen stiff in the frigid germ-free air, and then saddled and set upright on their feet alongside their owners. And there they had remained for over two thousand years, just as perfect as the day they died.

The reason for their preservation is simply that even the hottest summer does not thaw the earth of Siberia to any great extent, so that even a few feet under the surface the temperature remains perpetually below the freezing point. Germ-free in the beginning, the atmosphere of these vaults remained at deep-chill until they were opened, so holding Nature's garbage-disposal units perpetually at bay.

Essentially the same process occurred in caves at the opposite side of the earth, providing us with still another mysterious natural morgue. The great plains of Patagonia, forming the southern extremity of South America, face the south Atlantic Ocean over which icy winds constantly blow from the Antarctic. At various

94

places about Patagonia are limestone bluffs riddled with caves in which the local natives, before the coming of the Europeans, kept certain enormous beasts that have now vanished from the earth. The natives called these animals *Ellengassen,* and they were covered in long shaggy coats of coarse brown hair. They were related to the present-day tropical American anteaters and, like them, were armed with huge, recurved claws for digging. However, they also had a sort of armour-plating of thousands of little bones about the size of checker pieces buried in their thick skins. The natives apparently drove them into the caves, and then walled them up with piles of boulders to retain them as a source of food in lean periods. Sometimes the animals died or were butchered in the caves, and their skins and bits of their bodies were left lying about.

One of the results of this procedure provided a great surprise for the modern scientific world in the early part of this century. Some natives working on a sheep ranch near a place called Ultima Esperanza—the Last Hope—found in a cave a large part of the skin of an Ellengassen, still perfectly preserved in the cold, dry air. They lugged it back to their camp, and tried to soften it but, failing in this, spread it over a bush to dry. Some time later an Argentine naval officer named Moreno, who was carrying out a survey for his government, happened to come along and, being somewhat of a naturalist, recognized this skin for what it was. He purchased it and sent it to the famous Dr. Ameghino, his country's fossil expert, who forthwith solemnly accounced that it had only recently been taken from a live animal! Unfortunately, he was completely wrong, for the creature had of course been dead for several centuries.[70] Since that time, the mummified remains of similar creatures, which we now call somewhat incorrectly "Giant Ground Sloths," have been found in other caves even in the United States. The dung of one of these animals turned up as far north as Nevada.

I will never forget exploring an excessively dry limestone cave in Yucatan in pursuance of my normal business of collecting animals. I had gone in armed only with nets, bent upon the capture of bats which I had seen flying in and out at dawn and dusk; but extended search led me deep into the earth and still no bats were to be seen. I was about to give up when I threw the beam of my flashlight into a side chamber and got the most frightful shock.

Curled up on a sort of natural rock table was the vividly spotted form of an extremely large jaguar. The silence and stillness in that cave at that moment was absolutely electrifying. I'll swear that I actually could hear my own pulse beating; and I remained thus, frozen for minutes, but nothing happened. Then I noticed something very odd. The jaguar had a hole in it!

It took me several more minutes to puzzle this out, during which time I remained poised for instant flight; but the absolute stillness of the beast slowly convinced me of the truth. I crept slowly forward until I saw that the animal was deader than anything I have ever seen; in fact, it was literally mouldy and perhaps even "moth-eaten." This is the only naturally dead wild animal I had ever found in fifteen years of search in tropical countries.

For some reason, the great cat must have crept deep into this cave and then neatly composed itself for death, alone in its eerie, silent, and desiccated tomb. It was completely stiff and bone dry, and once I had it free of its rock pedestal to which it was rather firmly attached, it was so light I could pick it up with one hand. Its skin was almost complete and perfect, though some lesser creatures had bored two holes into its flank and the parts that had touched the rock below had disintegrated into dust. It was a natural mummy and contained the shrivelled flesh and internal organs as well as the skeleton. It might have been hundreds of years old.

Though dry air, peat water, and frozen soil are the most common methods employed by nature to preserve her privileged children, they are neither the most bizarre nor the most successful that she has used. Embalmed animals and specimens set in plastic—such as certain advanced educational institutions now prepare for purposes of classroom demonstration—are also known.

Some fifty million years ago, the climate of Europe was considerably warmer than it is today. As a result, the area that is now North Germany was clothed in forests such as are now found in Florida; containing palms, coniferous and broad-leafed trees. The conifers —that is to say such trees as pines, firs, yews, and so forth— exuded resin then, just as they do today. This excessively sticky, sweet-smelling sap trickled from rents in the bark of the trunks and branches, sometimes forming little blobs or icicle-shaped formations. Small animals walking over this or attracted to it by its smell became ensnared and were sometimes ultimately enveloped. Some of this resin then fell to the ground or into swamps and, being a very permanent substance, was covered up and buried. Later, some of the mud or silt in which it lay was dried and compressed into strata of rock, and the resin was finally dried out and turned into what we call amber.[71] This, when freed from the rock once more by the action of the waves on a coast, has been collected by men as a semi-precious "stone" for ornamental purposes since earliest times.

Millions of tons of amber have been found throughout the ages, but only a few thousand pieces containing animals have been preserved. Yet the animals are of extraordinary variety—over two hundred kinds of insects, some hundred species of spiders, large numbers of different centipedes and millipedes, some ticks, mites, and lesser creatures, a few small lizards, some bird feathers, and a variety of plant remains. All of these are, however, absolutely unchanged from the day that they became set in this natural plastic. Even the scales on a mosquito's wing-veins may be counted accurately! No more perfect or permanent method of preservation has ever been devised by man or nature.

Then again, in 1929 a landslide in a valley in the Province of Starunia in southern Poland brought to light a very peculiar deposit of great geological rarity.[72] This was a huge pocket of sand saturated with a mixture of crude oil and brine. Some of the local inhabitants, poking about in this black, gooey mass, noticed great bundles of fibrous material that looked like hair. Notice of this odd discovery fortunately reached the ears of scientists who subsequently investigated and found a number of large bones, more hair, and pieces of skin. A careful excavation was begun, and after the removal of rather large quantities of the oily sand, there appeared one of the most remarkable discoveries of all time. One complete and two partially complete rhinoceroses of a species that dwelt in Europe during the height of the cold, glacial phases of the Ice Age, and which were covered with a dense coat of thick wool and long fur, were brought to light. Most of the fur and hair came away in the oily mass that enveloped them, but their bodies were so well-preserved that they could be skinned just like a fresh animal, their corpses dissected, and the skins softened, stuffed, and mounted.

These beasts had died tens of thousands of years ago during some great flood, and their bodies had been washed down a torrent. This torrent had entered a more gently flowing river that must have wound across a fairly level plain, for it had developed great side loops in its course, in which the current formed whirlpools and eddies. The dead rhinoceroses were washed into one of these that happened to have been gouged out of a bed of sand through which natural oil was seeping in large quantities. This sand by chance contained also a high proportion of salt originally derived from the sea at some earlier time when the strata were laid down at the bottom of some shallow sun-drenched lagoon where evaporation was excessive. The corpses sank to the bottom and were rapidly covered over by the mixture of sand, oil, and brine which effectively sealed them away from the world. What happened then is perhaps unique, for the brine somehow penetrated the bodies, effectively pickling them, while the oil seeped into every possible entrance and waterproofed them both inside and out, just as is done in embalming. By chance, no further floods occurred before the loop in the river filled up completely and the main stream shifted and cut a new channel. The rhinoceroses were left sealed in their oily grave.

I don't know about you, but to me these "things" constitute items worthy of rather long pondering. We of the West have always tended to believe that physical death is the end of what we call life. However, when we come to examine even our own past we find that this is really a very modern notion. Wherever you look, and the farther back in time you go, the more frequently and universally do you encounter evidence of our ancestors having apparently thought otherwise. What they may have thought about the continuity of the spirit, soul, personality or whatever you wish to call the non-material part of all us living things as individual entities, we can only conjecture or endeavour to interpret from the remaining extant writings of the ancients. And, from these we can but assume that over the millennia they came to the conclusion that what we call death is but a turnover point. Of their ideas of corporeal continuity we have much more concrete evidence. This is demonstrated by the remarkable practices of burial or interment, and of mummification. Very few animals bury their dead and then only, it would seem, to prevent predators from picking up their *own* trails; yet man, it now transpires, began burying his dead deliberately at a very early period in his cultural evolution. And when you come to contemplate this, I think you will agree that it is really a very astonishing concept. Why did he do this?

Anthropologists leaning to the so-called "psychological" aspects of man's evolution appear to agree with religionists that the first thing that differentiated our species from the other primates was an awareness of ourselves. This could be so, but it appears to me to imply too strongly some form of divine or other outside influence; otherwise, how could somebody wake up one day and say something like: "Py Jinkoa, I'm *me*." No: the process must have been much more gradual, with countless generations of "naked apes" becoming ever more aware of not only their environment but of their own individuality. And, during this ages-long process, they must have learned to integrate what they observed of their environment with its effects upon themselves.

Just what did ultra-primitive hominids make of their dead? I've watched monkeys and apes confronted by deaths in their group. The former either totally ignored them, after one sniff, or they chewed on them a bit if they were hungry. The apes, on the other hand, often appeared to become quite distressed, even if the corpse was not of their family group, and displayed symptoms of

99

fear, rage, or puzzlement. They seemed to react in either one or the other of two diametrically opposed ways. Either they fled in terror, sometimes displaying gestures of disgust; or, if the dead was what *we* would call a "loved one," they would give every appearance of refusing to accept the fact that it was no longer animate; and by fondling and in other ways, try to treat it just as if it were still alive. The effect of such behaviour on the part of a middle-aged chimp when its companion—which I suspect was a sibling—died, really ripped my heart out. The poor dear would not let anybody near him, and after hugging and clinging to his dead brother, he solemnly tried to inter him under a pile of everything moveable in his large, outdoor cage. We eventually had to "gas" him with ammonia so that we could separate him from his charge, and he then further completely broke us all up by going through a solemn sort of ritual "dancing," accompanied by the most extraordinary sounds that I have ever heard from any chimp (or any other animal, for that matter)—and for days on end.

Where did this intelligent ape get these emotions and seemingly ritual ideas? Have such ideas survived as what we call "customs" until today in the form of physical bodily interment? Did humans emerging into the Stone Age encounter pickled people, and such other things as rhinoceroses preserved in oil, and frozen mammoths, and realize that if they could but bury their loved ones in the right place, they might not melt away? Could this not have been the first stage, and the notion that the spirit or the non-material spark of a living thing could also survive have come later? I have to state that I prefer this thought to any idea of outside intervention. It seems sequential and logical and avoids a lot of theorizing about things of which we have no proof.

CHAPTER SEVEN

PICKLED TREES
AND ASTROBLEMES

FUNNY HOW SO often little things lead us inexorably into the outer limbo of cosmic enormity. This by way of introduction to a rather long string of most extraordinary matters that, I must admit, somewhat unnerve me.

This "story" began, for me at least, some years ago when a perfectly splendid young couple—now married and with a somewhat prince-like five-year-old son—brought me some color transparencies of a swamp area in southern New Jersey. They were beautiful photographs (Plate VIII), but there was something "wrong" with what they showed. Jeri and Joni—officially Mr. and Mrs. Gerald Bentryn—were in those days members of a group of young friends with most exceptional interests. As a matter of fact, they were interested in just about everything and spent all their spare time and weekends wandering all over the New Jersey and northeastern Pennsylvania area, collecting animals like salamanders, plants of medicinal value, and digging up Amerindian and colonial artefacts, and any other old "remains" such as cannonballs and a really great collection of old bottles that Joni still adds to. I have met several lots of intelligent young people in my somewhat extended life, and in some score of countries, but this was the best bunch I ever encountered. They were alert and intelligent, and they applied

101

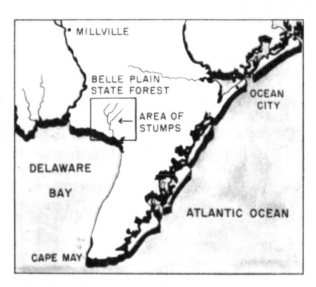

Fig. 24. *The Cape May Area of southern New Jersey. Box indicates area in which tree stumps are observed in a number of creeks and slews mostly connected with the East Creek (river).*

the knowledge they had learned at school; and as a result, they have all gone on to be professionals in the fields of geography, geology, archaeology and such. Despite the almost overwhelming efforts of our so-called educational system, these young people have steadfastly refused to become "stuffed shirts." This I find very refreshing.

The photographs in question were taken by Jeri on a canoeing trip through the swamps, glades, and open-water lagoons of the southern tip of New Jersey (see map, Fig. 24). As you will see, these show a seemingly endless parade of tree stumps, some of them up to six feet in diameter, sticking out of the swamp water, but all *broken* off at about the same level, and some three feet above the surface. All around stand smaller and presumably younger trees, forming a thick wood with a closed canopy. These were pretty pictures, but the thing that immediately struck me when I first saw them was that these tree stumps were most obviously not

102

the result of logging operations. Enquiry then elicited the fact that they were all extremely old cedars—old in the sense of maturity—and that they were also very 'old' in the historical sense. In other words, all these thousands of huge trees had at some time very long ago, and undoubtedly long before the arrival of the white man, been *broken off in situ* like a lot of gigantic match-sticks. What force on earth can snap off cedars with a six-foot diameter so comparatively cleanly, and all over acre after acre?

First, I asked this question of the Bentryn gang, but they, being truly intelligent pragmatists, had nothing to offer even after some considerable pondering. I then asked the "experts" in ascending order of magnitude from the self-appointed to the truly professional and presumably properly trained and informed. One and all of those who even bothered to listen, came back with a single suggestion; namely, a hurricane. Experts, I fear me, constitute near tragedy.

I happen to have survived nine hurricanes of various kinds on both sea and land, and in both the Orient and the Caribbean. A couple of these were what we used to call "real beauts" with the major wind up to 180 mph and the "blasts" within this running up to only God would really know what velocity. One in the Orient (naturally there called a typhoon) that I was subjected to, caught me on a local prau in the Java Sea *en route* from the island of Madoera to Borneo. It was quite impressive: we were underwater fifty percent of the time for twenty-four hours. But the one that really impressed me hit us when we were some fifty miles inland up a river on the Caribbean coast of Nicaragua. This also was a "beaut," and finally struck when we had parked our sixty-foot schooner tight in behind a bank of fifty-foot mangrove trees that shielded us from the oncoming wind. On the other side of this inland lagoon there was a wall of primaeval "primary" forest such as the average non-tropical person would call jungle. The trees rose to a hundred feet in height, with some huge emergents going up another fifty feet. These trees stood right in the face of the hurricane, on low, swampy ground only a few feet above sea-level and, like all such

tropical trees, they had widely spreading but not deeply penetrating root systems. So the winds came—first from one direction
and then from another, as is the way of these circular disturbances
—and the great forest bent before them for hours. Limbs blew off,
leaves flew, and some old dead trunks collapsed; *but not one single
living tree went down.*

Some years later, we were making a forestry survey of the
mountains of southern British Honduras in Central America, and
we ran into something very strange. On the southern flanks of all
the ravines running down the east-facing slopes of these mountains, named locally "The Cockscombs," we found the ground
surface littered with tree trunks, some of which had obviously not
died when they fell, since they had put out shoots that had grown
up to be trees of themselves, and to heights of fifty feet or more.
We enquired of the Forestry Department, for whom we were working, for any records they might have of any natural disaster in
this area that might have caused such a strange phenomenon.
From "ring counts" of the (what are called) epigenous trees that
had grown up from the fallen trunks, it was estimated that this
event must have taken place about 40 years before. The records
showed that a particularly concentrated and thus "vicious" little
hurricane with very high velocity winds had hit that area of the
southern coast just about that time and had whirled inland, but
nothing much of its effect had been recorded, for the simple reason
that practically nobody lived along that coast at that time. The
forestry people could therefore infer only that all these trees, caught
on those particular faces of the ravines in those mountains at that
time, had been literally uprooted on their steep slopes and thrown
down. And these trees were indeed all *uprooted—not*, be it noted,
broken or snapped-off.

Hurricanes, or *huracans*, as they should more properly be called,
since we got our name for them from the Arawak Amerinds of the
Caribbean, are spiral winds of concentrated energy that originate
in the doldrums just north and south of the equatorial belt. In the
Orient, north of the equator, they are known as typhoons; in the

southern latitudes, as wish-willies. Once generated—and it is still not known just how this happens—they wander off, in the northern hemisphere, first to the north and west and then swerve around to the north and east so that they end up in the north Pacific or Atlantic Oceans where they peter out and become ordinary cyclonic storms. In the southern hemisphere, they curl the other way, first to the west and south and then to the east and back north again.

To the constant surprise of the inhabitants of what are so ridiculously called the "temperate latitudes" (they are, of course, the most *intemperate* known) of North America, these aerial monsters take sort of sideswipes at our eastern seaboard year after year. Some of the heaviest have hit from New York to Nova Scotia and have caused a really frightful mess on low-lying coastal areas like those of Massachusetts, Connecticut, and New Jersey. But while they have washed out roads and bridges and countless homesteads, and have *uprooted* trees and telephone poles, clogged harbours, and flattened lesser vegetation, *never* has a healthy tree been reported to have been broken off near its base by any of these winds. Therefore, I am sorry to have to inform the "experts" that the breaking-off of tens of thousands of enormous, deeply-rooted trees along the New Jersey coast was *not* accomplished by a hurricane. Whatever broke off these trees and left these stumps * must have been a very great deal more powerful and sudden than a mere hurricane, the force of which mounts gradually. And here we run into some considerably unpleasant things.

To snap off a cedar of six-foot diameter, you have to give it one hell of a wallop; and once again, let me stress that I am *not* talking of debranching or uprooting, which a really good hurricane could do. If one or two trees were rotten about their bases, they might snap off, which would be very convenient for the theorists; but how could several tens of thousands of trees all happen to be rotten at just that level at the same time, and regardless of their age or

---

* Actually, in most of these creeks, slews, and lagoons, these stumps appear above the surface only in exceptionally dry periods, and nearer the present shoreline at very low tides.

girth? Come now! How far can you push such an argument? And what is more, there is not the slightest evidence of "rottenness" in any single one of the stumps standing in these lagoons! They are all what one may legitimately call "fresh snapped"—their fibres splintered but cracked off just like those in the end of a broken kitchen match as seen under a magnifying glass.

This constitutes a mystery indeed, but on investigation, it leads to even greater conundrums. The question as to what could have accomplished this gigantic reaping is one thing; but then comes the question, what happened to the trees? At first, one naturally says that, however they were "felled," they must have gone away somewhere. According to the hurricane theory they would have been presumed just to have fallen down, like the uprooted trees in British Honduras, and then to have either revegetated or rotted away. According to another theory that we will come to in a moment, they would have been washed away. Both theories are perfectly splendid, but in this case neither fits the facts. Unfortunately (for the theorists) there are no snapped-off tree trunks lying around on the surface, either with or without epigenous shoots. On the other hand, there *are* enormous masses of huge logs buried to an average depth of about twelve feet in the silt of nearby areas. These logs are *beneath* the roots of the trees that today cover the whole area. Where did they come from; and where are *their* stumps? Or do we have here two parts of the same problem?

When the Hollanders and then the British first settled along our eastern seaboard, they built houses of wood—log cabins and such. In imitation of some Algonquin housing, the Europeans first knocked together rectangular log cabins. Later, when they got better established, they started putting up frame houses such as they had built in their old countries, anchored firmly in country-stone footings. Later still, the Hollanders started importing bricks as ballast in such of their trading vessels as came here with empty holds. This is all perfectly straightforward, but for one item that has been considerably overlooked: the roofing used by the early colonists.

106

From early records we learn that at first flattened bark strips were used but that later, filletted, soft-wood planks were employed. As the Hollanders moved inland they came upon slate, and taking a clue from others who had come from other European countries where this had been employed for roofing for centuries, they adopted this material. However, somewhere along the line and apparently at a very early date, the colonists stumbled upon *shingles*. These devices were known from Roman times, their name being derived from *scandula* which meant "little bits, rising by *scando* or steps," as in *ascando,* to ascend. These are sort of fillets of wood, but with a wedge-shaped cross-section; and to produce these, logs have to be split in a very special way—i.e., radially, from the center to the outer periphery. Further, the logs to be split (and especially when this is done with a hand axe) have to be of a certain consistency. Green logs just don't make shingles. Drying them out does make them amenable to splitting; but some trees dry out so hard you can't split them at all, while others go crumbly.

It now transpires that some people discovered a gigantic "mine" of just the right kind of logs for cleavage into shingles, lying buried along the coastal strip of southern New Jersey.[73] How they were ever discovered remains a mystery in itself and is not on record, but by 1800 there was a thriving industry in this area based upon the disinterment of enormous cedarwood tree trunks which were perfect for splitting into shingles. As a matter of fact, this curious industry is still not dead, and the long-time inhabitants of the southern New Jersey Pine Barrens are still producing roofing shingles by this age-old method.

So what of this apparently inexhaustible supply of pickled logs buried in silt and muck to an average depth of twelve feet? Where did they come from, and how did they get so buried there? And here comes another funny thing. All these logs are "snapped-off" at their lower or thicker ends, and all have been stripped of their branches and their tops. Moreover, these trunks are of the same species and the same age as the stumps! The stumps now stick up some two to four feet above mean tide level (lagoons in which they may be seen in drier years rise and fall to a considerable extent in accord with mean sea-level). The *trunks* all lie horizontally some twelve feet below that level.

Even if the latter are not the missing trunks from the stumps, how did they get down there and where did *they* come from? Some positively cataclysmic force must have transported them and buried them; and don't try to say that they were just a lot of old trees that fell down over the centuries and sank into swamps. All of these tree trunks were fresh when they were buried; all were de-branched and snapped off at their bases; and all are pickled at the same depth, in the same way, and all, apparently, at the same time. So what agency caused this singular phenomenon? And, at this point I think I should ask you to take a rather deep breath before turning the metaphorical (or perhaps actual) page.

If there is one thing that riles geophysicists, geomorphologists, classical geologists, and geological historians, it is the mention of anything that might smack of a "cataclysmic theory." This, as first mooted by the great traditionalist, Baron Cuvier,[74] suggests that, apart from the theory of gradualism to account for the changes in the earth's surface, there have occurred from time to time sudden and violent happenings that have substantially disrupted the even tenor of events. There has been a whole gamut of such suggestions made by innumerable "crackpots," but there have also been quite a number put forward by serious scientists.[75] However, all such theorists have been soundly and roundly "clobbered" by everybody else, who state that there is no evidence for any such event ever having taken place. And I would have gone along with this, I suppose, had it not been for a scientist of the utmost probity who solemnly published a series of technical papers, and then a popular article in the *Scientific American*[76] which manifestly went to "prove"—as far as anything can ever be said to be proved—that at least one kind of cataclysm must have hit us, and time and time again, during past geological history, and at rather frequent intervals at that. This observation may sound positively garish, but one can take it at its face value. Here it is.

108

It was not until the end of the last century that astronomers first suggested that the pockmarks on the Moon were caused by the impact of meteorites—and possibly also the heads of comets—rather than by volcanic eruptions from below the surface. There is still considerable debate about this, despite our having now attained our Moon, but nobody any longer denies that some of these craters could be what are called impact craters. The mystery was, initially, why our sister planet should be so pock-marked while we were not. Then it came to the attention of astronomers that a bowl-shaped hole in the surface of Arizona, now called the Barringer Crater,[77] was not the result of some volcanic gas emission from below but gave every indication of being the point of impact of a large meteorite from on high. Even the local Amerinds stated that it had been a direct hit on their territory by one of their sky gods!

The crater is nearly three-quarters of a mile in diameter across its top, and is over 600 feet deep. There is an impact ridge of broken surface strata around its rim, and there is a scattering of meteoritic-type nickel-iron strewn all around it. Those who first became convinced that this hole was the result of a meteorite impact spent enormous sums of money delving below the crater in the hope of finding the main body of the meteorite that caused it; but to no effect, since as is now conjectured and fairly satisfactorily agreed, any metallic body of a size large enough to make such a hole would for the most part vaporize on impact, while that of its substance which did not do so would melt and then recondense and be spattered far and wide all around. More recent investigations have, with considerable certainty, dated the arrival of this object as having occurred about 25,000 years ago. (One wonders if the Hopi Amerinds were actually around then in order to have recorded the blow-up in their traditional legends.)

It took a couple of decades before those scientists particularly interested in this matter got around to issuing definite statements that there were other such meteoritic craters scattered far and wide over the earth's land surface that could be reliably demonstrated to be of a similar origin.

The story of this discovery, if I may call it that, is fascinating in itself but can only be touched upon here. Also, it is fully and properly told in this extremely well-presented and most interesting article by Dr. Robert S. Dietz, that appeared in the August issue of 1961 of the *Scientific American.* [78] In this article, several points are made that are of exceptional interest but which, when taken together, appear to have been completely overlooked. They present us with an inescapable conclusion, and one of a nature that is more than just unpleasant, and to scientists and laymen alike.

The first point that comes to light is that the land surfaces of our earth also turn out to be quite extensively pockmarked with meteoritic craters; and it looks as if, but for one factor, it *could* present today almost the same appearance as that of the Moon, or Mars. This factor is our comparatively thick atmosphere, which causes much more rapid and extensive erosion of the surface on our planet than do such long-term forces as "creep" due to heat expansion and contraction and such that act on the Moon, and which also appear to play a major part on thin atmosphered planets such as Mars. Further, our planet is more dynamic in other respects, in that it appears always to have been in a state of continuous upheaval with massive volcanicity, mountain building, the drifting of continental plates, and so on, going on perpetually. (How much of this, incidentally, is due to the presence of a liquisphere, in the form of water, still has to be determined.)

The result of this rather "lifelike" behaviour of our planet is that its surface features are being constantly changed, and things like meteoric craters get eroded away and covered up in comparatively very short periods, geologically speaking. Only the most recent blemishes remain visible to us—and the Barringer Crater is, as I said above, considered to be not older than 25,000 years. However, careful examination of aerial survey maps brought to light many more such craters that are not apparent on the ground, but the conformation of which were subsequently confirmed by geological inspection, drilling, and subsurface mapping. Then also, it was discovered that a particular species of mineral called *coesite* and a very distinct rock formation known as shatter-cones seem to be the result primarily of impacts from *above,* rather than from volcanic gas explosions from below. These cones and the *coesite* have now been found in an ever-increasing number of more ancient and deeply buried geological structures of a circular form, and associated with other known features of impact craters.

When all these were mapped—and more and more are being found and identified every year—a second fact became clear. Large meteorites, and possibly the heads of some comets (which are formed of ices),* have apparently been landing on the surface of the Earth, and on a fairly regular schedule throughout geologic history, certainly since before 250-million years ago, and right up until the present.[79] The last major event was the arrival of a hundred enormous hunks of a meteorite in 1947 on Sikhote-Alin,[80] which is the area that forms the eastern shore of that bit of Siberia that faces Sakhalin Island.

The next point brought out by these searches and researches at first sight appears ridiculously obvious. However, on second sight it presents us with something really worth thinking about. This is simply that, while we are now and always have been bombarded twenty-four hours a day by meteorites, ranging in size from microscopic particles to seemingly planetoid dimensions, the vast majority of these burn up in our atmosphere. Only the really big boys get through intact, and these Dr. Dietz has called Astroblemes. Yet, we now find that a really very considerable number of the latter *do* get through.

The size of some of these, moreover, is more than just impressive. For instance, there is the New Quebec Crater in the Ungava Peninsula which is two miles in diameter; the Ashanti Crater in Ghana, six miles wide; and the monstrous Vredefort Ring in the Transvaal in South Africa that is 26 miles in diameter and sur-

* Not necessarily "water" ice (i.e., H_2O) but frozen gases of many kinds.

111

rounded by effects extending that ring to 130 miles in diameter![81] These things must have made quite a "splash," just as they appear to have done on the Moon. And this brings us to the really pertinent aspect of all this.

Almost three-quarters of our planet's surface is covered with water—taking into account the larger lakes and landlocked seas. Now, the Moon and Mars appear to be fairly evenly spattered all over with meteoritic craters, and we find that the *land surfaces* of Earth are likewise splattered, despite the tough, erosive forces that work on these craters from the moment that they are formed. There is, therefore, only one conclusion, and this is that three-quarters of all the larger meteorites (and possibly comet heads or astroblemes) that have broken through our atmosphere intact, *have landed in water*. So back to Dr. Dietz's article, and I quote:

"A giant meteorite falling into the middle of the [North] Atlantic Ocean could generate a wave 20,000 feet high that would overwhelm vast areas of the continents surrounding [that] ocean, sweeping over the entire eastern seaboard of the United States and across the Appalachians."[82]

You can say that again, Dr. Dietz! And I would most strongly advise that any of you who are interested in this matter—and who shouldn't be?—go to your nearest good library and get a back copy of the science-fiction magazine entitled *Analog* and look through its cumulative index for an article (presented as fiction) entitled "Giant Meteor Impact" by J. E. Enever. This will really make you sit up and take notice. (Also, it gives you, in simple language, the mechanics of 20,000-foot waves, among other things.)

Now we can get back to our pickled trees and chopped-off tree stumps in southern New Jersey. These were not felled by humans, they did not rot off, they were not blown down, and they were all cracked or snapped off at the same level. What force could do this? So far, I can envisage only one sufficient force—namely, a *tsunami*, which is to say, a gigantic wave suddenly rushing ashore from out of the open sea. Some tsunamis are known to be caused by underwater earthquakes, and some of them have dealt enormous destruction to coastal areas all over the world. But what geophysicists are now asking is, just how many tsunamis are born of earthquakes and how many may be produced by meteoritic impacts in water?

A 20,000-foot wave hitting our eastern seaboard would not only top the Appalachians but, according to some oceanographers, rush across the whole center of the continent and peter out only against the east flank of the Rockies. A tsunami, alleged to have had a front two hundred feet high, rushed up the mouth of the Ganges and Houghli Rivers in India in 1863, killing tens of thousands and washing out a vast area.[83] However, even this enormity did not "snap-off" large trees. Let us, therefore, sort of compromise and suppose that a mere 1,000-foot wave hit the New Jersey coast—say, a thousand years ago. What would have happened? Everything would have been washed off the surface of the low coast, and the water would not have stopped until it hit the Appalachians. By that time, its force would have been considerably spent due to bottom drag and its bulldozing action on the stuff on the land surface which it traversed. But still, it would make a pretty clean sweep of everything.

Now, after the initial front of a tsunami (the big wave), there comes another one about half its height, and then a third, half that height, and so on until equilibrium is restored. Thus, the initial wave, when finally spent, will start *back* downhill, to the coast, and so meet all the lesser waves that have been following along behind it. Result: complete chaos and nullification of forward movement. Then, naturally, all stuff being carried along inland gets dumped, just as in rivers that suddenly slow down.

So, take a tall forest of great cedars standing just back from the New Jersey shore. A tsunami strikes; the trees are firmly rooted and bend away from the "n"-million-ton onslaught and—this being so abrupt—they just snap off like matchsticks leaving their

113

stumps behind them. Off they go inland along with everything else, but being large objects and "fuzzy" with branches, they slow down pretty fast and get stuck at the bottom of the flood. The lesser waves pass over them. These become increasingly devoid of debris, and they diminish rapidly in force. So the great trunks rest. But then, the counter-flow arrives from inland, bringing back with it all the lesser stuff plus sand and fine silt; and as these waters rock back and forth into the Atlantic, all this muck gets dropped on top of the trees. There's some ten or twelve feet of it by the time the water drains off and things return to normal.

Hence our pickled tree trunks that make such fine shingles; the sad stumps that still stand in the lagoons; *and,* one might suggest, the otherwise so puzzling "Pine Barrens." So, there have never been cataclysms?

CHAPTER EIGHT

PETRIFIED ORANGES
AND SUCH

$\mathbb{B}$ACK IN MAY, 1962, I received a letter from a Mr. J. S. F. Carter of Carter & Nansen Co., Inc., of New York, an engineering firm specializing in the installation of distillation and absorption plants. Mr. Carter, himself a chemical engineer, had spent many years in South America. His letter announced in most businesslike terms the following:

A number of years ago I was in Uruguay and, together with three friends, took a trip in a Model T to the north of the country, into Salto Province. Near the town of Constitución there is a river called Arapey, a branch of which has the most amazing properties. The water of this river will petrify a fairly large tree, and I have seen some at least 18 inches in diameter completely petrified within a period of a year. The small branches will petrify in three to four weeks. I saw, for instance, half an orange in which the pulp had been removed in some manner, but the rest of it, including the outside skin, the little center post and the small veins which run from the post to the outer skin, completely petrified, and at the same time retaining their original color. The local people told me that this happens regularly within three to four weeks. I suppose that the answer is the river water is very high in calcium salts together with some others.

In August of 1962 he wrote me again:

It so happens that an Argentine friend of mine, Dr. Parodi, is leaving for Uruguay in the next few days. I have talked to him about the petrification of wood and oranges and he is going to get in touch with a friend of mine in Montevideo, the engineer Valetti, who is Chief Engineer of ANCAP, their local alcohol, sugar, and cement government trust. ANCAP has a plant fairly close to the site of this river so that we should be able to get somebody to go up there and get some samples of wood, and also possibly some oranges which have been petrified. It so happens that Dr. Parodi is quite interested in this situation and he suggested that if there were no oranges evident in the water that the ANCAP people could "plant" some therein and let them petrify. After this has happened he would, of course, send samples up to me. Or if some oranges happen to be in the river he will have them sent up as soon as possible.

On the 20th of November Mr. Carter wrote:

On last Friday Dr. Parodi suddenly dropped dead of a heart attack so I certainly will not be able to talk to him again! As a result of this, however, another friend of mine left for Uruguay on Saturday and he is going to follow the matter up. It may be, of course, that ANCAP has been going forward with the work anyway. At least we should know before too long.

Unfortunately I had to leave on an extended trip abroad at that time and, as a result, failed to follow the matter up. Now I cannot trace the company, or Mr. Carter, in the New York area. (Incidentally, at the time of writing, there was not one single Nansen listed in the New York telephone directory. This we find to be completely incomprehensible.) We would very much like to have half a petrified orange that had clearly been "halved" by human agency. If it had "Sunkist" stamped on it, and the purple ink had also gotten petrified, we would be positively elated.

We have become increasingly suspicious over the years of the current beliefs on the time needed for the preservation of identifiable bodies—animal, plant, or artefact. The whole matter of such natural preservation is extraordinarily complex and will be briefly reviewed in a minute; so please consider a case that really jolted geologists, and which I personally witnessed in Mexico in 1940.

The police at a place called Navajoa in the State of Sonora had a nasty crime on their hands, involving several deaths. The allegation was that certain parties had driven inland towards the Sierras in a truck and butchered a whole family in a tiny settlement on a dry arroyo. My wife and I were living in the town and had become very friendly with the Jefé de Policía, a most splendid and enlightened man from the State of Nayarit who read Proust in French. We were collecting rare rats and chasing Nazis, and the Jefé gave us enormous help in both endeavours; so he came to us with his problem, since we were outsiders and therefore not involved in local affairs. He wanted help in getting casts of the truck tracks, but there had been a flash flood about a week after the crime had been committed, and now the arroyo was covered with concrete-hard silt. They had the tracks up to a certain point, but then they just petered out, and there were no return tracks. Everybody put their heads together and decided to dig farther up, near the settlement. This was done. It took pickaxes and crowbars, and we had to go down almost three feet; but, sure enough, there was the old road (a euphemistic term if I ever heard one) surface, and on it, tracks. But then we had to drive back to the town to round up cold chisels and light sledge-hammers because, in just a month, the silt deposited on the old road had turned into a sort of argillaceous marl and was as hard as some limestones. What had happened was this:

The night of the alleged slaughter it had rained and the road surface was soft; then for some days it was baked dry by the desert sun. Next came the flash flood and the silt. Then, this too was dried out, and apparently calcium-carbonate, or some such mineral dissolved in its flood-water content, had cemented its granules

117

into solid rock. In other words, we had here truck tracks *fossilized* in just over a month!

As I said *in re* Pickled Danes, objects can be preserved in many ways. You can have them preserved for millennia in frozen soil (muck) such as the mammoths in Siberia and Alaska; you can find them preserved in crude oil seepages such as the famous family of woolly rhinoceroses in Starunia in Poland; and you have them pickled in peat bogs. Then, you can have imprints like these truck tracks, and also the footprints of dinosaurs and such, produced in just the same way. Next you have casts, produced, for example, by things like shells trapped in a mud deposit, then themselves being completely dissolved, and finally having an entirely different substance deposited in the spaces left by the dissolution of the shells. Finally, you have petrifaction, which means the replacement, molecule by molecule, of the original materials by various other substances. The commonest sites of such replacement are the famous petrified forests, found all over the world. The most usual mineral to so replace the original material is opal, which is an amorphous form of SiO_2 and which has a curious ability in some cases of preserving the original colors of the objects. Mr. Carter's half oranges would seem to be of this order.

However, while fossil truck tracks only a month old were enough to give us considerable pause, the idea of the *petrifaction* of things like oranges in a few weeks presents geologists—and palaeontologists—with some very awkward questions. If fruit, let alone wood, can be so rapidly petrified, why can't animal bodies? And, if they can, why do we not find a higher proportion of fossil animals' complete bodies instead of mere skeletons—and particularly skeletons still in perfect order and properly articulated, rather than rent apart? Perhaps the chemistry of what we call animal (as opposed to plant) life-forms precludes the substitution of such simple mineral depositions.[84]

It is, however, a bit alarming to have to realize that things can be truly fossilized in a few weeks and that said fossils can then be buried under dozens or even hundreds of feet of overlay deposits, and literally overnight, by floods or by subaqueous disturbances. But it is the time factor that really gives us considerable pause. Happily we do not employ the fact of mere petrifaction for dating the "fossils" we unearth. Rather, the type of animal and its stage of development on the evolutionary scale is considered; then the stratum in which it was found; and finally the new physicochemical methods of dating geological strata are brought into play. And this brings up a whole slew of further questions.

Given the right conditions, just how long (or how short) a time *does* it take to "fossilize" anything?

There are a few other places where all manner of things, of both animate and inanimate origin, become turned to stone in a matter of months. The best-known example is an overhanging cliff at a place named Knaresborough in Yorkshire, England, where highly mineralized water drips constantly all year round from the outside of an arched and smoothly curved, natural sort of pent-roof structure.[85] Items suspended from wires just underneath this shower become encrusted with what is popularly called "lime," just as are things in many hot springs and in some caves all over the world. However, at Knaresborough, said items are not just encrusted, but actually turned to stone, and in a most curious manner. For many years this place has been a tourist attraction where hundreds of kids have had their favourite teddy-bears and other toys hung up to be "permanentized." And they are! Their outsides soon develop a thin encrustation, but the mineralized water in this case soaks into the heart of the objects where it dissolves anything soluble therein and then replaces this, *and also* fills any spaces between, with a kind of agate. The result is a semi-petrifaction; i.e., one containing sealed-in materials in their original form, not removed and replaced by molecules of some other substance as in true petrification; some materials dissolved and replaced by other substances; and finally, other unaltered material which is simply encrusted.

At this point our path bifurcates. In some circumstances, the production of such a sort of plum-pudding-rock does not stop

119

there, but proceeds over greater lengths of time until we end up with what we have come to call, simply, "fossils"—by which I mean things wholly replaced, like dinosaur bones. (Please understand we are not concerned here with casts or impressions, but only with "whole" objects.) The really amazing aspect of this has been brought to light by Drs. Ralph W. G. Wyckoff and Mahlon F. Miller of the Department of Physics of the University of Arizona.[86] These studies should be read in the original by any who might be deeply interested, but we have not the space to quote, so that the best thing to do is, I feel, simply to state, and try to state simply, just what they have demonstrated.

The bones examined were of the Cretaceous and Jurassic Ages, which is to say, by the modern revised dating, 71 to 130 millions and 130 to 175 millions of years old, respectively. After most careful cleaning to eliminate contamination, these bones were subjected to a prolonged series of chemical analyses. The result was that "More or less intact proteins, containing upward of 20 amino-acids, [were] recovered from individual bones [on an average] 150 million years old." [87] In other words, when mineralization (or petrifaction, if you will) of some parts of animal bodies takes place, other non-soluble parts become completely sealed-in, and in some cases even to the extent that such comparatively "ephemeral" organic substances as amino-acids may be preserved. This throws a somewhat different and most startling light on the whole matter of fossilization.

The next question must then be: Just when does merely getting buried, or immersed in water, initiate petrifaction? We have to be exceedingly careful here in our terminology and semantics, and mostly because of the proper definition of "fossilization." The mammoths and other animals found in the Siberian and Alaskan muck are true "fossils," but they would appear to have been fossilized almost instantly. Actually, they are "petrified," for the simple reason that ice is a rock, and ice in combination with sediments and other matter such as form this *muck* can be classed *only* as rock. Thus, we can actually have what may legitimately be called instant petrifaction! And this is where we have to be extremely careful with our language since the whole business depends upon the definition of the word "rock" and the "petri-" part of petrifaction. At this point we run, screaming, to the dictionaries.

The word "rock" today has all kinds of very different connotations (and quite apart from certain noises that are currently classed as music!). It also has a multiple origin. "Stone" is a synonym (the word "stone" is apparently of Germanic origin, the earliest form being *stān*),[88] and is defined as "any particular igneous or stratified mineral constituent of the earth's crust, including sands, clays, etc." "Rock" is derived from a Gallo-Roman word, *rocca*, which actually means "red." (The verb "to rock," on the other hand comes from the Norse *rukk* meaning "to move"; hence, very rightly, "rock music.") The "petri-" bit is simply the old Greek *petra* meaning a rock; hence Peter. This would at first seem all to be adequately satisfactory, but the crust of our planet contains enormous quantities of substances that are not igneous in origin and which need not be stratified, and which are often not even solid. These range all the way from gases, through liquids of ever-increasing density, to colloids, and on into amorphous plastics. And this is where we run into real trouble.

It is hard enough to explain to any other than geologists that frozen water is a *rock,* and that it behaves in every way like any other rock. But when you come to *oil,* you hit both a semantic and a physical problem. At what point in the drying out and compression process do the hydrocarbon petroleums become "rocks" as opposed to liquids? In other words, what is natural pitch (otherwise called tar, bitumen, or by all manner of other misleading terms)? This can behave like a colloid, and even, when sufficiently heated, as a liquid. Another problem with the amorphous colloids is presented by the "jellies." These are not oils, and they are usually unknown or overlooked, yet they play, and have always played, one of the most vital parts in the construction of the surface of our earth. They start off in a variety of

different ways but usually end up either as a "flint" or as a "coal."
And what was more important to man in his first million years
than these two things?

The vital point to grasp here is that while things can in very
special circumstances be preserved *in* oils, at least for limited
periods, they cannot be "petrified" in them. Jellies, i.e., basically
non-oily colloids, on the other hand, are the second (after the
liquids) greatest petrifiers. Flints and cherts are formed on the
bottom of seas as gelatinous, non-oily masses (or even layers)
and then themselves become rocks. In doing so they may replace
every other substance in a sea creature, turning it to flint, but
retain its every feature and sometimes even its internal complexity. Methinks that these petrified oranges were of this ilk, and that
the substance could have been a flint, like the agates and opals
which do this sort of job on the trees that make up petrified forests. Flints are marine in origin, but the substances that compose
them can be locked up in marine rocks that then become elevated
onto and into dry land *before* they gather as jellies, and then,
millennia later, when released by erosion and dissolution by acid
waters, go right back to work as petrifiers.

When we come to the other branch of this progression—
namely, the coals—we enter another world altogether, and the
one which most intrigues me personally. There are literally innumerable kinds of coals, and their origin, history, and composi-
tions form a whole "science" in themselves. They are, however,
now generally agreed to be derived from plants growing on dry
land and/or in fresh water; but one type, called the cannel coals,
has always constituted a puzzler. These are sort of waxy substances, ranging in consistency from an extremely solid form
called Gilsonite, to gooey masses that can be cut like fairly soft
cheese. The latter have for long been regarded as the "digested"
end-product of the spores of certain trees and other plants of long
ago—as diametrically opposed to the whole plants that would
seem to have formed the principal constituent of the other coals.

While not affirming that this explanation is invariably the case, I can confirm that it might be true in some instances, because I once stumbled upon just such a process. It happened thuswise:

For a number of years I lived on my own schooner in the Caribbean. I was doing a dual job, initiated primarily by my then life work of collecting zoological and botanical specimens for zoos, museums, and educational institutions. There are tens of thousands of cays and islands in the Caribbean, and it was my duty to visit as many of them as possible; and the things we encountered on the lesser-known and uninhabited ones would fill several volumes and definitely not be believed, even if I supplied adequate photographs in support of my diaries. One of them stands out in my memory and not only in connection with the matter of which I now write. This was a small cay—which is *not* an "island" but a tiny coral atoll—off the east coast of British Honduras.

Coral reefs that grow up around islands which are subsequently washed away, or which sink due to a lowering of the sea-bottom, or which become inundated due to a rise in sea level, are not themselves true islands. When the initial island (which *is* true "land") goes under, you are left with a ring of living coral that surrounded it at a discreet distance and which always keeps up within inches of the sea surface, so that you end up with a ring of reef with a lagoon inside. If then, the sea bottom rises again or the sea level sinks lower, the result is a circular or ring-like "island" on which coconut trees and other vegetation finally takes root. Usually, a narrow channel breaks through these rings, so that the sea flows in and out of the central lagoon with the tides. Sometimes, however—and particularly in very small atolls—there are no such breakthroughs, so that they contain lakes or ponds (not lagoons) which, over the years, have lost their salinity and, being replenished by rain, become freshwater sumps.

The "island" of which I speak was of this nature. Its coral "ring" had risen so far out of the sea, and so long ago, that real soil had formed on it, and it supported mainland-type trees and

123

bushes as well as the maritime coconuts and seagrapes. In fact, it supported a pretty good tropical forest about a quarter of a mile wide all around this "ring." The central "sump," pond, or lake was completely fresh and about a quarter of a mile long.

This was one of the most eerie and fantastic places I have ever encountered (see Plate IX). Its "waters" were jet black as seen from above. All around it stood a dense forest about seventy feet tall, but in the central pond stood a forest of bleached, silvery-white dead trees, all just about equally spaced and retaining only their larger branches—a sort of ghost-land. There was absolute silence in this place, and even the soft but constant trade wind did not penetrate there, yet there was lots of small life in the pond. As a result, and it being my job, I went into said "waters"—with nets and bottles in hand. I went straight down!

Very luckily I was within calling distance so that help arrived before I went under permanently, which I would have done in a few more moments if I had panicked or struggled, because I found myself not in water as I had thought, but in a viscous, clear, pale-yellow fluid of about the consistency of a substance called water-glass that used to be used for storing fresh eggs before refrigeration came along. Being a great deal denser than water, it actually buoyed me up, but due to its exceedingly cloying property, I could not get my legs up and "float" on my back. My gang had a really hard time pulling me out.

This exercise annoyed me not a little, and I was greatly puzzled; so I spent a long time investigating this place and taking samples from the pond. And I discovered that the whole of its surface was actually composed of some organic substance derived from the spores, pollen, and other detritus of the reproductive parts only of certain trees growing around, most of which were tropical evergreens. Their leaves also fell into this lagoon, but these sank to the bottom. The droppings from the inflorescences floated, and then, while rotting, they were all moved slowly to the northwest due to the prevailing and almost constant air drift from the trade winds that blew from the southeast. I had entered the pond at the northwest side.

Fascinated by this discovery, we dug in the soil around the edge of the pond and, as we went down, we encountered successive layers of, first, almost clear jelly; then, dark-brown stuff of about the consistency of "Jell-o"; next, a grayish-brown gunk just about as rigid as mozzarella cheese; and finally, a jet-black layer looking for all the world like "black-top" on a modern highway and which could only be incised with a heavy machete. In other words, we had here a clear demonstration of the creation, today, of at least one form of cannel coal.

This dissertation may sound irrelevant, but what I want to show is just what had happened to the spores and flowers and fruits of the trees that fell into this pond and caused the initial "jelly." They were not "fossilized" in the popular sense, but they were eventually "petrified" in that they ended up (in mass) as a form of "rock." It would seem that this could have been at least one of the processes by which some coals were formed. Now take this one:

In 1806, an Englishman named Thomas Ashe travelled through what he considered to be the "wilds" of North America, particularly the area now covered by the United States. In his book *Travels in America,* published in London in 1808,[7] he wrote as follows:

A gentleman now living close to Cincinnati, on the upper bank, . . . had occasion for a well, and persevered in digging for water, though he met with none at the depth of sixty feet; continuing on, his workmen found themselves at once obstructed by a substance which resisted their labour, though it evidently was not stone. They cleared the surface, and soon made it appear to be a stump of a tree which had been cut down with an axe! The incisions of an axe were perfectly visible, and the chips made by its action lay scattered about its roots.

125

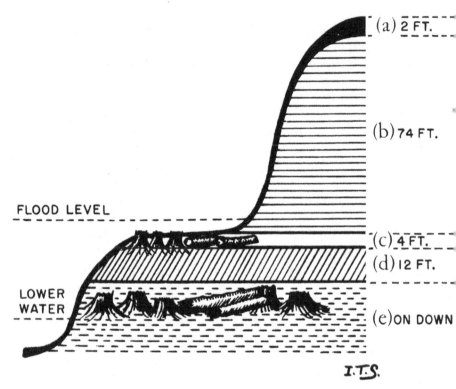

Fig. 25. *Cross (transverse) section of Mississippi River bank (west side), south of Memphis, Tennessee, showing positions of stumps and cut logs:* (a) *recent (1838) topsoil and sod;* (b) *sterile clay, stratified, varying depths;* (c) *light, compacted silt, with oak* (Quercus aquatica) *logs and pine* (Pinus tarda) *stumps;* (d) *sterile clay;* (e) *mixed silts with carbonaceous matter and sand—top strata containing cypress stumps and logs, swamp hickory, and cottonwood*

The stump was three feet in diameter and two in the perpendicular above its knees. It was nearly the colour and apparent character of coal, but divested of the friable and fusible quality of that mineral. I have these facts from my very intelligent friend, Dr. Goforth, and twenty others of honor and veracity who saw the chips cast out of the well before the men broke

up the body to which they originally adhered. The roots and
stump from being turgid, tough, saturated, and in part,
petrified, took considerable time to remove. Ten feet beneath,
water sprang up.

But this is not the only such case. In Silliman's *American
Journal of Science* there appears a letter from a Professor William
Carpenter of Jackson College, Louisiana, to the celebrated Professor
Silliman, published under the title "Account of the Bituminization
of Wood in the Human Era." [90] The bottom halves of trees and
stumps which appeared as the Mississippi River eroded a bank were
"bituminized" (see Fig. 25), i.e., they were described as being
"glossy black coal" with no wood fibers discernible, though the top
half was soft, soggy, and rotted. There were *axe marks* in the coal.
Carpenter stated that "The axe marks must, of course, be comparatively recent, though they were evidently made before the change in
the wood commenced." Both Carpenter and Silliman were baffled,
and Silliman noted, "I should like to compare this bituminized wood
with well characterized lignite."

The most pertinent question left unanswered—if it ever was
asked in these cases—is: "What kind of axe made the marks?"
Chips cut with a steel axe are quite different in form from those
resulting from a stone axe; and don't imagine for a moment that
stone axes don't give chips! If this stump that lay sixty feet below
the surface was cut with a steel or other *metal* axe, we are presented with a conundrum indeed. Either the axing had been done
after Europeans arrived—and if such was the case, surely there
would have been some record of floods or some such that piled
sixty feet of silt over the area—or else there were some people
running around with hard metal axes prior to the arrival of Europeans. If, on the other hand, the cutting was done with a stone axe,
the time factor is anybody's guess. Even then, it is a bit startling to
learn that a tree stump *in situ* can be carbonized to the consistency

of a coal in the limited number of millennia allowed for the habitation of this continent by axe-wielding men.

Thank goodness we now have radiocarbon dating so we can exactly pin down the time that it *does* take for things to get fossilized in various ways. But one thing is now clear: you don't need thousands of years to fossilize things; and they can be petrified almost instantly. Moreover, their original substance can be preserved almost indefinitely, provided the rocks in which they are enclosed are not themselves altered by metamorphic action.

CHAPTER NINE

THE ZODIAC

ASTROLOGY IS NOT a science, nor is it even a "useful art." In fact, if its showing over the past half century is any criterion, it is an amusing sort of game, but it can be a damned dangerous one to boot, and especially when it encroaches upon the province of prediction. This is a sad commentary on an exercise that so many people spend so much time on, and which so many other people innocently accept as gospel, in the belief that it is either a science or an ancient art. It is doubly sad since it *could* form the basis for a new departure into reality, just as alchemy formed the stepping-stone to chemistry. This, however, would mean abandoning its whole current basis and substituting another. As of now, astrology runs entirely on misconceptions and false premises, while there is lying around, and right under the noses of its practitioners, a solid, proven framework of tested knowledge on which it could be so re-erected.*

* Since the investigation described in the next paragraph was published,
a most remarkable book was published in France by one Michel Gauquelin,
which was entitled in the American translation (Stein & Day, 1969),
The Scientific Basis of Astrology. Trained as a psychologist and statistician,
M. Gauquelin is currently working at the Psychophysiological Laboratory at
Strasbourg University. The book is divided into three parts, the first is a survey
of the history of astrology. The second describes extensive research into the
alleged "findings" of astrology. In this the author was aided by a number of
the leading professional astrologers in Europe who lean towards as scientific an
approach as is possible to the subject. The third covers the extraordinary volume
of orthodox scientific work that has now been done on what can only be
called the cosmic influences of astronomical bodies on the electromagnetic,

A few years ago, the United States government gave a six-figure grant to one of the larger commercial complexes specializing in electric, electromagnetic, and related technologies to study, over a period of three years, the possibility and validity of suggestions that the 11½-year sunspot cycle might be correlated with and thus responsible for erratic and anomalous radio reception on earth. When the technologists' report was submitted, both officialdom and orthodox sciencedom received a considerable jolt. The findings were to the effect that, while such anomalies on earth did appear to show predictable rhythms, these did not seem to coincide so much with the detected solar periodicity but rather with the movements of the planets, their conjunctions and oppositions and so forth. The concensus was that the effects were produced by gravity rather than electromagnetic interference or boosting.[91] The popular press gave out with a consorted howl of glee, especially in such countries prone to mysticism as Germany, but the astrologers were strangely silent. This may, of course, have been due to the fact that they live in a world of their own and one of makebelieve at that, and so could not accept anything said by either science or technology, even if they stumbled across it in print.

To scientists, however, this tentative finding initiated some very profound thinking. True scientists are always interested in the unknown, the unexplained, and the frontiers of knowledge, and on this occasion they started to take another look at astrology and with some enthusiasm. But alas, they immediately encountered all the old bugbears. And then they ran head-on into a much greater obstacle.

In trying to make some sense out of the outpourings of astrologers, it had long ago been observed that these folk, in making their

chemical, and biological continuity of both inanimate *and* animate entities on this earth. The second section utterly demolishes astrology; and with the concurrence of those astrologers who aided Gauquelin in his statistical researches! The third section, on the other hand, proves beyond any shadow of doubt that there could be a true science concerning itself with the actual influences—rather than a lot of imagined ones—of stars and galaxies as well as the planets of our solar system, that interfere with, if not actually regulate, life on our planet. This book is an absolute "must" for everybody in any way interested in the subject; and both pro and con.

predictions and developing their charts, have ever failed to take into account a number of most vital and potent factors which *do* affect our environment and everything, living or inanimate, "born" within it. True, in casting a horoscope, modern astrologers take into account the locus of birth on the surface of the earth and thus of its position *vis-à-vis* what they call the heavens, but they have never taken into consideration the basic ecological factors of the environment at that point. Latitude and longitude are naturally important; but altitude, temperature (both mean annual overall and monthly), barometric pressure, and all the other simple factors operative at any specific time in any specific place, let alone the particular readings at the time of conception, throughout the period of gestation of the embryo within the mother and at the time of birth, are blissfully ignored. This wouldn't matter if one were dealing only with a cosmic event, but these factors are known positively to affect not only every individual but whole races—and of all animals, including man.

Further, there are two sets of such factors. The first is what is now called the biorhythm displayed by all living things,[92] dependent upon seasonal fluctuations, and such. The second is the ever present incidence of erratic and anomalous environmental factors. For example, while such animals as oysters taken from the east coast to Chicago continued to open and close on their original time schedule, according to season (sunlight, etc.) and latitude, they gradually changed that rhythm to fit the time zone into which they had been transplanted. What happens to a Sagittarian born (or conceived) in a violent and prolonged electrical storm in West Africa, if transported to Texas? And what of the mother's state of health, physical and emotional? Come now! All Sagittarians born in the same place at the same time cannot all face the same prospects when these countless other factors have not even been taken into account. And they have *not* been by astrologers.

Then, there is another thing. Just when is an animal, and especially a mammal, born? Is it when the young first appears; when it is completely out; or when it is separated from the mother, or the allantois or afterbirth? Is it when it takes its first breath of air as opposed to fluid? And who ever pinned down any of these to the second, or even to the minute? I was born twice, in a manner of speaking, during a four-hour period straddling midnight and had to be hauled out with a pair of tongs. Nobody has ever been able to figure out whether my birthday is the 30th or 31st of January, since Scots law, which is founded on Roman Law and not precedent, is not precise on this matter.

As if all of this were not bad enough, it must then needs be discovered and demonstrated that the astrologers' much beloved zodiac has nothing whatsoever to do even with ancient astrology, except that its various "houses" might reflect the most notable characteristics of certain peoples occupying the various sectors of the early Portolano compass which was divided into twelve rather than the later ten sectors. In fact, the zodiac was nothing more than travelling directions for anybody setting out in any direction from the head of the Persian Gulf. So, just what *is* this "zodiac"? *

As I have so often said, and possibly though in no way regretfully, *ad nauseam,* the best place to start on anything is the dictionary. If we don't know precisely what we are talking about, we simply cannot even attempt to communicate. So, to the dictionaries!

In these it transpires that the word "zodiac" is derived from the Latin *zodiacus.* This sounds reasonable, but it doesn't really get us anywhere since the Romans borrowed or adopted almost everything from the Greeks. So, reverting to the Greeks, one finds that they had a word which may be transliterated into the Roman alphabet as *zödiakos* which meant to them "a circle of animal signatures." This expression in turn derived from their word *zödion,* which was a diminutive of *zöon,* which meant "animal," but also particularly

---

* There are several so-called "zodiacs" originating from various parts of the world. There are Ancient Egyptian, both western and eastern Indian, a Chinese, and both an Aztec and a Mayan Mexican. There are also indications of similar beliefs elsewhere as in West Africa and the South Pacific, but these are only "similarities." It is only that one, developed by the Sumerians, that has had any real influence on "Western" thought.

Unfortunately, it has been everlastingly and wholly misinterpreted, misunderstood, and misused. It is nothing but a "road map," just like the oil companies put out today. It is still valid and real but it was never intended to tell your fortune, or do anything other than to get you where your boss wanted you to go to make money.

denoted small animal figurines, sculpts, or symbols. (One should note well that the science we call in our language today "zoology" has a similar base and is, of course, to be properly pronounced "zoe-ology" and not "zoo-ology.")

It now transpires that the Greeks somewhat prior to the time of Hipparchus—circa 130 B.C.—got some ideas from Mesopotamia. Of these, several were astronomical and of great use to a maritime nation for navigational purposes. One was this so-called "zodiac." It was a very neat project; simple, practical, and applicable even by illiterate mariners. It was simply a wheel, marked off into 360 equal parts around its circumference, and then divided by twelve spokes, each subtending an angle of thirty degrees. The ingenious Greeks seem immediately to have made a sort of hand-cranked computer (an example of which was dredged up from the bottom of the Aegean in 1900, and which has now been cleaned and resuscitated, and which is called the Antikythera from the locality where it was found),[93] in order to put this idea to work. You see, the Greeks, like us, had only ten fingers, and although they did not have the idea of a zero to make multiplication easy, they were stuck with the *decimal* system. But this blasted zodiacal wheel was based on the *duodecimal,* or base-twelve system!

Actually, the decimal system is an awful nuisance anyway, because while you can halve it, you can't quarter it; and when you try to divide it into thirds, you end up with the sort of ridiculous nonsense that Wall Street has to try and cope with, such as 33.3 and 66.6 recurring percent. The duodecimal base, on the other hand, is a positive delight since you can divide by both two and three—you know, 3 fours are 12, and so on! Point was that somebody had figured out that the earth was a sphere and that you could therefore slice it any which way you wanted and come up with a circle. By the grace of some Almighty God, however, these ancient people happened to choose deliberately to divide the circle into 360 degrees, instead of 350.

These sensible people appear to have been those we call the Sumerians, who popped up at the northwestern head of the Persian Gulf circa 4000 B.C., and are in part also called the Chaldeans.

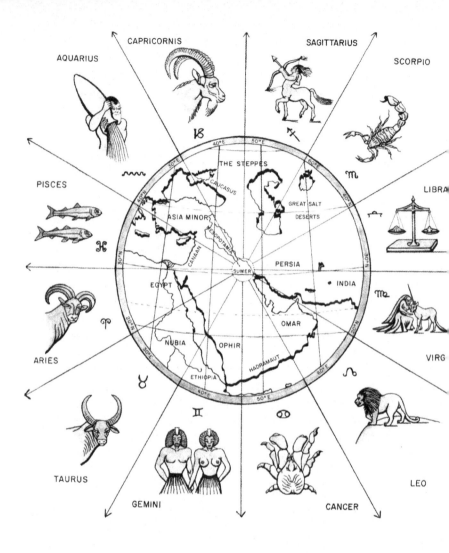

Fig. 26. *Map of the Near East, centered on the city of Ur in ancient Sumeria, surrounded by the twelve "zodioi"*

Nobody quite knows what to do with these people. Since they appear to have given us the practical arts of writing, mathematics, trigonometry, and so forth, as well as this duodecimal system for counting days as well as chopping up the circle; and all at about the same time, prehistorians have fallen back on the dreary suggestion that "they must have come from somewhere else, with a full-blown culture." This may well be true, but it is still ridiculous, because where then did *that* culture come from; and how long did it take them to develop all these intellectual arts? The Indus Valley perhaps? Actually, the Sumerians themselves put on record that they got it all from some chaps who appeared *out of the sea!* [94] Nonetheless, the western Near East, which is to say the Hebrew-Aramaic-Semitic, the Hittite, Cretan, Minoan, and even the Egyptian civilizations of the eastern Mediterranean got this Sumerian technology, and along with it came this zodiac. But just what *was* this thing?

The answer is extremely simple. If you copy the zodiac wheel, as used today, on a piece of clear plastic; stick a pin through its hub, and then stab that pin on to the home-base of the Sumerians (see the accompanying map, Fig. 26), you will immediately see what this is all about. Sumeria lay at a point which we today designate as the junction of 46°E. longitude and 30°N. latitude. (There just might be some significance in this, in that 30 degrees is exactly one third of the way from the equator to the North Pole, while 46° is twice 23° which is approximately the angle of the tilt of the earth to the track it makes around the sun. But this is another exercise.)

Imagine therefore that you are residing at the head of the Persian Gulf about 6000 years ago. You will find that whichever way you might have wanted to travel from there—except down the sliver of the Gulf itself—you would have to traverse several hundred miles of desert before hitting a coast. Now, all deserts look alike, and especially flat ones. Unlike maritime navigation, there are no steady winds, currents, coasts, tides, or other even fairly stable natural phenomena to aid one. On deserts, where the winds can come from anywhere and at any time, and where there are no landmarks, the only things you have to guide you are the stars. So, the Sumerians devised a star map for desert travellers, divided it into *twelve* segments, and gave each a simple symbol so that illiterate cameleers, horsemen, donkey-drivers, or plain foot-sloggers could keep going in at least the correct general direction that they desired. And the Sumerians were consummate astronomers, geographers, and also most knowledgeable students of international affairs.

What is more, they appear to have been basically, if not exclusively, an economic empire, so that their principal interest was in trade and commerce. They appear to have acquired a wealth of knowledge of the peoples living all around them, and from their immediate borders to hundreds and even thousands of miles beyond. They knew the principal products that each country had to offer, and also what each needed from them. They were not interested in the religions of other peoples, though the "totems" of those peoples were often the very animal, plant, or mineral that formed the basis of their economy. Thus, the Sumerians designated each land by its principal product.

These segments were originally devised to cover twelve equal parts of a belt of the celestial sphere extending between eight and nine degrees on each side of the eliptic—so covering that part of the sky within which the apparent motions of the Sun, Moon, and the principal planets took place.[95] Actually—and this is another case where the astrologers have gone off the rails—these constellations in the twelve sectors have, due to what is called precession, shifted in the last 6000 years almost precisely 180 degrees, so that, for instance, the Aries original signature is now in the so-called "house" originally assigned to the scales, or Libra.[96] They say that they make adjustments for this, but no two lots of these soothsayers seem to be able to come up with the same adjustments.

So, take your zodiacal wheel and center it on Sumeria, and then arrange it so that the north-to-south line runs due north between Capricorn to the west and Sagittarius to the east. Imagine then that you are a merchant starting out from Sumeria to prosecute trade to the northwest-of-north. You will point up the left-hand side of the Mesopotamian valley until you hit the mountains and, if you get there, what will impress you most? *Goats*—both wild mountain goats, ibexes, and domesticated goats, since the last were the first animals to be domesticated—and by just those people you will find living there. Thus, the land of the "Capricorns" or "Goat-horned Ones." Further, to aid you in your travels, the scientists back home have given you a pretty picture of a bunch of stars that you must find at night and which they have linked together by straight lines to form a *goat*. So let us proceed around the zodiac as if we were merchants setting out for the next sector to the left, or west, as viewed from our home base in lower Mesopotamia.

Here we hit mountains once again; but this time we can follow the great rivers Tigris and Euphrates right up to their sources in what is now eastern Turkey. Now, these rivers have always flooded annually and regularly and since before even Sumerian times, so that there was always a tradition among the indigenous peasantry of Mesopotamia that there must have been a great god somewhere "up back" who periodically poured water from heaven into these waters. Hence Aquarius, bearing his water-pot on his shoulder. Further, one should note that the Dravidians in India, the Chinese in Han, and the Egyptians also had the same idea about their great, life-giving rivers. Also, if you will read what astrologers have to say on the character of the people who lived where these "gods" were alleged so to deliver their bounty on so regular a basis, you may perhaps see why these mystics attribute the characteristics that they do to these "Aquarians." They were mountain folk and they were always amply supplied with water; and when the snows melted each spring, the excess water quickly ran away downhill. Thus, they could not care less where it went or what it did when it got down onto the lowlands. They had better things to think about, and to do. They weren't *against* anybody; they just were not interested. This is perhaps the basic outlook of all mountaineers, regardless of the dates of their births, on our or anybody else's calendar!

Moving, then, to the next segment to the west (actually WNW), what do we find? If you left from Sumer, you would trek across a couple of hundred miles of particularly dreary desert and come to

"The Land of Palms," namely Palestine. There you would meet a bunch of fish-eaters. These were sturdy, patient folk; and, what is more, they had been going off into the sea beyond for millennia and without fear or cavil. Look at the map: the world of the fishermen, and of the fish-eaters goes right on out into the Mediterranean.

Try the next segment slightly south of due west. Once again, and of course, following the constellation so neatly joined together to look like a prancing ram, you will traverse an equally dreary desert but soon begin to hit tribesmen wandering about with droves of skinny, short-haired sheep. They even worship the brutes—see fatted calves, golden rams, and so forth. This goes on all the way across the peninsula of Sinai and on through lower Egypt to North Africa. Sheep, sheep, sheep, and more sheep; and, apart from the sport of kings, nothing *but* sheep, even unto the wild ones of the mountains of North Africa that look like goats but which aren't, being aoudads.

So on your next trip you start out towards what we call the southwest, which we have been told is the land of the Bull. This time you have to pound off on an 800-mile walk across a ghastly desert until you come to an arid coast—the central east shore of the Red Sea. So what did you want to go there for? Answer: one of the most valuable commodities then known, to wit, cattle. But to get these you have to cross a sea to the Land of the Great Oxen —namely, Nubia.

Let us not forget that the progenitor of our western cattle was the aurochs,[97] but that this itself remained an animal "of the chase" until its final extermination. The first cattle to be domesticated were the humped breeds of northeastern Africa, and it was from that area that the Ancient Egyptians and the Mesopotamians, and even the Dravidian Indians got their cattle. Take a look at the great friezes of these enormous creatures in Egyptian frescoes and you will get the clue: marching along in seried ranks, their horns on high, their dewlaps flapping, and their huge heads crowding aloft, one in front of the other, and all driven by one small black Nubian. Today, we pay in six figures (American) for

138

pedigreed bulls of breeds from Europe. No wonder the Nubian bulls were so very much desired by the ancients. (Incidentally, this stock appears to have been boated around Arabia to Mesopotamia and India.)

Now we come to the more esoteric and interesting side of the zodiac. No one merchant traveller could go and do business in all twelve of these "segments" in one lifetime; so let us assume that you are the old man's son, and that you choose to go first to the Land of the Twins. This is south-southwest, and thus necessitates a *thousand* miles of travel across a desert. This is an enterprise of enormous extent (even if camels have by your time been domesticated), and it simply is not worth undertaking unless the potential profits are very great indeed. That they were so is evinced by the fact that for millennia people did make just this passage, right across Arabia to the Straits of Bab El Mandeb and then over said strait to the Land of the Twins. Why? Because Ethiopia was the fabled Land of Ophir, or of gems and other equally valuable items that came in small packets and which could be easily transported. But why should this land be called that of the twins?

The tradition among the priesthood of Ancient Egypt was that their Pharaonic aristocracy came originally from somewhere around the southern end of the Red Sea. By all descriptions they would be called by us today Hamitic people, and they apparently were the end product of a very long cultural history. Among their many customs—that were, incidentally, quite foreign to the indigenous inhabitants of the Nile Valley—was one of great significance. Apparently, these extraordinary people had discovered that inbreeding within a family group was the *best* thing, not only to preserve but to better the "stock," *provided* the genetic factors were what were desired (or "good") in the first place. Thus, not only did they disbar out-breeding with any others, but they insisted upon full brother-sister marriage and breeding. And, just as with domestic animals, their "stock" duly got better and better; and it went gaily on for over 4000 years! So, please note, the "Twins" displayed by astrologers and everybody else on the zodiac, always show a male and a female holding hands. Token brother-sister marriage is still practiced in Somalia.

We come next to the quadrant named by the ancients that of the Crab. For long this presented a considerable puzzle. Why would anybody want to make a thousand mile trek to southern Arabia? Obviously only for profit; but *what* profit, and on *what* trade?

This segment of Arabia is known as the Hadramaut and is today a rather nasty, arid area. However, up till not so long ago it was one of the lushest and most fertile areas in the world. This was the land of frankincense and myrrh, and—what most people don't seem to realize—of *oil!* Also, and only somewhat incidentally, of pearls! In fact, this was one of the most worthwhile areas of the ancient world for any trader to visit. As long as you could get there without dying of thirst or being waylaid, with a caravan of the metallurgists' products in gold, silver, electrum, copper, bronze, zinc, or what-else, you could get many times their value in a wide range of items not available back home. But what about the crabs?

There are crabs galore in all the seas of the world, as well as, to a limited extent, in the open oceans; and they swarm in tropical rivers, on tropical lands, and even in jungle trees. A crab, as a totemic symbol, is found all over the world. Most crabs are good to eat, and many kinds are frightfully impressive. Take the king crabs of the northern Pacific, one of which had an arm span of 13 feet. But there is one crab that is truly outstanding. This is found all around the Indian Ocean. In body bulk it matches even the largest king crabs, and in weight it tops them fourfold because it spends most of its life out of water. It is a hermit crab, but about the size of a football. It is named scientifically *Birgus,* and it feeds on coconuts, which it cracks open with two trip-hammer, spiked claws (see Fig. 26 and Plate X). It has been alleged to be able to crack the skulls of exhausted, shipwrecked mariners, who have passed-out due to thirst, famine, and exhaustion on beaches around the lower reaches of the Red Sea and the southern Arabian coast. Not pleasant.

These crabs are very good to eat, and it appears that the early inhabitants of the south Arabian coast made them a staple of their diet so that vast quantities of their shells are found in middens that these early inhabitants left on that coast. The *Birgus* became the symbol of that area, and this was preserved in carvings and depictions into a later period when the country became a great empire where, incidentally, some of the first true cities were built with true "skyscrapers." In other words, anybody setting out for this land, six thousand years ago, would say that he was heading for the Land of the Crabs.

The next segment, travelling counter-clockwise around this zodiac, brings us to that designated Leo, the Lion. At first this too looks funny because it covers only the northeastern slice of Arabia. What on earth, you may well say, can this have to do with lions? We must, however, appreciate the fact that the names originally given to the twelve sectors of the zodiac were basically *economic* by definition. The animal symbol assigned to each was the most notable and prominent feature of their economy—even unto virgins. Only Libra and Aquarius lack a straight animal sign; but then, water (not bread) is the *real* staff of life. The Sumerians were not interested in the religious connotations placed by other people on their principal products, other than to advise *their* travelling representatives that they should respect the attitudes of the locals to these. Lions were then found very numerously in this sector, which includes what we call today the Trucial Coast and Oman. But they were valuable not merely as items of the chase, but for a quite contrary reason. These were the lands where lions were raised and trained *for* the chase, and also for controlling mobs, *and for war*. The Assyrians, Kassites, Babylonians, and even the Egyptians got their hunting and martial lions from this area.

Moving next to the northeast, we come to the sector given the sign of Virgo, meaning the Virgin. This would be very puzzling were it not for the fact that said virgin has always been depicted as wearing a *sari* and petting an unicorn. At first this looks a bit balmy, but let us consider some facts. If you look at the map again, you

141

will observe that, if you go east from Sumer, you have to travel across the deserts of Persia, Laziristan, Baluchistan, Pakistan, and Sind before reaching non-desert India. Now: there were two commodities to be traded along that route—namely, child brides (i.e., virgins) and unicorns (i.e., the horns of the Indian rhinoceros), which then, as now, appear to have been held in high repute for medicinal purposes. This is all perfectly logical and plain—but for the traditional form of the unicorn.

This has always been depicted as a rather delicately formed *horse* with a single, spirally-twisted horn sticking out of its forehead—certainly never in any way like a rhinoceros. So what went wrong here? From a zoologist's point of view the explanation is very simple and straightforward. It is simply that the desert areas that had to be traversed to get to India were the homelands of a wild ass (the onager) and a wild horse which was partially domesticated, also of some truly domestic horses, and of something else that *looks like a horned horse.* This was a species of antelope related to the oryxes of Arabia and East Africa, which have a *pair* of long, rapier-like horns that are ribbed throughout their length (see Fig. 27). One of these animals, seen from the side, looks as if it has only *one* horn and this is the way the ancient artists depicted it.

Fig. 27. *The Arabian oryx antelope, of which the Persian was a subspecies, shown with head exactly in profile. Note that there appears to be but one horn.*

Actually the horns of the oryxes slope backward, in line with the plane of the face; but possibly because there was some knowledge of the upright position of the "horn" on the snout of the rhinoceroses, its direction was increasingly misrepresented. The clincher, of course, is that rhino horns are neither ringed nor do they have spiral ridges, like some goats and antelopes. Also, it is quite possible that the horns of the oryxes had an intrinsic value of their own.

To the east-northeast of Sumer lay a mountainous land which seems then, as it still is, to have been inhabited by many tribes of wild, freedom-loving individualists. However, the designation "Libra" for this sector probably has quite another connotation. The clue to this is the *scales.* By some adversion these have become the symbol for "justice" (which we of the West regard as synonymous with freedom) but they now appear originally to have been the symbol for "honesty."

The lands in and bordering this *Libra* sign formed the kernel of the area in which the earliest metallurgy was developed, and which was a major source of gold and other precious metals. Now, both for alloying metals and for trading in them, *scales* were used; and for these, standard weights had to be used; and these, in turn, had to be universally respected. When trading goods for gold (and thereby employing it as a medium of exchange) you just *had* to be able to trust the scales, or rather the "weights" that merchants and governmental officials used on them. The invention of the balancing scales has been sorely neglected. It was one of the major inventions of man.

Let us be very sure from now on to stay with the map—and particularly with its physical features—because you will notice from this that the segment designated *Scorpio* slices through a mountainous region to the deserts of central Asia. These are the most ghastly deserts in the world, being alkaline. Then, coming to consider the original reason for this "sign," we must take a number of matters into consideration. Scorpions are one of the commonest forms of life throughout all the twelve signs, but they are more noticeable in this otherwise almost lifeless country.

Those wise ancients of Sumer did not just hand out land-sailing directions to merchants on a frivolous basis, however, and their choice of the scorpions for this direction undoubtedly had a very pertinent significance. Various suggestions as to why this sign should have been chosen have been put forward. One is to the effect that it was really a simple way of saying "Don't" or "Keep Out," since the whole bit was hostile and sterile. Another contends that the scorpion symbolized *poisons* generally; and this area, with its naturally "poisonous" soil, would indeed seem to have been the dissemination point for all kinds of mineral and vege-table poisons which were sought by such early peoples as the Han Chinese, the Dravidian Indians, and the early Mesopotamians.

So, we finally come full circle, *via* the sign that is the most ob-vious of all, and which, even if none of the others should fit this analysis, would prove its validity. This is the land of the centaur, or Sagittarius.

Fig. 28. *Central Asiatic mounted archer, circa 2000* B.C., *from contemporary depictions. These nomads were so completely "integrated" with their horses that the eastern Mediter-raneans may well be excused for believing that they con-stituted but a single animal.*

Prior to the development of the atom bomb, there were really only three major advances in warfare. The first was the long-bow, which seems to have been contemporary with, if not to have antedated, the stone axe;[98] the second was the mounted archer, i.e., Sagittarius (see Fig. 28); and the third was the gun.[99] It was the second, moreover, that really changed the world, because it broke up the ancient hegemonies, and for the very simple reason that they had no defense against a mounted archer.

This was a development of the nomads of Central Asia, who practically lived on the backs of their horses. They were carnivores and they lived off the land, while their sturdy horses didn't even need grass in emergencies and for prolonged periods. These nomads invented the stirrup and the short bow, constructed of layers of horn and wood with a short but enormous pull and which shot tiny arrows to great distances with enormous penetrating power. They fired from their horses at full gallop, and they used the good old (to us) "Red Indian" trick of wheeling around foot-soldiers and the grounded archers—right-handed bowmen one way, southpaws the other—while their buddies chased the enemy's gallumphing cavalry all over the lot, picking them off piecemeal by "cutting-in," but never getting close enough to be touched themselves. These tactics were what finally stopped the Roman legions; they also forced both the westerners and the far easterners to adopt armour, and to retreat into walled towns and castles. No wonder the Greeks were impressed, and thought that these "monsters" were half man and half horse.

One might well wonder why even traders from the high civilization of lower Mesopotamia would want to pound over such great mountain ranges just to get to the land of these terrifying horsemen. And we might, therefore, infer that the "centaur," as occupying this sign, was also nothing more than a warning sign. However, it has now been shown that there was considerable trade between these two areas and that, scattered about the lands of these nomads, were several most advanced cultural centers, and from the end of the Neolithic Age in that area. In fact, throughout early history these people constantly poured outwards in great waves—to east, south, and west—and they brought with them not just destruction but also a lot of material things, and even some fine arts. Ever hear of the Medes and the Persians?

Thus, having come around the full circle of the so-called zodiac, we find ourselves holding but one conclusion. This is that the *original* zodiac was, to early land travellers, what the later wind roses were to mariners. This map was centered on Sumeria and was based on economic enterprise. Further, it is manifest that explanatory texts went with this device and that these recorded the most outstanding personality traits of the peoples to be encountered in each direction. However, the travellers who used this map were illiterate and so had to be given simple symbols—a mountain goat seen in profile for Capricorn; a ram seen from the front for Aries; and so forth. Having done this, the priests of Sumeria, who were true astronomers, took a bunch of stars that could be recognized in each segment, joined them up arbitrarily with lines to look like goats or sheep or oxen, and then trained these travellers to spot them, and so to send them safely on their way. Then, they did something else.

They integrated, as far as was then possible, the most propitious dates between which said travellers should *arrive* at their destination. And this is where the astrologers have most surely gone off the rails, because they have never realized that the distance to the desired destinations, and in each of these twelve sectors, from the point of departure, varied widely and wildly; and they make the monumental mistake of trying to start their assessment *from the center,* when those who devised the whole thing were only trying to put on record the best time *to get there.* It is useless to head off for the headwaters of the Euphrates just because you were *born* between late January and mid-February. That was the time you had to *get* there.

CHAPTER TEN

LITTLE GOLD
AIRPLANES

A COUPLE OF YEARS ago, an old friend of mine named Emanuel M. Staub, of Philadelphia, one of this country's leading jewellers, sold his business and was clearing out his shop. For twenty years, Manny had been one of a very few artisans entrusted with making casts of the priceless gold objects and jewellry in the collections of leading museums. The beautiful displays that you see in many of our great museums are often his work. These are gold-plated copies, while the originals are kept locked up in vaults.

Manny has never thrown away a mold, so that while cleaning out his shop he was somewhat jolted to find the small item shown in Plate XI. Manny made a copy of this and sent it to me with a note on its origin. The essence of this note was to the effect that about fifteen years previously the government of Colombia (South America) sent a sampling of their fabulous state collection of gold artefacts on tour to the United States. This great collection is kept in the State Bank in Bogotá, and it is not only one of the greatest treasures in the world but absolutely unique in the field of art.

The selection from this collection brought to this country was put on exhibit in six of our leading museums, ending in the Metropolitan in New York; and, when it was there, a gentleman named Al Jahle obtained permission from one Señor Sanchez who was in charge of the exhibit, to make casts of six of the items, using a new plastic that he had developed for dental surgery and which could not possibly harm the specimens. Mr. Jahle, I should add, was then a senior technician of the Cardiology Department of Hahnemann Hospital in Philadelphia and the inventor of the first electric heart-stimulator. He sent his molds to Manny Staub and asked for casts, and this little mystery artefact was among them. So much for the background.

This neat little trinket is ambiguous, to say the least. It was one of a group of somewhat similar figurines, all of which were listed in the catalogue that accompanied the exhibit, as "zoomorfica," meaning simply, animal-shaped objects. This was fair enough considering the age of these gold pieces, which has been pinned down to between 750 and a thousand years. However, the collection also contained dozens of most clearly identifiable animals, all rendered with the greatest accuracy and attention to realistic detail. The startling question asked about this particular trinket therefore was rather naturally: What animal? So, let us look first at the biological possibilities.

There are several types of animals that fly: birds, bats, insects, and several "gliders," like flying opossums, squirrels, some little lizards in Indonesia, and even a snake. There are also some other creatures that *come out of water* and "fly": the flying fishes. Then, there are others that "fly" *through* water. These are the skates and rays and some other selachians—a group of animals that are not really fish, but which are closely related to them, and which includes the sharks. These skates and rays, or batfish, literally "fly along" under water, in a horizontal position, by undulatory movements of the edges of their huge pectoral fins. These fish have upright *fins* on their tails, but invariably have long, tapering "tails" behind these. Many have delta-type "wings," with a pair of fleshy, horizontal appendages behind, called claspers, which are used during mating. What is more, several have prominent eye-like markings on their "wings," probably to detract attackers from their

148

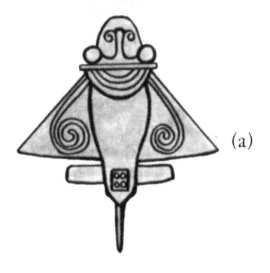

Fig. 29. *Little gold trinket* from the Colombian National Collection: (a) *as seen from above*, (b) *the side*, (c) *in front*, (d) *behind*

real eyes, which look out sidewise and are under ridges on the tops of their heads, and which are way out front. I therefore first thought that this artefact was an ancient artist's conception of such an animal. But when we photographed the little model, blew it up many times, and traced its outline, all kinds of things immediately came to light (see Fig. 29).

Seen from above, the gold model proves to have practically no fish-like attributes at all, but rather, to show some most explicitly mechanistic ones. What appear to be structures which are now called "elevons" when on airplanes (being a combination of ailerons and elevators), have a slight forward curve. These latter, however, are attached to the fuselage rather than to the wings, and would seem to be elevators rather than ailerons. In any case, they certainly look more like airplane parts than like the claspers of a fish. Then, if the centers of the two "squirls" on the wings * are meant to indicate the eye spots on a ray, what is one to make of the two very prominent globules to right and left of the straight bar across the back of the "head"—especially if the two little twirls out near the front of the head are meant to be the *real* eyes of such a fish?

This is all odd enough, but when we come to view this object in profile, or sidewise, we get more profound shocks. First, why should anybody—skilled artisan or uneducated idiot—want to make a solid-gold model of a fish (or moth, or anything else) with its

---

* Since this was first written I received a most interesting letter from a Mrs. Elfriede Tingleaf [100] of Tonasket, Washington State, who has spent half a lifetime copying and recording Amerindian rock carvings. She points out that in the "language" of these petroglyphs—and they are now acknowledged to be sort of primitive hieroglyphs—both the large and small spirals on the left side of this artefact indicate "ascend or go up," while those on the right mean "descend or go down." She goes on to point out that: "No matter which way you turn this little model, the spirals read the same." Since many, if not all of the ancient Amerindian conglomerate petroglyphs appear to have been maps, these symbols would seem to have referred in those cases to trails going up or down on the surface of the land. If the Central and South American artists who made these little "plane" models were Amerinds, they might very well have employed such symbols for some things that they wished to indicate went up and down, in the air and/or water.

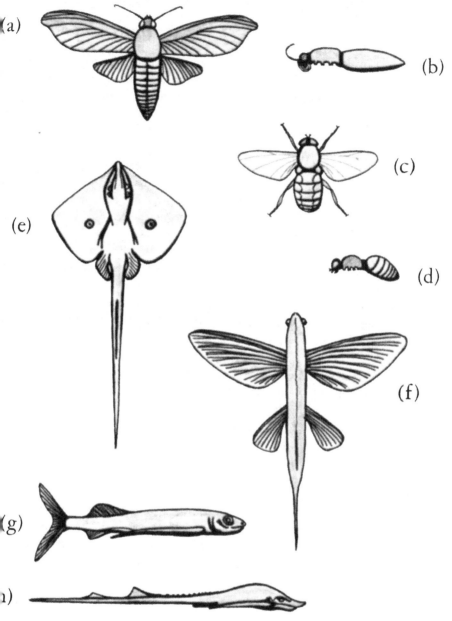

Fig. 30. *Known animals that have been put forward as possible "models" for the little Colombian gold trinkets:* (a) *a hawk or sphinx moth;* (b) *the body (or fuselage) of same, seen from the side;* (c) *a house fly;* (d) *fuselage of same from the side;* (e) *a ray (selachian fish);* (f) *a Pacific flying fish;* (g) *the same seen from the side—pectoral and pelvic fins in outline;* (h) *the ray seen from the side. Note especially the dissimilarity of the "tails" of all of these.*

head three-quarters cut off? Second, why make the nose precisely rectangular (as seen from the side, Plate XII) like an old-fashioned Rolls Royce, and then put louvres on the top of it on both sides? Then, why tilt the "windshield" (or bit of flesh at the back of the head, after chopping it almost through) forward, and put a couple of eyes (headlights?) at either side, when a fish's eyes are far forward and near the center? Next, what about the "seat" in the "cockpit"? What's this supposed to be—fishwise? Then there's the "scoop," under and a bit forward of the cockpit; and seen from the front, it *is* a scoop, not just a ridge for punching a hole through to string the thing on a necklace.

Now consider the fins or wings. Note that, from the side, they are absolutely horizontal, but when viewed head-on from the front (Plate XIII), they curve slightly downward. Then, those little elevators. They stick straight out at a slightly higher horizontal level, are square-ended, and of a definite geometric shape— *not* curved fins. And the four little knobs above them—what are these?

On the tail, we come to something equally intriguing. Fishes have tails of all sorts, and all are upright (except for the flatfish, which are really lying on their sides). However, none of them has only a single, upright, perpendicular flange.* But planes do! What is more, this tail fin has the exact shape of the upright "fin" on many modern planes. It also has a strange marking on it.

When everything is considered, this enigma just does not look like any kind of known animal; but it *does* look astonishingly like a small airplane. The worlds of fishes, bats, birds, and insects do not offer any reasonable or even possible inspiration for the maker of this artefact (see Fig. 30). We submitted these pictures and a cast of the object to a couple of aerodynamics people, one of them no less than Arthur Young, who designed the Bell helicopter and other aircraft. His reply read as follows: [101]

---

* Some so-called heterocercal tails of fish do approach this outline on occasion, but there are a number of aspects of these that, in combination, never coincide with the rest of the features of this model.

Little Gold Airplanes

Have received the small "flying" object, and your request
for an opinion. This small, solid-gold object certainly suggests
an airplane, especially in the vertical tail surface, which is
not present in any bird or insect. But the wings are in the
wrong place—[they] should be further forward so that its
¼-chord coincides with the center of gravity—for anything
other than a tail-engine jet. Also, the nose is very unairplaneish.
So I have to confess that, while it *suggests* an airplane, it
does not resemble one. Perhaps it is an artist's "impression."
Anyhow, it is quite fascinating. Whatever it is, the front end
is inexplicable and, of course, in this area, no one is an expert.

We also are most certainly not experts in this field either, but
what we still want to know is why some artisan a thousand years
ago went to the trouble of making this thing in the first place;
and why he made it just the way he did. The nose is definitely a
sort of rectangular box, as seen from the side. Then again, if all
this front end was but a sort of "glove compartment" and the
heavy machinery was abaft of what appears to be the cockpit, the
thing *would* have been perfectly balanced—fore-and-aft, that is—if
held between its two wing-tips. The thing *is* manifestly an "artist's
conception"; but what did that artist know of the machinery of
anything so bizarre? What kind of power plant, if any, did it
have? Or was it a glider?

This was the first dependent problem that we went to work on,
and it called for a further appeal to the engineers. I always become
happy, and almost to the point of elation, when I can toss a problem to this fraternity, since they have proved over the years to be
the most open-minded and pragmatic of realists, wholly devoid
of traditional strictures and philosophical cant. Perhaps this is because they *have* to be right, or lose their jobs, and/or commit
suicide. Take bridge-building for instance. If the damned thing
falls down, either before or after they've got it built, they've had it!

Aerodynamic engineers are given a bit more leeway because
they are asked to design and construct things to find out what

153

conditions said machines will have to contend with *before* we know what said conditions might be. This is a real challenge. In this case, however, there is a lot of accumulated knowledge to go on, in the form of airplanes that have already been built and which have both fallen down or *not* fallen down. This is not to say that these gentry didn't get into an argument, as I will now demonstrate. As a result of the elevation of these questions, I turned the matter over to Jack A. Ullrich, who was one of the first rocket-plane pilots in Germany, and who flew all types of prop planes and many early jets, and who has a very considerable engineering background, including aerodynamics. His preliminary report reads as follows:

> The first impression I got from this thing, not knowing its origin or anything else about it, was that it represented some form of aircraft; and a high-performance one at that. With its delta-wings, it looked like an F-102 Fighter. Since first impressions are often the best, let me start off by assuming that it *is* an aircraft, and then let me try to analyze its external features, and then make some tentative suggestions as to what might be hidden in its interior as a propulsion unit.
>
> Starting at the nose, we find, first, two decorative "whirls" on the top and then two things that look like eyeballs arranged laterally at the back end of said "nose." Such items are not normally found on aircraft as we know them. They could be due to what is called "artistic license" but the funny thing is that, if such things were put on modern airplanes, said planes would still fly. Many modern aircraft have more junk than that hanging on their outsides, and they still manage to "stagger" into the air. Take a look at some of the fighter-bombers flying today in Viet Nam. They are literally "hung up" with stuff, hanging on their outsides.
>
> Reverting to the model, the cockpit is broad and, depending on the overall size of the craft which, of course, we cannot estimate, could accomodate one, two, or more persons. Again, I refer you to the F-102, which is about the size of a C-47, and you may then see what I am talking about. The body could have been streamlined with a bubble over the cockpit.

In fact, since the delta-wing configuration implies high-performance—by which I mean speed—it would be a necessity. Otherwise, the occupants would not "do so well" with the resultant air turbulence.

The body of this "plane" is nicely tapered and has enough volume to allow installation of a power plant, which should be, in this type of thing, a turbo-jet engine. It would not make sense to put a reciprocating engine, or anything like that, into a fuselage such as this. (Propellors do not give the performance required to match a delta-wing construction, though they can be made to perform with such a structure up to several hundred miles per hour. But we are talking here of much greater speeds.) But this object spells out but one thing to me—namely, JET. But I wish to analyze this further. If it be a jet, where the exhaust should be—i.e., near or under the tail—detail is lacking in this little image. But what if there was *no* exhaust? Maybe it could have had a propulsion system other than that which we call a jet; but I will not speculate on that.

The only difference I see between this and today's delta-wing jets* is that ours all have a different type of fuselage, which was developed more or less by accident and which is called the "coke-bottle fuselage." This specific shape has been created in order to make it possible for the plane to pass through the atmosphere at very high velocities and, at the same time, to decrease buffeting.

Consider next the underside of the object: an air-intake for an engine may be indicated on the belly-side, under the cockpit. Then again, this may be nothing more than a protrusion to allow it to be drilled and a chain put through it so that it could be worn as a pendant.

As I mentioned at the start, this thing appears to represent a high-performance type aircraft, and for those of you not acquainted with these matters and specifically not with the F-102, I would ask you to look at the widely circulated designs of the proposed SST of Boeing.

* See Plate XV, Swedish delta wings.

Aircraft with this type of wing need great power for take-off and they rise at a remarkably steep angle in order to get lift. They then fly very fast and land at high speeds. What I mean is, no slow cruising or gliding for these. This is why cargo transporters cannot be constructed on this type of configuration, and the only way the SST can make it is with brute power.

This is why we have no delta-wing gliders, since the glide-angle ratio would be prohibitive—somewhere on the order of 5:1, which means that for every five yards forward motion, the plane sinks one yard. The most efficient glider configurations are seen among birds, which have very high aspect-ratio wings—by this I mean wing-span versus width of wing. Powered aircraft do not have high-aspect ratios—with the notable exception of the U-2, of Gary Powers fame.

Unpowered gliders—i.e., sail planes—*do* have a very high ratio, and the best performance was exhibited by a flying wing design of the brothers Horten in Germany during the 1940s. Their glide ratio was 1:45, greater than an albatross, and which I do not think has been exceeded till now. This is diametrically opposed to the performance of delta wings. There isn't a rubber band made that could launch this thing in flight.

Looking at this model from in front, I note something particularly. Most planes have their wings slightly dihedral—in other words, when you look at it from the front, the wing-tips point slightly upwards. This helps to control the plane so it will be flying properly in relation to the horizon; with the exception of the high-performance aircraft, whose wings point downward; in other words, the wing-tips droop a little bit. (I'm not referring to the B-52 type of wing which is extremely flexible, but to fighter wings, such as you see on the F-84, and the F-105 fighter bomber made by Republic Aviation.)

Now to get to the rudder. The rudder is conventional, but where body and rudder meet there are a few strange humps, which are mystifying and I shall allow myself no opinion on them. We have also *elevator* surfaces at the tail which modern delta fighters do not have at the rear end of the fuselage, as the model has; but, if and when they do have these surfaces,

they are on the tip of the rudder. It is shaped like a "T" when
you look at it from the front. Let me explain that modern
Deltas can do without these surfaces entirely, since they now
have what are called "elevons," a contraction of the words
aileron and elevators. And these elevons are located at the
wing's trailing edge and perform the function of both aileron and
elevator. Then again, these two things sticking out at the
hind end of this little model here, may not be elevators, but
possibly extended speed brakes, though their surfaces are
parallel to the wing surfaces, which they should not be, for
this way they will not grab the air and act as brakes. Perhaps
it would have been difficult to do it some other way. I have
no way of judging this. If they were elevon surfaces I think
they should have been swept, as is the wing, since it would
have made no sense to sweep the one and not the other.

While Jack Ullrich was chumbling over this report, I appealed
to another old friend, Adolph Heuer, who is an engineer and has
built all his own farm machinery, *and* an automobile that is still
twenty years ahead of the most advanced current experimental
models. He was with the U.S. Air Force Quartermaster Corps
during WW II in charge of plane loading. He took a completely
contrary view of the balance of this little plane to that taken by
Arthur Young, whose report he had not seen. (He also came up
with something quite else, as we will see further on.) His basic
analysis led him to feel, like Jack Ullrich, that the thing was a
high-boost, steep-take-off plane in which the engine could have
been either in front or in back of the cockpit. He envisioned it as
being some form of jet- or rocket-propelled device, and wondered
whether the four little knobs or louvres just ahead of the tail fin
might not be some kind of air *intake* to feed the fuel passing backwards through the base of the tail to a single, small propulsion
vent, such as we have in modern single-engine jet-planes. (I should
note here that everybody has always assumed that there was a
transparent dome over the cockpit.) However, before proceeding

to Adolph Heuer's separate set of general observations, it is better that I interject here a second memorandum from Arthur Young.[102] This goes as follows, and is reproduced with Mr. Young's permission—provided only that it is *in toto*:

Your last letter prods me to pull the stops out and make further speculations about the airplane-like object. These speculations depend on estimates of the center of lift and center of gravity of the craft represented. Of course, not knowing the construction, it's impossible to tell where the center of gravity actually was, but the likelihood is that it is even further ahead than it is in the solid metal model because the tail surface (which is likely to have been of less density than the nose section which "looks" heavy) has the greater moment. About the center of lift; I said before that it could be no further forward than the ¼-chord (25% back from the leading edge), due consideration being given, of course, to the delta shape of the wing. But the fact that the center of lift, as suggested by Mr. Ullrich, could be further back, only makes the discrepancy greater. To maintain level flight (that is to be sustained by the wing), the aircraft must have the center of gravity and the center of lift coincide. It is one of the functions of the horizontal tail surface on an airplane to insure this coincidence.

These considerations lead me to say that the object in question is not an airplane. This does not mean it is not some kind of aircraft or flying object. What kind? Here is where the considerations above provide clues to interesting speculations.

Since the surface is far back, it must be intended for a *dart-like* flight, a descent through the atmosphere; and the delta-wing and tail [i.e., elevon] surfaces not intended for lift but for control. We might then make sense of the proboscis-like nose. This is a jet or rocket which jets forward and is intended to *slow it down,* rather than to make it go forward. But there remains a curious unexplained feature: There is a V-shaped groove transversing the fuselage and

158

just ahead of the wing. This is a conspicuous feature and has no counterpart in conventional aircraft. And if one is to explain something it is important to take account of its unusual features. I puzzled over this for some time; then it hit me!

The whole nose section hinges 180° so that the jet or rocket ejector can be pivoted around a hinge line at the bottom of the V-slot into a position to point the thrust rearwardly. In this position the weight would be at the correct point for the delta surface to act as a wing and we would have an airplane of sorts, complete with propulsion means. Putting these speculations together we can guess that this is a *convertible aircraft* of a type that (to my knowledge) has not been proposed. It is a craft capable of two configurations: (see Fig. 31)

Fig. 31. *Mr. Arthur Young's alternate suggestion as to what the artist was trying to depict. This is on the assumption that the power unit was in the front, and that the pilot was housed in the main, central body of the fuselage.*

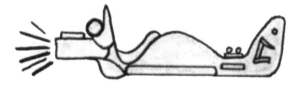

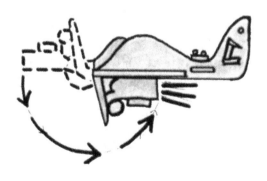

(a) With the propulsive nose in the forward position
it would have a configuration suitable for descent and slowing
down, for in this case the surfaces supply dart-like stability
and the nose supplies reverse thrust for slowdown. After
slowing itself down from, say, five miles per second to a
few hundred miles per hour, it could land as an airplane.
Such a device suggests that it would serve as a vehicle for
entering and leaving the earth's atmosphere in support of a
larger space vehicle which remained in orbit.

(b) With the propulsive nose tucked under and back,
it can take off as an airplane and rapidly ascend, depending
more on the thrust device than on the wing; since, in this
configuration, it would have too much drag for extended
horizontal flight.

Adolph Heuer was the first to have sight of Figure 29 and it
was he who first pointed out the pertinent fact that the wings were
not perfectly horizontal but turned ever so slightly, but precisely,
downwards out near their tips. As a result, we yelled for Jack Ullrich, who literally came running (on rubber) all the way from
Connecticut. Confirming this revelation by a tedious lot of precise
measurements, he agreed with Adolph that a steep-rise, super-
powered craft such as this would have the tips of the wings slightly
elevated. What, then, did the down-curve mean?

To make a long story short, the only known answer was that
this thing could have been constructed to dive *into water* and then
get out of it again into the air! This, of course, brought on all
manner of further enquiries. Was the scoop under the front of the
cockpit a water as well as an air intake? Alternatively, if the front
hinged back as Arthur Young had suggested it *could* have, would
not it be the nozzle of a jet when underwater? This led us to en-
quire about submarine-airplanes or aerial-submarines such as all
manner of popular publications have been talking about for years;
but this proved to be an awfully tough nut to crack.

Finally, we got a "blueprint" of one such device—a privately
built job that actually so performed off the coast of New Jersey in
1966—and with propellors, yet! [103] Another model was alleged

to have made one dive; regained the air; but then disintegrated on re-entering the water, killing both pilots. This was a Navy job. Both had slightly down-curved wingtips. Such was the status of this business about a year ago (as of the time of writing) and we all felt pretty unhappy about it. But then another colleague, Mr. Barney Nashold, popped up with a "real beauty."

What happened was that he wrote me almost casually, saying that, while puttering around the South American ethnological collections on public exhibit in the Chicago Natural History Museum, he spotted the object shown in Plate XIV. This is somewhat gloriously, though apparently rather tentatively, labelled a "Flying Fish." Wonderingly, we made application for further details; and to our modest surprise, Barney Nashold duly came back with data and photos on no less than four of these items from that museum. But to make matters worse (or better), the original discoverer of all this, Manny Staub, who had moved to Washington, D. C., by

Fig. 32. *Map of eastern Centroamerica and northwestern South America to show locations of Sinu and Coclé*

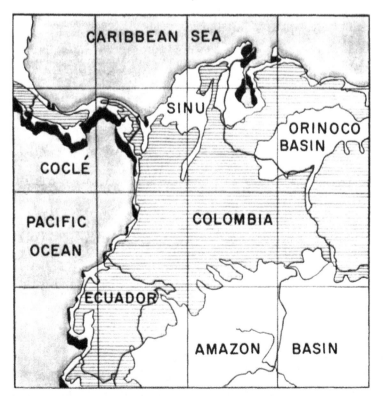

that time, sent us photos of *still another one,* which is on public exhibit in the Smithsonian Institution—and labelled, simply, "A cast gold ornament"!

The core problem in this mystery is, of course, the *age* of these artefacts. Quite a large number of radiocarbon dates have now been obtained from organic materials and charcoal found intimately associated with this gold work, and from an area spreading from Costa Rica to the borders of Venezuela, and south to Peru (see Fig. 32). These have given a very considerable range in time, but all the dates derived from those cultures and subdivisions of cultures in which these seeming aeroforms have been found, seem to come out somewhere between 500 and 800 A.D.,[104] making them *a minimum of 1000 years old!*

I would have thought it unnecessary to point out that we got our first heavier-than-air machines off the ground only about 70 years ago; but we discovered to our amazement that the average reader—and notably the younger people—of an article that I published on this subject in a popular magazine, was totally unimpressed. Puzzled, we ran a survey, only to become even more astonished to discover that many people simply failed to see anything odd about 1000-year-old airplanes, while some youngsters, when pressed, proved to think—albeit rather vaguely—that both airplanes and television had been known for centuries! (This does not say much for our education system; and anent this, I should put it on record here that I once went on a TV program to compete for a thousand dollars and found myself opposed by a high-school teacher. We were asked the question: "In which year was the Atlantic first crossed by *radio?*" My opponent wrote on a blackboard, "1774 A.D." I am still reeling from the implication of this.)

That the older generations are just as firmly convinced that we did *not* have airplanes, or TV, a thousand years ago, of course, explains *their* indifference—their reply naturally being "Don't be ridiculous." Therefore, when such items as these turn up in deposits that have been dated, to the oldsters' satisfaction, to the ancient past, they just as naturally class them as mythical or religious figures; and when they look like possible animals, they call them

162

zoomorphs to sort of "get off the hook." However, there are darned few archaeologists, prehistorians, historians, or even art experts who have any zoological training, and I am not sure that there is so much as a single living member of any of these disciplines who is a systematic zoologist, trained to identify and classify animals. Hence, they often talk the most unutterable rubbish in this department.

Laymen, which is to say everybody other than professional archaeologists, prehistorians, and zoologists, must, on the other hand, bear a corollary fact in mind when assessing the interpretation of these items. This is that artists and craftsmen from the very earliest times—*vide* the early Stone Age cave painters of the Old World —were the most consummate artists; and when it came to depicting the animal life of their areas were a darned sight better than most of our best modern illustrators (as photography has now demonstrated). In other words, they knew their animals intimately; and even when exercising what we call "artistic license," they, like that late, great genius, Walt Disney, *never* played hob with the basic theme or indulged in flights of fancy—such as adding extra legs. When they were depicting mythical beasts, on the other hand, they went hog-wild; but such depictions and sculpts are readily distinguishable.

When a zoologist comes to contemplate these (seeming) aeroforms, he will immediately find that he has a very limited number of major categories of animals to choose from as possibilities. These are, as already stated: (1) bats, (2) birds, (3) pterodactyls and one other kind of extinct reptile, (4) two kinds of "fish": first, the true flying fish; and second, the batoid selachians, or skates and rays, and (5) insects. These are the only animals that have either true wings and which actually fly or which make flying motions. There are, of course, gliders, skimmers, and parachutists, like the so-called "flying squirrels," but these can in no way be correlated with the structure of the little gold airplanes. The most likely suggestions are delta-winged birds like starlings, certain insects, and two kinds of fish. However, the form of the tail eliminates the first two without further ado. Then again, the batfish are similarly

163

eliminated, since they have long tapering tails. But there are two small groups of relatives of these fish, called the wobbegongs and the electric rays, that display *some* of the features required. However, their overall outlines and the arrangement and proportions of their "wings" *do not conform;* while the tails of the former are bifurcate. Also we *know* that these ancient artists knew perfectly well what these creatures looked like. So, with what are we left? Only the flying fish.

This in many ways is the best candidate, but once again, every one of their morphological features is just plain "wrong," *vis-à-vis* these little artefacts, and are quite impossible for a zoologist to "stomach." Instead of writing a detailed analysis of these features herewith, I suggest that you take a look at the outlines of a flying fish (Fig. 30g and h), alongside those of one of these artefacts, since I feel sure that, provided you are not a professional archaeologist, you can conduct this exercise for yourself. Anyhow, the flying fishes' tails, like those of the wobbegongs, also have two tines— one going up, and the other down.

Thus, I am sorry to have to tell archaeologists and prehistorian art experts that these things do *not* represent *any* kind of animal(s)—even with their heads three-quarters cut off! I am also afraid that I am constrained to observe further that they would be pretty rotten efforts on the part of such consummate artists as made them in an endeavour to represent any "god" or other mythical beast, while they are damned good models of certain specialized types of high-powered heavier-than-air machines (See Plate XV, A and B).

The only other suggestion as to what they might have been that I have ever received (that made any sense, that is) was that they were fishing lures. But I don't fancy that even a wealthy Amerindian chieftain would have his made of gold, even if they were but "models" of his lures. Also, why have them constructed this way instead of in the form of the animals that were the natural food of the fish that he wanted to catch? And where did his craftsman get *his* model to copy?

164

CHAPTER ELEVEN

A LITTLE GOLD
'DOZER

T

HERE WILL PROBABLY be
those who have hoped that we would, by now, be done with such
"ridiculous nonsense" as was presented in the last chapter. But
I'm sorry to have to announce that this is not possible because a
somewhat similar, and in some respects even worse, case has come
to light.

The little gold "airplanes" came from, as Fig. 32 shows, northern
Colombia. As far as dates can be correlated with other professional diggings, they appear to have been modelled somewhere between 500 and 800 A.D. on our time scale. This in turn correlates
with the radio-carbon dating of some posts dug up at diverging
points along the famous Nazca Lines on the coast of Peru.[105] Now
we come to another thing from another area, that is asserted to be
of roughly equivalent date, and again according to modern radio-
carbon assessment. In my personal opinion, this find is even more
startling than the delta-winged airplanes.

It is a piece of jewelry made by a consummate artist; in gold,
containing a huge green gemstone, and obviously intended to be a
pendant. It is four and a half inches long (see Plates XVI, A and B,
and XVII) and was described by its discoverers as a crocodile, but
later by others as a jaguar.[106] It is, however, covered with mechanical devices, including two cogwheels. This is rather a long

165

story but for once a fairly straightforward one—provided, that is, one preserves what sanity one has and starts off with some form of the famous "open mind."

In the late 1920s, what archaeologists call a "site" was located on the land of a family named Conté, in the Province of Coclé, which is on the southern coast of Panama to the west of the Canal Zone. This site was near the town of Penonomé, the exact location of which may be seen on the accompanying map. Here were found hundreds of graves containing great masses of pottery, some funerary urns of children (a most important find, as it turned out three decades later), and masses of gold ornaments, body shields, and jewellry. The Peabody Museum of Harvard University carried out somewhat extensive diggings on this site in 1930, 1931, and 1933.[107] Later, the Museum of the University of Pennsylvania made a further investigation of the site from the 25th of January to the 14th of April, 1940; [108] and then, it is reported,[109] the Peabody again tackled the business in 1951.

The site is on a level plain, cleared for pasturage, about a hundred miles west of Panama City and ten miles back from the Pacific coast. There is nothing on this plain to indicate that there are burials beneath, because the people who did the burying did not erect stone edifices or any other kind of permanent memorials above ground. The site came to light only because a river known as the Rio Grande de Coclé flooded in the year 1901 and cut a new channel that disclosed these graves. They are now known to spread under at least six acres. The graves appear to have been sunk, and then filled, over a period of several hundred years; and from radio-carbon datings obtained from the ashes in the cinerary urns mentioned above, to have been dug between 200 and 1000 A.D. In some instances, there were several graves, one on top of the other, and of different dates. There is another site in Coclé province near a place called Nata, but the material from there seems to be of somewhat later date.

The jewellers of this area reached a pinnacle in their artistry about 1000 years ago, but they were apparently still going strong when the wretched Spaniards arrived. These *bandidos* proceeded to rob and ravage the country starting in 1519, and they toted off literally tons of gold in the form of ornaments, body "armour," and jewellry. There are certain peoples in history to whom I take the gravest exception because of their gross and, in my opinion, immoral behaviour; and those sixteenth-century Spaniards now top my list. With a cross in one hand and a sword in the other, these money-grubbing, barbaric, uneducated goons proceeded to muck up the second best group of cultures man ever created, and all in a few decades. Despite their robberies in this area, the site near the town of Penonomé on the land of the Conté family was saved because it was not visible above ground, and it has proved to be the most productive of the finest jewellry and other gold artefacts.

It must be explained that here, just as in Mayaland farther west, and in the Andean area of South America, jewellry substituted for coinage; while the elaborate metal body coverings—in the form of breastplates, helmets, calf and shin encasings, huge arm-bands, and so forth—were not constructed for protection, as was the iron armour of mediaeval Europe or as were the walrus-ivory and elephant hide outfits of the Orientals. They were ornaments, pure and simple. And among this wide variety of bodily adornment, great emphasis was placed upon collars, breastplates, and especially upon pendants. The last have turned up literally by the millions, and in every case they constitute the best of workmanship. The most interesting thing about these ornaments, however, is that the consummate artists who made these exquisite things for century after century, depicted just about everything they could lay their hands on. What is more, their knowledge of their local fauna and that of the adjacent seas and oceans was almost phenomenal, in that a trained zoologist today can almost invariably spot and place a proper name or identification on all the animals represented in this jewellry, and in many cases even down to species. At the same time, these old artists often embellished these animal designs with

167

all kinds of weird and sometimes monstrous appendages, curlicues, and fabulous excrescences.

These latter degraded items have come to be called *zoomorphic* designs by archaeologists and modern art dealers and museum people. But I am afraid this designation is nothing more than an easy "out" employed when anything turns up that manifestly cannot be clearly identified as a known animal, a god, or some purely mythical beast. Of such "monsters" there are aplenty, but they are readily identifiable in that all of them are based on a human or humanoid frame of reference. The *zoomorfica*, on the other hand, are quite otherwise. It is true that the ancient Amerindian artists often did "zoomorphize" certain things—which is to say they modelled them in the form of the animal that they knew best and which looked to them, in shape or outline, just like that which they wished to depict. In other words, as was pointed out in the last chapter, if these artists wanted to model a flying fish, they did just that; if a moth or a hummingbird, likewise; but if they were confronted with something that flew but which was manifestly no known animal, they went right ahead and did with it what they could.

Now, it may be perfectly true that this class of items are *zoomorficas;* but then, why aren't they either true representations of known animals such as these artists turned out by the millions, or truly mythological things such as there are also aplenty? These people weren't a bunch of bumpkins banging away at bits of soft gold. The artisans who made these things were highly skilled technicians, way ahead of their European contemporaries in some casting methods, soldering techniques, and certain forms of filigree work never found elsewhere outside Southeast Asia. Further, there is no real reason to suppose that the artisans who made these things were themselves the designers of these objects. They may have been, but as it would seem from several glaring bits of realistic evidence, they were not. Instead, it appears much more likely that the designers were artists and ran large "shops," and simply gave in-

168

structions to their workers to make this, that, or the other, and thus, thus, or thuswise. It would seem also that if a model of an animal was needed, these headmen did not have to give any instructions, apart from stating *which* animal. When it came to mythological and religious items, the designers doubtless consulted the priests, and then probably gave very detailed instructions. So then we come to these *zoomorfica* items that are of neither of these categories. What were these, and why did they come out the way they did?

Before we go any further, I had better give you another thought —and bluntly. Our great museums and other collectors of ancient art—and this goes for all countries in the world that have such —actually have very little idea just what they have got in their collections. And I don't mean just what the specimens they have *are;* but rather, specifically, just what specimens they *have!* Hundreds of thousands of items are on exhibit for the edification of the public that are either not labelled at all, or are mislabelled, or misidentified. What is more, many that have been "identified" are catalogued as things that they most manifestly are *not,* and could not possibly be. Tens of thousands of others have defied identification and so have simply been stored away. Get inside any great museum and get permission to inspect their basements! The basic reason for this is simply that in this day and age, curators are far too specialized and, at the same time, have seldom if ever even heard of any agreeable explanations of these things, other than those given in the textbooks and constantly rehashed in the publications of their colleagues. An example:

Some years ago a Roman villa was discovered in southeastern Sicily, and on its being excavated, there was brought to light the largest and most perfect mosaic floor ever found in a private Roman residence. The world's press went wild over this, and both stuffy and popular magazines published many color-spreads of it. The reason for this outburst was that these mosaics displayed a number of young females with the sort of skinny figures common to such

169

magazines as *Vogue,* but all wearing "bikini-type" swimsuits. One enjoyed this modest diversion, but what interested us much more was that some of these "models," just like their modern counterparts, were shown leading and fondling wild animals.

One of these animals was covered with black spots on a yellow ground. It was, of course, immediately called a leopard—and by everybody, and even in the most erudite publications. But not by the wildest stretch of even a non-professional zoologist's imagination could this have been intended for that animal; and because of half a dozen features that had been most carefully and accurately depicted by the chap who laid the mosaic. It was absolutely and without any possibility of a doubt a *cheetah,* and a damned well-done cheetah at that. There was also in this mosaic a very careful depiction of a species of gazelle, which is a form of antelope, and of a species that is still found in Tunisia and Libya. This was labelled a "deer," but with the added nonsense that *it came from Africa.* It just so happens that there are *no* deer in Africa and never have been! This is the sort of "official" rubbish that the layman has to contend with.

So, what can one expect of a curator of an archaeological collection of ancient artefacts, some of which definitely do *not* portray animals, but have all the aspects of machinery? Poor "expert:" if he can't tell a cheetah from a leopard or an antelope from a cervid, how in the devil can he be expected to differentiate between a delta-wing jet plane and a flying-fish? So, at somewhat long last, we may get back to this "crocodile-jaguar-what-have-you" item.

During the diggings on the Conté estate in Coclé Province of Panama, a few truly magnificent pieces of jewellry were brought to light which were set with gemstones. Such added ornamentation is exceedingly rare among the pieces found in this area. In three cases these stones are said to be cabochon emeralds, but it now appears—at least according to the gemologist and jeweller Emanuel Staub—that these stones are actually very fine jadeite. This fact in itself is rather interesting, since the so-called "jade" of the New

World is almost all a related mineral named nephrite. However, a very few objects of genuine jadeite, which is found otherwise only in eastern Asia, have turned up in Central America, and notably among Mayan relics. It is now believed that the Mayas obtained this mineral from a source—the location of which has since been lost—in what is now Guatemala. It should be noted that artefacts of the Coclé type have turned up in Guatemala, so that there would appear to have been interchange between these two regions in early days. Among the objects set with gemstones that came to light near Penonomé was this piece initially called a crocodile and then a jaguar. This contained a huge gemstone over an inch long, domed, polished, and not faceted, as our latterday gemstones tend to be.

The story of this object from the time it was unearthed is somewhat obscure, but it is now owned by the Museum of the University of Pennsylvania in Philadelphia. It has been on public display therein for a number of years where it is described as "A jaguar with a large emerald set in its back and [which] holds a stylized snake in its mouth." [110] At this point I just have to draw a line, or lower the boom, because it's the same old story as with the little gold airplanes all over again.

A jaguar, indeed! Did you ever see a large spotted cat without spots, but with a straight tail, rectangular in section, and bearing two cogwheels on an axle going through its tip, and a rocker arm between them? Did you ever see *any* cat with, in addition, two more rocker arms sticking out of its rump and holding triangular "mudguards" behind its heels on either side? Did you ever see a cat with two enormous, globular eyes *on the top of its head,* like those crazy goldfish developed by the Japanese for fun? Did you ever see a jaguar or any other cat with a row (both above and below) of evenly matched teeth, all shovel-shaped and slightly recurved? Please look carefully at the accompanying drawings (Fig. 33).

It may be interesting to note that nobody appears ever to have

171

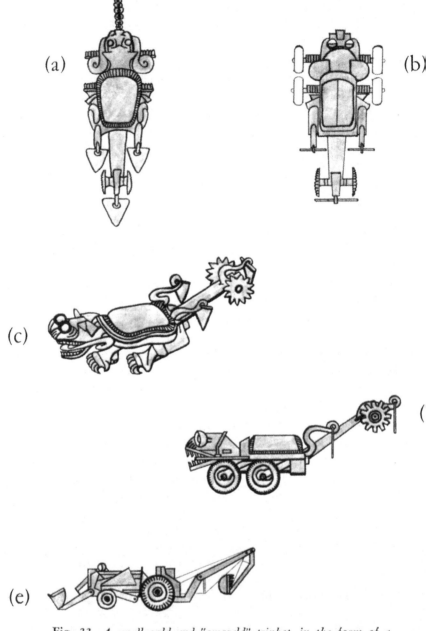

Fig. 33. *A small gold and "emerald" trinket, in the form of a pendant, from Coclé on the south coast of Panama, circa 700 A.D.: (a) hung as a pendant; (b) as seen from above, "squared-off," with "mudguards" hanging down, and possible riding wheels indicated; (c) object as from a photograph taken in the University Museum of Philadelphia; (d) the same, rectified for lateral view, also "squared-off" and with wheels added; (e) a modern back-hoe with dozer-bucket scoop as front attachment*

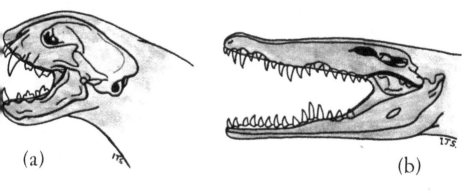

(a)

(b)

Fig. 34. *Lateral views of* (a) *a jaguar's head and* (b) *a croco-dile's* (Crocodylus moreletii) *head, with skulls outlined for comparison with the "head" or front end of the Coclé artefact*

taken a photograph of this object in profile. Small wonder, perhaps, for should they have done so and published the result as a "jaguar" they would doubtless have found themselves in a most embarrassing situation, for even an archaeologist ought to know that *no* animal has rocker arms, axles, and cogwheels. As to its being a jaguar, please glance at Fig. 34. So let us examine this lovely little thing in detail.

First, it is most unlikely that it was "hung on a chain which passed through the loops created by the curved claws of the animal's front paws." [111] To the contrary, there is an indication that there was a small hole centrally placed under the forepart of the thing by which it might well have been suspended as shown in Figure 33(a). What is more, the claws of *both* the *front and back* feet curve right around and backwards so they form tubes of equal diameter which look as if they were constructed to hold axles. Next, we must understand that this object was made by jewellers, and Amerindians at that. These people never were much for sharp angles, preferring, rather, curved and rounded edges and corners. However, as we saw with the airplanes, they rounded things off but did not totally ignore or destroy rectangular construction. So, and once again, when we view this object directly from the side

173

(Fig. 33c), we discover that it is altogether different from that which pictures of it taken from other angles would suggest. If we then "square off the angles," as it were, we end up with something as depicted in Figure 33(d). By this time, any resemblance to a jaguar, or any other animal, has completely evaporated, and in its stead, there emerges something alarmingly like a certain type of machine, only recently developed by us. This is a machine known to all farmers and construction men as a backhoe. Cast your by now doubtless somewhat jaundiced eye on to Figure 33(e). Notice that, in the model depicted, there is one pair of typical tractor wheels that are larger than the other pair. However, some models made in Germany have wheels of equal or subequal diameter and which are much closer together and further forward. Bear in mind that anybody, having never seen *any* powered machine, might well think it to be some ghastly kind of animal, since it made noises and apparently moved of its own volition.

At the "front" end—or left side, as here depicted—of the Coclé thing, we note a sort of gaping mouth armed with a very regular and even set of "teeth," both top and bottom. Neither jaguars nor crocodilians have a set of dentures of this nature (see Fig. 34); the former have small ones in front, then very large canines, followed by a gap, behind which come cutting teeth, running fore-to-aft, and with more than one prong. The jaws of crocodilians are long and slender, and when viewed from the side, the edges in which the teeth are inserted go up and down with notches. Besides, all the teeth of both animals are pointed, whereas the "teeth" on this object are strap-like, with dull chisel-shaped ends, all slightly recurved. This is precisely the shape of the prongs on our modern mechanical bucket-grabs.

At the other end of our modern backhoes there is, of course, an arm, like a crane, from which depends a scoop. Some of the larger machines developed in West Germany have a pair of pulley wheels at the end of this arm over which heavy cables pass downward to the scoop which is on a shorter arm. This sort of assemblage is pretty well reproduced in the Coclé object in which, it should be noted, the main arm is angular with very severe straight edges and is rectangular in section, while it tapers from the main body backward. The model-maker was very careful to make this portion of the object this way although, as I have said, Amerindian artists were not much for straight lines and sharp angles. If this was supposed to be (or was modelled on a theme of) a jaguar or a crocodile, why on earth did not the artist make the tail round in section and in other ways of the shape and proportions of either one or the other? Such questions are nonetheless obviously rhetorical, since no animal has two cogwheels and a rocker arm at the end of its tail!

There are other items on the Coclé object that should be particularly noted. For instance, there seems to be an engine hood in front and two louvers on either side of this. Behind this assembly come two huge spheres which we must presume the "zoomorphists" take for eyes. However, you will see from the picture of a jaguar (Fig. 34a) that the eyes are rather small and directed forwards and downwards. On the other hand, the headlights used on heavy construction equipment are very large floods, and are normally placed just where these things are. There are then curved and slotted guards (modelled to represent the feet of an animal) that would have covered the axles, should there have been such passing through the neat circular shafts immediately behind and beneath these. But what is much more interesting is that these "guards" have their own sort of axles, and these are *square* in section. When the legs are looked at directly from the side it will be seen that their "joints" are hinged the wrong way for an animal but exactly the right way if they were heavy-duty shock-absorbers. But perhaps the most significant features of all are the three S-shaped "arms," each with a dependent triangular plate. There are two of these at the back of the main body, one on each side, while the third one is median and goes up and over the end of the "tail." When the object is hung up, "head first," and viewed as shown in Figure 33(a),

175

these flaps add very greatly to the design, as do the two curlicues on either side of the head. However, you will see by looking at the object from the front (Plate XVII) and from the side that the latter are thin plates issuing from the "mouth" (into which they are, incidentally, soldered) and which extend backwards on precisely the horizontal plane. These things have been solemnly suggested to be "a formalized snake" [112] held in the mouth! Words fail me.

When I first got photographs of this object, I was staring at them somewhat gloomily when a very old friend of mine walked in. He is an engineer by training. He took one look at these illustrations and burst out laughing. Somewhat nonplussed, I rather tentatively asked him what the joke was. His only reply was to grab a catalogue of heavy farm machinery, find a number of backhoes, and then point out to me the model nearest in outline to this Coclé object. He happened to own such a machine and pointed out to me that it had two tabular "mudguards" extending back from the back end of the front grab-bucket, above the front wheels to just behind the driver's seat. (This seat can be reversed, incidentally.) But he then went on to tell me that *he* had constructed and suspended three "mudguards" at the other end of his machine in just the positions shown in this Coclé object. These were large metal flaps, which, like the heavy rubber ones that hang down behind the back wheels of trailer-trucks, were devised to prevent mud and water from splashing back at him when he was working on ponds and drainage ditches.

It was this same neighbour of mine who first speculated upon the reason for the insertion of this huge green gem in its particular position on the object. It would seem to have particular significance, and he wondered if it might not represent a power unit. Further, if the "head" was hinged so that it could be lowered, the whole construction could be worked like a combined dozer and bucket-grab. Should such have been the case, the heavy guards in front of the "headlights" would become much more logical, since they would hold off material falling from above as the scoop "bit in" at ground level. (I should put on record, however, that another friend suggests that the green dome could have been a fuel tank.)

The photograph (Plate XVII) taken from the front shows the object resting on its *hind* "feet" and its "tail." Thus, it is considerably elevated and shows the front "mudguards" partially from below. It also shows upwardly recurved plates on the heels of the feet. What on earth could these be on a jaguar or crocodile? On the other hand, they would be essential if axles ran through the holes under the claws. And something else most strange is the rather precisely angular, sub-rectangular plate with a slight keel, on what would be the "chest." This, we find when the thing is tipped forward, is placed exactly where a heavy-duty "skid" would be needed if the dozer blade were operated over rough ground or rocks.

If you are ever in Philadelphia, which is a delightful city despite the rude jokes made about it by non-Philadelphians, go and take a look at this blasted thing in the University Museum before you make up your mind that I am talking nonsense. Please understand that I do not in any way claim that the analysis of this object as given above is the only possible one, the right one, or even valid. It is merely a suggestion, but before tossing it out as being plain rubbish, I do ask you to consider its two opposing aspects; and the first thing is the abject absurdity of trying to tell us that this thing is even a *formalized* jaguar or crocodilian.

The real trouble is that we have been conditioned to the belief that, up until some two hundred years ago, people had not discovered any kind of *power* sources other than themselves and animals. That the ancients, and particularly the Romans, had mechanical devices is admitted—things like levers and wheels and pulleys and the catapults of warfare. However, a true "dark ages" apparently descended upon the Old World well *before* the rise of the Romans and not *after* their collapse. Moreover, it seems to have descended upon the New World at about the same time, so that there were only memories left; but these memories were kept alive there for some two thousand more years because their local priest-hoods were not extinguished until the arrival of the Spaniards. The priests of the truly "ancient" (to us) world were manifestly a technological class (and possibly worldwide), and they kept their knowledge to themselves—and so closely that, when threatened by aggressive temporal power, they had no defense but a sort of "scorched earth" policy. And these spiritual hierarchies went down like ninepins between 1500 and 500 B.C. in the Old World. Man had to start all over again, and he is only now just beginning to understand some of the "mysteries" that the intermediate genera-tions created.

CHAPTER TWELVE

FRIGHTFULLY
ANCIENT ELECTRICS

$\mathbb{B}$ACK IN 1938, a German archaeologist by the name of Dr. Wilhelm Konig was working in the national museum in Iraq, where he devoted some time to the close examination of artefacts found in a small tower which formed part of a Parthian settlement at a place called Khujut Rabu, a few miles from Baghdad. It is not clear whether said Dr. Konig was going over material that he had personally dug up or specimens unearthed by others and lodged in this museum. However, he came up with an item that caused quite a furore. There are now innumerable second-hand reports on this, but after comparing these with some of Dr. Konig's own original statements, I feel that the following is the simplest and most succinct and accurate that has been published in popular form.*

The Parthians, who lived as an independent nation southeast of the Caspian Sea until 226 A.D., used, if they did not invent, a practical electric battery at least 200 years

---

* This is reproduced by the kind permission of the editors of *Fate* magazine—that somewhat remarkable little pocket-sized popular publication that, for well over twenty years now, has somehow managed to preserve a fair balance between the *tangible*, "fortean" items (in which we are interested), and the *intangibles*, such as ghosts and the like. This account was written by Mr. H. C. Goble, and published in the March, 1958, issue.

before the birth of Christ. Twenty years ago, Wilhelm Konig, a German archaeologist at the Iraq Museum, began excavations in a hill near Baghdad. A Parthian village had been discovered there by accident. During these excavations a peculiar object turned up. It strongly resembled a modern, dry-cell battery. Konig learned that four similar objects, plus rods suggesting present day bus-bars, had been found in a "magician's" hut at Seleucia, some miles down river. On going to Berlin, Konig found in a museum 10 more dry-cells like the one from his original digging, but these were broken down into their component parts, as though someone had been interrupted before assembling the pieces into a working battery. This came to the attention of Willard F. M. Gray, of the General Electric High Voltage Laboratory, in Pittsfield, Mass., who volunteered to build a duplicate of the Parthian battery. Willy Ley gave him dimensions, diagrams, and a metallurgical analysis.

The duplicate battery, in which Gray used copper sulphate instead of the original electrolyte (which is, of course, still unknown) worked perfectly, and is in the Berkshire Museum at Pittsfield, Massachusetts, at the present time. There is no information giving its exact output, but it seems reasonable to assume 1.5 to 2.0 volts per cell, unless the long-vanished electrolyte of the Parthians was vastly more efficient than any known today. (Which, of course, it might have been.)

The cell consisted of a cylinder of sheet-copper, about the same length and width of two modern flashlight cells placed end to end—or about 5 inches long and 1.5 inches in diameter. The edges of the copper cylinder were soldered with a 60-40 lead-tin alloy (comparable to the best of modern solders). A copper disc was crimped into the bottom of the cylinder and on top of this was a layer of pitch or bitumen to insulate it from the electrode. The electrode was an iron rod placed in an asphalt stopper which was shoved into the top of the copper cylinder. The unknown electrolyte, of which no traces have been found, filled the space between iron rod and copper cylinder walls. Gray proved that copper sulphate would work very well as an electrolyte, but it could

equally well have been acetic or citric acid, both well-known
in Parthian times. Or it could have been an unknown
compound far more powerful than anything known today.

It is assumed, although no reason is given for this
assumption in the material thus far published, that the
current from these batteries was used for electroplating by
Parthian metal workers. However, since the Parthians never
showed any remarkable abilities except in military tactics,
it is thought that they must have obtained knowledge of the
battery from the Sumerians, via the Babylonians. It was not
much before 250 B.C. that this nomadic, warrior race got out
of the saddle to settle down and to build cities—so it seems
unlikely that *they* invented this battery. But obviously
someone invented it—and it wasn't Volta in the early 1800's!

Before I plunge into this maelstrom of controversy, I ask to be
permitted to make a couple of modest points, and first, about these
Parthians. According to the latest findings, these people were originally nomadic tribesmen from the plains north and east of the
Caspian Sea, who moved south into Persia (now Iran) some time
later than the "famous" Medes and Persians.[113] Who they were,
where they came from, or what they did subsequently, while probably of considerable interest to prehistorians, need not concern us
in the present context. But one aspect of their placement does indeed do so. This is that they moved into, and resided in, the original
"hotbed" of metallurgy,[114] which appears first to have been in
that great arc between what is now Turkish Kurdistan and Iranian
Khurasan, and which extended south to the province which is now
named Khuzistan, at the head of the Persian Gulf. Thus, they
spent several centuries of residence in the area where metallurgy
appears to have been "invented," and where such processes as
electroplating, alloying, and the use of the "scale" or "balance"
were first adopted. Wild horsemen they may have been originally,
but such ancient and profitable enterprises could not have escaped
their attention.

As Dr. John M. Allegro [115] has now demonstrated through his extraordinary philological studies and interpretations, *Sumer* was the nodal point of all our so-called western cultures, and just as we pointed out earlier, it was for so many other aspects of learning and invention, like the "zodiac." As this scholar further makes clear, writing was invented only (as he puts it) "a couple of minutes ago" in the chronology of thinking man. He then goes on to say that, prior to the invention of this method of recording knowledge and thoughts, civilized man passed on his "records" by using his memory as his library and his tongue as his pen [116]—and for many millennia, it seems. This is why the Sumerians appear not only to pop up rather suddenly, but with what was obviously a most ancient and highly developed technological (as well as spiritual) civilization.

Despite the fact that these "Baghdad Batteries," as we call them, exist in museums and are completely accepted as *being* batteries, nobody seems to be willing to accept the plain fact that they clearly demonstrate knowledge of the existence of electrical energy at least three thousand years before it was applied as a "force" in the West. Moreover, there has been ample evidence that it *was* so applied in ancient times; and in both its static and frictional manifestations.

Indirect evidence is supplied by the history of metallurgy—*and cosmetics.* The earliest traces of metallurgy, *per se,* have recently been found in what is now eastern Turkey.[117] These are objects of apparently tempered—rather than simply beaten or pounded—native copper. Something much more sensational, however, is the discovery in South Africa of an iron mine radiocarbon-dated * at 41,000 B.C.! [118] These incredibly ancient South African miners were apparently after not only, or primarily, iron ore, but a substance found in association with it named *specularite,* which has been known from the very dawn of history as the basis for a most astonishingly vivid and durable cosmetic! (Aurignacian man, of the Old Stone Age of Europe, used mineral-based paints for his magnificent cave painting, and notably red-ochre, which is one of the oxides of iron.) That Early Stone Age people were mining

* By organic materials found in said mine.

metals is bad enough, but that they could separate two minerals like *haematite* (iron) and *specularite* should give us pause to consider and reassess a lot of our most cherished beliefs. A proper explanation of all this would require a small book, so suffice it to say that the history of metallurgy includes the development of the process of electroplating. This, in turn, implies knowledge of electrolysis, and this calls for batteries. Just when *did* man first separate metals, and then "re-combine" them by this means? Apparently a very great deal earlier than we have previously thought.

Thales of Miletus mentioned such processes in 600 B.C.,[119] and it would seem that the generation of electrical current by friction is more than just implied in several of the even more ancient Veddic Indian writings. (Back to the mercury engines that were said to power some of the *vimanas*.[120]) Since this expression by the Greek, Thales, has been fully accepted for a century by us and we now have the batteries, I fail to understand why certain other ancient items, and notably sculpts, petroglyphs, petrographs, and paintings, that would seem to show clearly electrical "machines," are either ignored, meticulously explained as being something quite different, or are "damned" out of hand as being figments of a pseudoscientific or otherwise disordered mind.

I am not interested in beliefs or even, for the most part, in theories, and I will have no part of intangibles. What I am presenting to you in this book are concrete realities, and almost invariably ones that, however reluctantly, have *had* to be accepted by orthodoxy as existing. What I mean is: while anybody can legitimately question the statements of ancient Dravidian poets to the effect that their princes put atomic energy to work, it is quite useless for anybody to try to deny that the Near-Easterners knew of static electricity three thousand years ago. Yet there *are* those who so deny this fact, and notably many who should know better, having particular specialized knowledge of the life and times of the ancients of that area. Let me give you a couple of classic examples.

At a place named Dendera in Egypt there is a temple that was built in the Graeco-Roman period, dedicated to the goddess Hathor. This is a sort of museum in that each of its rooms is devoted to a

Fig. 35. *Relief from the Temple of Hathor at Dendera, showing priests carrying devices attached to a braided cable to an altar*

specific cult, the traditions of which are depicted on its walls in the form of incised petroglyphs. In the room designated No. XVII, there appears the accompanying depiction (Fig. 35). This was duly described by the Egyptologists Mariette [121] and Chassinat.[122] However, nobody did anything further about this until the Swedish writer Ivan Troëng, resuscitated it in his book *Kulturer Före Istiden,* published in 1964.[123] Under a reproduction of this wall in the temple of Dendera in that book there is a caption that reads: "This picture from Hall 5 [sic] of the Dendera Temple obviously shows electric lamps held up by high-tension insulators."

Troëng is a most remarkable sort of "excavator" of odd facts in the fields of archaeology, prehistory, and ancient myth, legend, and folklore, and his books are an absolute delight because they

184

plunge, bald-headed, into anything and everything that looks in any way "suspicious"—if I may put it that way. I can't say that I agree with him on all (or even many) counts, but more because I have not had the opportunities that he has had to inspect what evidence there is firsthand, than because his statements are so often at complete variance with the established beliefs of the experts. Nonetheless, he has certainly stirred up the amateurs and profoundly provoked a lot of said experts!

There was a minor outburst among both these fraternities when Troëng republished this pretty little picture. But then a funny thing happened. Its publication, of course, did not come to the attention of the Egyptologists; but by some lucky happenstance, it greatly stimulated a number of real "experts" in quite another field: namely the electronics engineers. These specialists, being unencumbered by the niceties of classical archaeology, and still less Egyptology, took one look at this picture and gave out with a concerted "howl." What is more, when they were shown the "official" explanation of it they one and all became not a little hilarious. This is an exact copy of a statement on the subject, kindly supplied by Dr. John Harris of the Ashmolean Museum of Oxford University, England, to Janet Gregory, the representative of our Society (SITU) in England.

> The drawing reproduced [see Fig. 35] is of a relief, not of a painting, in one of the cult-rooms of the Graeco-Roman temple of Hathor at Dendera (no mystification)—Room XVII, according to the notation of B. Porter and R. L. B. Moss, *Topographical Bibliography of Ancient Egyptian Hieroglyphic Texts, Reliefs and Paintings*. VI. Upper Egypt; *Chief Temples*, p. 68 (186). The scene was originally published by A. Mariette, *Denderah*, II, pl. XLIX (from which the copy is taken), and subsequently by E. Chassinat, *Le Temple de Dendera*, II, pl. CXLIV (overall sketch) and pls. CXLVII-CXLIX (photographs of this detail). The objects represented are an

elaborate form of the "snake-stones"—pairs of (granite) stelae with snakes on them—discussed by H. Kees, "Die Schlangensteine und ihre Besiehungen zu den Reichsheiligtumern," *Zeitschrift für Agyptische Sprache,* LVII (1922), pp. 120-136. Their precise significance is difficult to summarise in brief, since in the course of time they acquired a wealth of religious associations, but essentially they were apotropaic in character—*e.g.,* as guardians of doorways (in much the same way as obelisks and flagstaves). I append what Kees has to say about the scene in question * and the one parallel to it: Mariette pl. XLVIII; Chassinat pls. CL, CLI-CLIII, from which you will see that the stones are here connected with Horus *sma-tawy* ("Uniter of the Two Lands"), to whom the accompanying inscription refers. The objects supporting the stones, are incidentally, *djed*-pillars (symbolic of stability), and the double outlining of the larger figures is simply to indicate that there are two of them standing side-by-side.

---

* Kees' original goes as follows:—Dabei ist aber festzustellen dass die Vorstellung von der Schutzschlange in späterer Zeit an dem Orte, wo sie uns am stärksten betont erscheint, nämlich in Dendera sich wiederum mythologisch mit einer Horusform verbindet, nämlich des Person des Harsomtus. Dieser ist zweifellos ein alter Schutzgenius in Schlangengestallt, er wird denn in Dendera auch haufig genug mit dem Namen der Schutzschlange 🐍 [i.e. s3-t3] belegt und um den Zusammenhang vollends klarzumachen, besitzen wir Bilder aus Dendera, die das Hervorgehen des Harsomtus in Gestalt des Schutzschlange aus der Lotusblüte nach dem Vorbild des Sonnengettes darstellen und zwär in einer Form, die unmittelbar als Illustration zum "Aufstellen der Schlangensteine" dienen kann. Die nahe Beziehung zum Himmels und Sonnengot ist hier also auch für die Entstehung der Schutzschlange gewahrt und hervorgehoben, voll entsprechend den alten Anschauungen von der Zugehörigkeit der Schutzsymbole der *snw.t* zu Rê oder Horus.

This may be roughly translated as: Yet it is possible to establish that the Snake (god) Patrons, wherever they appear prominently such as in Dendera, are definitely connected in the mythological sense with the identity of Harsomtus. He was obviously a genius in the art [of the snake cults] since he is so often mentioned in Dendera in relation to these. Harsomtus' connection with the snake cult is further established by other pictures of him in the form of a patron climbing out of a lotus blossom—a religious motif forming, no doubt, the basis for this illustration of the "Snake Stones." The close proximity of the gods of the Suns and the Heavens are no doubt responsible for the origin of the Snake-Stone tablets, the artists being fully aware of the ancient concepts of the signs for Patrons [i.e., saints?] pro or con the God Horus.

This is all perfectly splendid and doubtless quite correct—at least from an Egyptologist's point of view, that is—but I am afraid that it just does not wash. Indeed, these two "snake-stones" (sic) *may* have been set up on their stable (*djed*)* pillars on either side of the portals to temples, and notably at the entrances to certain rooms in them allotted to this snake-cult; but the ancient Egyptians were very careful and pragmatic recorders of all things, both in their glyphs, paintings, and sculpts, and probably because of their incredibly long-time use of hieroglyphic writing, which just *has* to be precise. There is no evidence that these two things that the "priests" are shown carrying in this picture *are* stones in any case, and even if the double lines do indicate two men carrying each, this would be quite a feat. Further, why attach braided cables to these *djeds?* If the apparent "light bulbs" *are* snake-stones, why make them that shape? Certainly, the two symbols on said "stones" may represent snakes, and by their particular conformations represent the uniting of the north and the south (of Egypt), with or without the able assistance of this Horus character. The real trouble is that snakes just happened to be the symbol of static electricity; while this Horus was a gag phrase for meteorological manifestations such as lightning!

Naturally, when the Western world started to dig up and study ancient cultures, scholars were confronted with the necessity for interpreting what they found. All they could think of in those days by way of explanation for anything enigmatic was mythological. And then, when they finally deciphered ancient writings, they found abundant confirmation of the explanations that they had been offering. However, what they did *not* then know (and it has not been until the last decade that this has been shown) was that the ancients deliberately hid the facts of their secret mystery cults in their texts by an exaggerated form of punning, and by double-

---

* For those who are exceptionally curious, *djed* is not a noun in this case, but an adjective. It is descriptive of a type of pillar which Egyptologists interpret as being symbolic of stability. Anything mounted upon said pillar is anticlimactic! Therefore, this is not THE *djed* pillar, but rather A *djed* pillar.

talk, and by using all manner of symbolism, while they also used the names of heroes, demi-gods, and gods to indicate to the initiated the technological matters that they were actually describing and discussing. If you want to know just how far and wide the ancients went in this respect, please read the book already mentioned, entitled *The Sacred Mushroom and the Cross*,[124] by Dr. John M. Allegro.

Meanwhile, we are well advised to listen to an analysis of this glyph from the Dendera temple by an electromagnetics engineer. This chap had only the depiction to go on when he wrote the following, and he knew nothing of ancient Egyptian history or mythology, and he had not seen Professor Harris' analysis; not that any such knowledge would have influenced him in any way, as he now assures me. His initial comments went as follows: [125]

> The items, as depicted, are most fascinating—certain elements, especially the cables, are virtually an exact copy of engineering illustrations as currently used. The cable is shown as very heavy, and striated—indicating a bundle of many (multi-purpose) conductors, rather than a single high voltage cable. As a matter of fact, a single (high voltage) cable would be much thinner; if the insulation was required to be that heavy for extreme high voltages, or moderately high voltages at high currents, rest assured that no technician would be holding the associated device. Corona leakage would "get" him most swiftly. The supporting stands would be much taller and heavier, to withstand such voltages.
>
> It is much more likely that the cable is, as stated, a multi-conductor, wrapped and insulated with an outer jacket. If this were a "light bulb," the maximum size of both would be explainable by heavy current demands; but high voltage insulators of such large size would not be required. It would seem to follow that moderately high voltages are in use; a connector is obviously employed; some type of supporting base to glass seal seems apparent. However, the two "bulbs" are not identical, as shown by the designs on their sides and the base stands. I do not think that they are transparent, as

the "technician's" body is not visible through the device; it would seem more obvious that these are identifying markings, or codings (as a type number on a TV camera tube), probably indicating use of the device.

Since the cables seem to originate at the "altar," one wonders if this is a manually controlled setup, or remotely controlled. Further, with both devices set at an angle, and shown aimed *at the wall,* could they not be the ancient equivalent of the modern TV projection system? One should also note that the two "technicians," especially the one on the left, seem to be wearing a mask device (eye shield?); and unless the drawing is badly reproduced, both have some type of apparatus in their ears, suggesting the equivalent of modern TV cameramen's gear, complete with radio receiver and/or earphones for direct instruction during a "show."

Frankly, this makes a heck of a lot more sense to me than all this jazz about "snake-stones" and lotus flowers, and lovie-dovie demi-gods. In fact, it's really rather amazing that an "explanation" of the Mesopotamian batteries as being mythological representations of a pregnant uterus or something, has not yet surfaced, since there would seem to be more justification for such, than for calling these Egyptian light bulbs "granite snake-stones." Clear away all the dross engendered by the poor scholars of the last century who had never heard of, let alone conceived of even the possibility of a TV tube, a high-tension cable, or any other such currently commonplace devices, and you will find that there is a perfectly logical and very simple explanation of many things depicted by the ancients that have puzzled, confused, and upset latter-day scholars. Little gold models of delta-wing jet planes and 'dozer backhoes are bad enough, but when one comes to work out the "wiring" (i.e., circuitry) of some of the designs painted on ancient South and Central American pottery, one may become a bit confused until one finds that they too are perfectly straightforward—provided one has the guts to accept that their designers also knew of, and manipulated, electrical power.

The Old World, and notably the Near East, is literally littered with evidence of the use of electrical power by the ancients, and not only in the form of things such as we call "Leyden jars," but also of really large and potentially powerful generators. Incidentally, there is a suggestion that the "Ark of the Covenant" of the early Hebrews was an electrical device [126]—but that must wait for another day to be told with appropriate details. So for now, I shall confine my observations to ancient Egyptian expertise though, admittedly, said Ark probably originated in Egypt.

The other most outstanding example that I have run across of the possible generation of electrical power in Egypt is the accompanying depiction of part of an eighteenth dynasty papyrus scroll (Fig. 36). This shows the same damned *djed* pillar, and also an *anhk,* and a number of other rather "annoying" bits and pieces.

Fig. 36. *Part of an eighteenth dynasty papyrus scroll depicting sacred baboons (allegedly) "worshipping" the sun. Note that the device bearing this "sun" and that object itself occlude the "mountains" so that they represent a solid opaque structure* (see Fig. 37).

This item was "explained" by one Erich Neuman [127] in absolutely classical and "classic" terms—you know the Germans when they really get going!—under the title of "The Great Mother: An Analysis of the Archetype." Well! This is complete drivel, so I will quote just one brief passage, as follows:

> *"Sarco-phagus,"* devourer of flesh; the coffin that, in the
> form of tree and pillar encloses Osiris in its wood, just as
> Nut, in her character of coffin, encloses the dead. The
> original sheltering of the dead in the body of the maternal
> giant tree appears in [our] ethnological sketch from East
> Africa [see Becker [128]]. But Nut, as tree of heaven, is also
> mistress of the celestial beasts of the zodiac. . .[129] etc.!

One becomes worried about poor old Osiris, sealed in his tree-stump; while this Nut (and what an appropriate name!) galavants around as the mistress of a lot of goats, bulls, crabs, centaurs, scorpions, and such. But perhaps we become a little too frivolous. Nonetheless, this Osiris was nothing more than the top priest-technician who is constantly shown (sort of) raping his lab-assistant—this Nut—in what appears to be a fairly modern bathtub. Admittedly, there is a lot of symbolism in this male-female getting-together, but this is nothing more than an esoteric way of passing on useful information on the exigencies of positive and negative electricity. However, there is another thing which is particularly significant about these two Egyptian depictions. This also has been completely missed. But then, Egyptologists are not zoologically trained. It is the presence of baboons in both and, moreover, running the mechanical gadgetry therein.

Be pleased to know that the ancient Egyptians trained baboons, and notably the Hamadryads, to sweep floors, weed gardens, collect and stack firewood, wait at table, and perform a lot of other menial jobs in temples.[130] (Parenthetically, a railroad switchman in South Africa once trained a baboon to throw the switches; and when he suffered a heart attack one night, his "pet" baboon made all the right moves, and also several that he had *not* been trained to do; and so brought an express train to a stop just in time.) [131] In fact, baboons were the "grease-monkeys" of the priest technicians of ancient Egypt because, being sort of *professional* "morons," they were more reliable than the lowliest fellahin, because the latter might start day-dreaming and forget his chores.

The following analysis of this second Egyptian "thing" (see Fig. 36) was written specially for this book by one of my colleagues, Michael R. Freedman, who is an electrical and electro-magnetic engineer on both the theoretical and practical sides. He states:

This remarkable depiction, with the singularly grandiose title of "The Great Mother: An Analysis of the Archetype," is, you will note, described as the life symbol ("anhk") and a rising sun, supposedly *in the mountain of morning* (could this mean a mountain in the east?). Said figure has been dated somewhere between 1555 B.C. and 1348 B.C. In line with our recent expositions concerning ancient electronics and advanced technologies, we looked at this figure with a somewhat wary eye. In doing so, however, we note that the entire conception bears a remarkable similarity to the famous Van de Graaff electrostatic generator [see Plate XVIII(A)]. This instrument was "first" developed by the eminent professor whose name it bears, and some colleagues at Princeton University in 1931.[132] It seems to us that the good professor just *may* have been a "johnny-come-lately" —and by some three thousand years!

The principle of static generators has been known for many years. Prior to 1931, machines such as the type seen in the second photograph [Plate XVIII(B)] were used. These consist of two glass discs rotating in opposite directions. The friction thus produced creates static charges which are picked up by metal collector brushes. A Leyden jar condenser stores the accumulated charges, which can be dissipated, when desired, by grounding. Such "accumulators," known as Wimshurst Static Machines,[133] or Influence Machines, can be made so as to generate up to 75,000 volts

or more. Professor Van de Graaff apparently was not satisfied
with the capacity of the above-described machines in his
studies of high-energy physics and the acceleration of charged
particles. So he invented his generator—a forerunner of
today's huge betatrons, capable of accelerating particles to
nearly the speed of light. (It might be noted here that the
cyclotron was developed in *1930*. Such units use alternating
currents and electromagnets to develop energy levels up to
over six billion electron volts.)

The construction and operation of the Van de Graaff machine
is quite simple. It consists of a large hollow metal sphere
mounted on top of an insulating column. An endless belt
runs inside the column between a motor-driven pulley in
the base and an idler pulley in the sphere. As the belt
goes up, its charge is passed to an electrode in the sphere.
The belt assumes the opposite charge as it goes down. The
first charge appears on the outside of the sphere as a
"potential" and as the belt travels, more and more charge is
transferred. A machine with a column four feet high is capable
of generating about half a million volts—depending upon
the speed of the belt (approximately 5000 feet per minute,
or 60 mph).

In point of fact, the charges developed by this generator
are *static;* i.e., the electrons are not moving constantly as
they would in the familiar electric circuit. As the electrons
are pumped into the sphere, the potential (or static charge)
rises—sometimes to several million volts—until the charge
reaches a high enough level to cause a most startling flash
of artificial lightning to jump between the terminal sphere and
the nearest object connected with the ground. Should there be
metal or some other good conductor nearby, the charge
will be dissipated sooner than if there were only poor
electrical conductors in the vicinity of the sphere. Nowadays,
miniature Van de Graaff generators can be bought for as
little as fifty dollars. Such units are capable of voltages as high
as 200,000 volts; but, because of the extremely low currents
involved (on the order of two-millionths of an ampere), these
"toys" are quite safe. But, what better "toy" for an Egyptian
priest of ancient times?

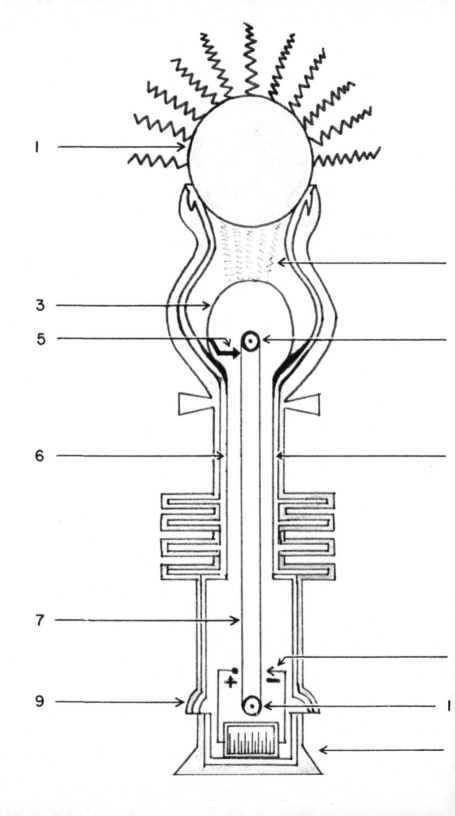

Figure 37 shows our conception of a cut-away view of what this XVIIIth Dynasty depiction might really represent. In this case, such an instrument could be used to control both the Pharoah and the fellahin, simply by illustrating, most graphically, the *powers of the gods;* of which, of course, only the priests knew the real secrets. Merely by placing a metal rod or metal-coated stave in the general vicinity of the sphere, said priest could produce a most wondrous display, with electric arcs and loud crashes. Even with nothing more elaborate than a ring on his finger, a priest could point to the "life-symbol," be struck by a great bolt of lightning, but remain alive and no worse for wear, thus illustrating the omnipotent powers of the gods—not to mention of himself—in preserving life for the faithful.

The reconstruction in Figure 37 shows the entire apparatus as a self-contained unit insofar as the priest need not "interfere." When a sufficient potential is deposited upon the surface of the "ankh," a similar "thunderbolt and clash" will occur as it

Fig. 37. *Suggested interpretation of same as a static-electricity generator (by Michael R. Freedman). The operating principles are relatively simple and require only a minimum of machinery; there is no reason not to believe that such knowledge could have been secretly held by the priests of the eighteenth dynasty.*

First requirement is a suitable source of electromotive force, in this case a battery of cells (11). The second requirement is that of an endless, moving belt (7) attached between two pulleys (4, 10). One of these pulleys (10) must be provided with a motor or other device in order to drive the belt at a fair rate of speed. The charge is deposited upon the endless belt by means of an electrode (8). Electrons attempting to jump between the negative and positive terminals are "caught" and transported upwards by the belt. A discharge electrode (5) is provided within the metal spheroid (3) to conduct the charge from the endless belt to the surface of that spheroid. The charge will continue to build on the surface of the sphere until sufficient force exists to allow this charge to bridge the air gap between (3) and (1). When this point has been reached, an electrostatic lightning display may be seen between the two spheres, and if such charge is powerful enough, and proper conditions exist, a glow may be set up surrounding the sphere (1). The sphere (1) is provided with a path to ground by way of the outer skin of the entire unit. Insulating material (6) coats the necessary surfaces to prevent premature dissipation of electrical energy. Vents for battery vapors (9) are provided.

discharges through the "sun." This would not-so-calmly illustrate how "life" reaches out to the sun for its perpetuance, in accord with the accepted religious dogma of the 18th dynasty Egyptian devotee.

However, this hypothesis poses two questions. First, what provided the initial electrical potential for the building of a high-level charge. Could this be where our Baghdad Battery fits in? This sounds reasonable enough to allow us to indicate such at the bottom of the apparatus. But, second: what provided the motive power to drive the endless belt? A hand crank turned by some lesser priests (or baboons?) behind or below the machine, with the appropriate gear ratios to permit the necessary speeds, could conceivably generate a sufficient voltage for the displays discussed here. As we have not even the tiniest shred of evidence as to what *electric* (or other) motors were developed or used by the ancient Egyptians, we should perhaps stick to this simple "crank" idea.

I could carry on with this business almost forever, but I will refrain for now at least, and offer but one further thought. This is simply that not just "ancient" man, but "primitive" man, and even "subman," *must* have known of electricity in at least two forms. First, there was always what the north-country English so succinctly call "thoonder, and lytnin' and all-sorts." Secondly, there are a whole bunch of fish, and of varied types, that collect and discharge electricity at really very astonishing potentials. There are the electric catfish of South America, the electric rays of the Mediterranean that Roman Senators suffering from rheumatism used to stand on as long as they could "stand" it,[134] and then a fish named *Gymnarchos niloticus* that can really give you both a shock and a "shock." No person and no animal that has ever dabbled in the Nile remains for long unaware of the potential of this splendid creature, and even frightfully holy cats (of Bubastis, of course) have been known to give up so dabbling, for life, after getting a full charge from one of these fish.[135] I know of at least two ancient Egyptian paintings that might have been intended to show these fish in a sort of aquarium.

CHAPTER THIRTEEN

ONE-WAY STRETCH

A NUMBER OF YEARS ago, that much appreciated and greatly respected science-fiction writer, Robert Heinlein, came up with a story entitled *And He Built a Crooked House*.[136] Heinlein's gimmick in this delightful yarn is best laid forth in his own words: "That's the grand feature about a *tesseract* house, complete outside exposure for every room, yet every wall serves two rooms, and an eight-room house requires only a one-room foundation." (But read the story.) "Tesseract" was a coined adjective for the form of the Roman *tessera* which was the word for the small, square (and usually cubical in depth) bits of stone used in the laying of mosaics. The point is that pictures made with such stones, when looked at from various angles, often seem to present different countenances, just as if they had a third dimension. One of the lead characters in Heinlein's story was an architect who had designed a four-dimensional house. Much as we love science-fiction and Bob Heinlein in particular, we are, however, happy to be able to state categorically that such is "impossible" within our spatial frame of reference; at least according to one Dr. Büchel [137] whose definitive pronouncement upon this matter was admirably expostulated in the *New Scientist*.[138] This went as follows:

"Have you ever wondered why ordinary space is three-dimensional? Although this may seem to be a ludicrous

197

question, it has been the subject of considerable thought by scientists and philosophers since the time of Aristotle. Before scoffing at their apparent folly, remember that myth and common-sense often succumb to scientific scrutiny. However, you do not need to worry that space has been five-dimensional without your knowing, because general physical arguments have revealed that *three* is the *only* combination that works. Dr. Ira M. Freeman has recapitulated the reasoning in a translation of W. Büchel's article "Warum hat der Raum drei Dimensionen?" (*American Journal of Physics,* vol. 37, p. 1222). Dimensions larger [i.e., more numerous] than three can be discounted if we accept that the gravitational force varies as the inverse square of the distance between two masses. This law, originally derived by Newton, will only allow for stable elliptical planetary orbits if spatial dimensions are three or less. Similar arguments apply for stable atoms. Unless there are two or three dimensions, electrons will collapse into the nucleus as a consequence of the inverse square law nature of Coulomb forces. In order to eliminate spatial configurations of two dimensions, Büchel invoked biological arguments. He claimed that nerve fibres would interfere with one another, unless they had the extra dimension. "The existence of a highly developed organism having many non-intersecting nerve paths is thus possible only in a space having at least three dimensions."

This is all perfectly splendid, but I am afraid that I have to report that it is apparently not the whole picture. Bob Heinlein's story was presented as an exercise in imagination; Dr. Büchel's thesis as an exemplification of reality. I am not prepared, nor competent, to dispute the latter gentleman, but I am wondering if he took all the necessary factors into account in order to arrive at his construct. I am wondering in fact if Bob Heinlein may not be a better solid-geometer than the gallant doctor and have conceived of a few extra concepts or "possibilities." Please understand me: I am not suggesting or advocating fourth, fifth, or more "dimensions" within *our* space-time continuum. What I *am* wondering about is whether our currently accepted definition of, and methods of measuring, as simple a thing as "length" are invariably valid, for if they are not, at least one other factor—*not* a "dimension"—would seem to be called for. To this end, I would very much like to know from physicists just what could be the cause—or rather, *a* cause, or *any* possible cause—of the anomalies that I am now about to describe.

Before launching into this I would like to say that it is quite useless for anybody to say that these anomalies did *not* occur, or, furthermore, that there *cannot* be an explanation. This business happened right in our own backyard, and four quite separate groups of people witnessed it, and at different times, and all with an adequate number of independent witnesses. Also, three of the principals were professional construction men and carpenters, two with their own businesses, another was a chemical engineer, and still another an electronics engineer. What I mean is, we weren't just a bunch of bumpkins slapping together some bits of lumber with inadequate tools. All of us were involved in a fully professional job under the supervision of two very experienced construction men from two separate companies. Moreover, we helpers did the initial and all subsequent cutting of the lumber (as to be described in a moment) under the eyes of professionals. But let me first list the persons concerned, giving their status, and then tell you why we were assembled, and what we were doing.

They were: (1) Mr. Oties H. Cramer of Blairstown, New Jersey, long-time professional carpenter (since the age of 16) and owner of his own construction company, specializing in homes and their internal finishing and decoration; (2) Mr. William H. Kise, an employee of Mr. Cramer's and also a professional carpenter of long standing; (3) Mr. Edgar O. Schoenenberger (the Deputy Director of our Society), a master stonemason and (then) owner of his own construction business in Long Island; (4) Mr. Ernest L. Fasano, an executive supervisor of a chemical company specializing in ceramo-metals; and (5) Mr. Michael R. Freedman (a

Director of our Society), a Navy electronics technician. Then, as witnesses, were Marion L. Fawcett (our Executive Secretary); Miss Julianne E. Bordano; my wife, and myself. Later two others, both engineers, went over the whole business (physically) some days later and tried to reproduce the anomalies. These were Mr. Adolph Heuer, Jr. of Knowlton, New Jersey, and Mr. Richard E. Goddard, a physicist, from Boston, Massachusetts.

The reason the above persons were assembled at our headquarters was to finish up the interior construction of a new building we had put up on our Society's property (see Fig. 38). This structure was actually first built in 1920 and was originally a two-storey chicken-breeder—the front and the upper storey being of wood, with a back-sloping, corrugated iron roof. However, in 1928 a tornado came right across the land, clearing out two lines of large apples trees in the orchard and blowing the whole of this structure away (with everything in it), except the back concrete wall and the two ends. These remnants then just lay there until 1968 when we cleared ground and started re-building. This building, as we have now reconstructed it, measures 60 x 20 feet, overall, on the outside, and we have built a concrete-block front to it. This structure is built into a large hummock of Ordovician slate. I only give all this detail since anything that might have any significance in this extraordinary affair should be put on record. And, to this end, I will now give some more details of what might be regarded as entirely extraneous information.

I have these details from a Mr. Allen Noe, now an inspector of federal government arsenals, who happened to have been born in the upstairs bedroom of the old house that my wife and I now occupy as caretakers at our Society's headquarters. His family then owned these fifty acres and maintained on it a highly productive fruit farm. In 1929, Allen, then aged eleven years, was painting a chair on the front porch of the old house, whilst his elder brother was building a wigwam against the southern face of this building. Their eldest brother was working at a farm next door, to the south. Their father had gone to town, and their mother was in the old house. The sky clouded up very rapidly in the late afternoon, and then it went blue-black with an intense ruddy glow coming through from the south beneath the clouds. In a very short time a tremendous roaring was heard and Allen Noe remembers dashing into the house where his mother was trying to get the windows closed against the approaching "storm," when this tornado hit, completely cleaning out a path across the land, including the entire chicken house. So sudden was its arrival and so fast did it pass that it was some moments before Mrs. Noe realized that her other son was missing. On dashing out of the back door and seeing the chicken house completely gone, and knowing where the lad had been playing, she naturally assumed that he had been plucked up along with the two thousand white Leghorns. But, to their amazement, this young Noe crawled out of his wigwam, which was quite untouched, and asked, simply, what had happened? Meanwhile the eldest Noe boy had come running across the fields to say that a large barn had been demolished, and that a fellow worker and one of their horses had been killed by flying lumber. The other horse was unharmed. Lumber, roofing, and perfectly plucked chickens were strewn for seven miles to the northwest. Allen recalls laconically: "We got mighty sick of chicken that year."

The first odd thing noted after the passing of the tornado—and this was not confirmed until *we* took over 25 years later—was that the two-foot-thick concrete base that remained, and which has a three-foot-deep footing down to bedrock, was "out" by eight inches at the south end of the east face. We naturally assumed that this was nothing more than an initial error in the original construction, but I happened to meet the old gentleman who laid that concrete. He was a German master stonemason, and he assured me that the two back angles were absolutely precise right angles; and if *that* gentleman said so, I am afraid that I can but accept it. So, one end of the south wall, although footed three feet deep and anchored to bedrock, had somehow been pulled eight inches *toward the oncoming tornado*. However unlikely this may sound, I am prepared to accept the fact that it *might* have been due to this cause, because tornadoes and hurricanes can do the damnedest things, as I very well know from personal experience. In some ways I am sorry that this discrepancy exists because it has led several sensible people to suggest it as the explanation of the completely different anomalies that I am now going to describe.

Actually, these anomalies cannot possibly have anything to do with this angular discrepancy, as any geometer or physicist can tell you, because they are purely linear, and have nothing to do with any angular alterations. In other words, they are anomalies of one dimension only.

Without the accompanying photographs (see Plate XIX, A and B) all this would be very difficult to explain because there were four quite separate "areas" where these anomalies occurred. We spent almost two (cautious) years putting up this building; volunteer members of our Society giving of their time when professionals were available to supervise them. The interior is divided into four parts: reading from left to right on the plan, a 20 x 20 foot extension to our library, but with living space for two and further adequate space for holding our Board Meetings of 20 persons; second, a projection room for movies and stills and housing a special device for the projection of "solids," both maps and drawings, and objects; third, a further extension of the library, with stacks and a reading desk; fourth, a garage to house a specially equipped Land Rover, and for the storage of field equipment.

The anomalies started coming to light when Otie Cramer, with his assistant Bill Kise, were putting up the library shelves against the back wall in the main room. Please understand that these two are true experts and have been doing just such work for many years. Bill measured up the back wall and then cut the lumber. When pieced together and laid on the brackets already installed, all these (horizontal) shelves proved to be between four and six inches too long. Not wishing to waste Otie's time, since he was working on some more intricate bits on the other side of the room, Bill remeasured most carefully, and then trimmed the planks. This time, all of the shelves were two inches *too short*. As a result, he was plain out of lumber, and its being after the yard had closed, he was forced to appeal to Otie for instructions. Otie told me later—and he did not report all this to me until after we had hit a similar problem—that he gave Bill some pretty extensive hell; in fact, he accused him of all sorts of things, and he tells me that he even said that Bill could consider himself fired! Otie then instructed Bill to recut some of the longer planks and so get at least two shelves up without patching-out. Poor Bill! The same thing happened all over again! So Otie took over; but again the same.

Otie got very mad indeed, and put up the four shelves himself, working from left to right, and extending them to the right wall with bits and pieces, by marking them off, rather than by measuring. At last they fit (fitted, or fut, or however you care to express it), and that ended Oties' worries, and he finished up the job.

About two weeks later, another crew moved in under the supervision of Eddie Schoenenberger to finish up a number of bits and pieces, notably on the south wall. Here we had put up a temporary shelf over the counter and the sink, made of two twelve-inch pine planks but only an inch thick. We knew this could not stand the weight of books to be put upon this six-foot length, so we ordered two *two-inch-thick* redwood planks. All we had to do was cut them to slide in between the two uprights as shown on the plan (Fig. 38). Chocks for them to lie on were already sturdily installed. Using a power saw, two volunteers, guided by Ernie Fasano, cut these planks to exact measurement. One came out two inches too *long,* the other one and a half inches too *short!* So, they put them back on the "horses," remeasured both the space and then

Fig. 38. *Plan of the Annex Building at SITU Headquarters, showing the three areas of measurement anomaly*

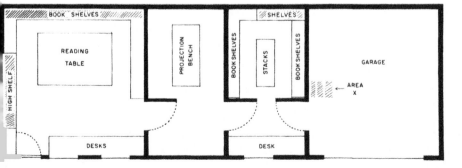

the boards, and then carefully cropped the overlength one. It came out almost two inches too *short!*

Since they had ruined the only two heavy boards we had, they appealed to Eddie, as the expert, to tell them what to do. And Eddie too went into a controlled rage; accusing the amateurs in his quiet tones of being unable to take a correct measurement, let alone learn to use a power saw. At that juncture I happened to wander in and so witnessed the following little charade. Eddie measured the space and then the boards. They were identical, so he held up one of the boards. It was two inches short! Somewhat mystified to say the least, he put the board back on the horses.

Having witnessed something of this nature once before, I made so bold as to offer a suggestion. This was intended to save face for both parties, and to show my superior something-or-other. So I told them a story. Way back in 1938, my wife and I went to that lovely little South American country now named Surinam. We were on an expedition to collect animals for various scientific institutions and museums. We had with us one Frederick George Allsop, an Englishman who had lived in Haiti since the age of twelve, an engineer, and when we met him, the airport manager in Port au Prince. Fred was with us for some ten years. He happened also to be a cabinetmaker by hobby, and I had decided to make a complete set of travelling equipment, for all our collecting and other gear, out of the local cedar wood. Nearly two hundred boxes had to be made with great precision, with all manner of permanent compartments, special hinges, locks and so forth. We rented a house in Paramaribo, the capital, and went to work. Fred and I did the planning on paper, then I ordered the lumber, measured it up and cut it—whole batches of a similar length at a time.

Everything went along all right until Fred started assembling the units. Then he increasingly berated me for "forgetting the thickness of the wood." Somewhat piqued, as I had also done a lot of carpentering in my life, I pointed out that *he* had given me the measurements; and I invited him to check on what I had done.

He did, and he found that I had cut the boards exactly to the length he had requested on paper! Somewhat mystified, he went back to the bits of the box he had started to assemble, and they also were all perfectly correct—*except for the bottoms.* Fred had a really vile temper hidden under his phlegmatic British exterior and used to go bright red when he realized that he was the culprit! *He* had cut all these bottom pieces.

It took us two days to solve the mystery. We had brought our own rather large and very fine set of tools with us. These had been purchased in England. However, in view of the mountain of work to be done, we had bought a second set from a large German hardware store in Paramaribo, named Kersteins. This lot included a number of metal rules. We were working in inches, and only then did we discover that the Dutch inch is not the same as the British inch—to the extent of half an inch per foot!

In view of this parable, I suggested to Eddie, assorted helpers, and, by this time, several onlookers, that I go get all the other rulers I had down in the old house—some two dozen, as they included my art implements. We then compared all the rulers and tried again. We got some long light boards and tried measuring them with various of these rulers, but in every case we got anomalies, and both ways and in all kinds of combinations—too long first, and then too short later, or vice versa—and coming out at various lengths, until we ran out of long enough lumber. So we tried one last board, and instead of measuring it, we held it up and marked it off with a pencil. It fit, fitted, or fut exactly!

This was more than just puzzling, of course, but I did not know then of Oties Cramer's troubles; and I did not learn of them for another two weeks when something else happened. My assistant, Michael Freedman, was due out of the Navy in which he had been doing his stint aboard a "Tin Can" for his appointed four years. We were all pressing hard to get this new building finished for his return, and so my wife, aided by the female resident members of our staff *and* a professional seamstress, measured up the four windows and a tall hanging closet for drapes, and also covers for two double beds, and then went to work with the machine. As pairs of drapes came out, they took them up to the new house for hanging. First one pair and then another came out four inches *short*. Positively infuriated, these professional and amateur seamstresses got into a terrific argument, ending, in one case, in tears of frustration. But still it did not dawn on any of us that there might be a correlation between this business and the seemingly unmeasurable shelf planking. It ended up by their having to stitch the drapes top and both sides and then take them up to the house, hang them, and trim them below, *in situ,* with all the due allowances for turn-ups, etc. This time they fitted. They had to!

Two weeks later still, Mike Freedman finally got home. It took him a week to settle in and get organized, but then he set to work on the electrics, planning the wiring and so forth, as he is an electrician and electronics technician. In planning the layout for the wiring to be installed by a commercial firm, he started drilling holes through the beams supporting the roof. These stand upright sixteen inches apart, all along the building. Roof timbers are held apart by short pieces of two-by-four called "cats," and in order to drill his holes exactly where he wanted them, Mike had to knock out some of these. Then he tried to put them back again. *None of them fit.*

It was a mild fall day, and we had all the windows open. The new house is 250 feet behind the old house where four of us were working, but we heard Mike's expletives, loud and clear; and so I went to investigate. He told me what was happening, and I must say that I felt a sort of chill creeping over me; but, playing it innocent, I asked Mike to show me what on earth he was talking about. He did, standing on a stepladder and using both the old cats and some new pieces of lumber (see Plate XIX, B). None "fut"! So I got a pencil and marked the latter off, cut them myself, and had Mike bang them in.

Mike is a very pragmatic chap and he was not happy. I said nothing immediately as I was just as unhappy myself, but it was then that I got on the phone to Oties Cramer and asked him if he had had any trouble with linear measurements while on our job. Only then did I learn that he had, and just what he had encountered—as described earlier—and that he was not just puzzled but somewhat distressed by it all. When he had heard me out, his first remark was to the effect that he had not wanted to bother me with this, as he thought that I would think him either balmy or totally incompetent. When I recounted what else had happened and the number of outside witnesses to each incident he gave an audible sigh of relief. He also came up and took a look around.

Then came another chap, a very old local friend who I have had occasion to introduce several times in this book—Adolph Heuer. Adolph is interested in everything, is enormously well read, and has not only a truly open mind but a deadly aptitude for putting an intellectual finger on the pith of seeming inexplicable matters. Being basically an engineer, he pondered this "cockeyed" building, asked questions, and then went away. Two days later he came back with a number of strips of wood, the tips of which he had painted black. He had laid out the distances between the straight inside edges of these black tips in standard American inches from measurements he had taken with his own metal ruler, in this new house, on his first visit. All these "measurements" conformed exactly to the spaces that had previously proved to be so anomalous—and both on the day that Adolph brought the rods and a month later, during which time they (his rods) were stored on a shelf up near the ceiling where they were subjected to the full heat from a big hot-air heater. (Physicists please note.)

Almost exactly one year later we decided to construct an extension to the library and reading room, between the projection room and the garage, as shown on Fig. 38. We planned and built floor-to-ceiling book-shelving, a set of stacks, and sundry office-type conveniences at the front (window) end of the room. The construction of the new wall was extremely solid, and both it and the ceiling were lined and insulated. I had decided to break down my office in New York and use the shelving and furniture from it for this new room at our headquarters up here in New Jersey. Some of the shelving was metal, the rest extremely well-seasoned boards that had been in use for 25 years.

Now, it happened that another of our members, Richard T. Grybos from Chicago, had volunteered for the summer—after receiving a BA in geography and before entering government service—to catalogue our map collection. Rich is also a handy man with tools and likes to take his daily exercise with them; so he volunteered also to handle the interior work in this new room, with assistance from the four others resident here.

When he came to the back wall he called for help to anchor some uprights, and then proceeded to cut and lay a series of six shelves of eighteen-inch planking, making a very neat job of it all. We started to move books in that evening but when we came to this section (see shaded area at back-right of this room in plan) we found, to our considerable annoyance, that this was the one place where the largest (tallest) books had to go. The upright spaces between the shelves were all too narrow; so Rich and Mike Freedman numbered them and took them down. Next day, and in my presence, when they went to put them back *none of them* fit, fitted, or fut!

So what have we here? I have given the facts as we have them. Unfortunately we did not photograph all of these events as they occurred, but I think that all of you will forgive us this apparent lapse. When things like this happen, one simply does not realize the significance of the fact at the time. Then again, not knowing of Oties Cramer's experiences till later, and being doubly suspicious of Eddie Schoenenberger's due to my own earlier troubles with the damned "Dutch inch," I still did not cotton on to the fact that this was a glaring example of a truly "unexplained" until after it was all over. Likewise, and, I suppose I should admit, with typical masculine superiority, I had put the seamstresses' troubles down to some inborn feminine inability to measure correctly or to make allowances for turn-ups and so forth. (How naive can one be? How would a fitter ever get a hemline straight if this was the way of their sex?) No: this was nothing but a masculine "superiority complex" and plain stupidity. But then came Mike, and this was what finally jolted me out of my complacent complacency.

That amateurs are often unable to cut a piece of wood to measure, I am prepared to accept, knowing some of the lumber that I myself have ruined. That professionals *can* make such mistakes I am also prepared to believe, having had to deal with them during a now somewhat long life and in all manner of different fields, like even unto building boats! But when an electrical engineer fresh off a modern naval vessel can't get a piece of mere wood to go back where it came from, that did shake me; and when he gave me said pieces of wood and asked me to try, and I could neither get them in because they were too long or make them stay in due to being too short, I quit and went out and sat in a deck-chair and did some profound thinking.

Here, dear readers—and all the rest of you, from theoretical mathematicians to hard-nosed (or hatted) citizens who actually have to *do* things, like putting up high-fly buildings or building the *Queen Mary*—is something to ponder. I've spent my life investigating unexplaineds and it seems that there is no end to them, but I must admit that this was a completely new one to me.* I had heard vaguely of some such before, but I had always put them down to the sort of thing that I described anent the damned Dutch inch. Now, having witnessed this series of cases right (and literally) in my own backyard, and with just the people I could most wish to have present, I am doing a lot more than simply wondering.

Just how many cases of a similar nature take place with ordinary citizens employed professionally, or as amateurs or hobbyists, who indulge in such simple linear measurements to get their jobs done? And how many cases that might occur ever get reported, even if the witnesses are satisfied that the cause was not just "bad" measurement or calculation? And how many peo-

* Despite Murphy's Laws.

ple would listen to such reports if they *were* made? What classical physicist would ever even consider such seeming nonsense? I certainly wouldn't if I were paid to teach mechanical drawing or undertake researches in that field. Good Lord! You can't have linear measures expanding and contracting instanter. The whole damned works would collapse. Yet again, I wonder. Might this not just be why some *do* collapse—like bridges and so forth? Pity the poor engineers.

It has been my personal pleasure all my life, and it is now the objective of the Society which I administer, to investigate any practical, concrete, material, tangible, measurable *things* that have not been explained, but always with a view to explaining them if possible on equally materialistic lines. Such explanations fall into two distinct categories: the possible and the probable. Most start off by being both impossible and highly improbable but mostly because of our previous lack of knowledge of them and our abyssmal ignorance of just about everything else. However, on "taking thought upon the matter" and burrowing around in what *is* known and published on corollary subjects, possible explanations for a very high percentage of these "nasty things" come to light. This cockeyed measurement is a tangle all right; but it is in its infancy as far as we are concerned, and, frankly, I haven't the foggiest notion what to suggest at this stage by way of even possible explanation. Sorry if this is an outrageous "cliff-hanger," but perhaps it will draw out some more reports from which a pattern might emerge. Then we could start theorizing and take our ideas to the appropriate specialists, though who these might be in this case I have even less of an idea.

CHAPTER FOURTEEN

RAIN-MAKING AND
CLOUD-BUSTING

Before I GET cracking on this rather cheery subject, I absolutely must do what I can to clarify another one which is always getting in the way, and which is a positive pest in this case. This is an *intangible*, if there ever was one, called "coincidence"; but which we designate simply "K."

Everybody, from the veriest moron to Albert Einstein, has from time immemorial invoked this "force" as a last resort to explain anything that he or she has been unable to do so otherwise—which is a sorry commentary on our intelligence. Nevertheless, by placing such a flat statement firmly on the record I may perhaps be excused for pointing up the fact that we don't know much about anything, or anything much about everything. What people presumably mean by "coincidence" has never been defined, and only one man that I know of has ever tried to investigate it *per se*. In fact, while it is dragged into everyday life, and even into scientific investigation—almost *ad nauseam*—it has no validity, or even any real existence as of now. As an item, K may best be equated with that almost equally abstruse bit of chicanery so beloved of insurance companies and expressed as "An Act of God." (And, anent this, I have always contended that we have got our metaphors mixed here somewhere because, if God is the "Good Guy," why is he held responsible for all super-disasters?)

This coincidence business gets into the act, and in a most noxious manner, in practically every case of the unexplained; for, in the vast majority of cases, it is given as the *final explanation,* and not only by ordinary folks, but almost invariably by "experts," and in some cases even by real experts. However, as I pointed out above, none of these good people can have the foggiest notion what they are talking about and simply because they still apparently cannot define this "thing" or "force." Mathematicians and advanced physicists have tackled the issue in a circumstantial and very circumspect way by trying to establish laws of probability (done), improbability (partly done), possibility (assumed), and impossibility (absolutely insisted upon, though without one iota of supporting evidence or even any reasons given). And, speaking of the last, I cannot refrain from referring to a modest interchange that I had a couple of years ago with a frightfully clever scientist of positively terrific standing.

Said interchange was brought on by an article I had published on forteanism,[139] in which I noted that anybody who still continued to state that anything *must* be impossible, is an idiot. This scientific pundit wrote, somewhat furiously and as from a considerable throne in an ivory tower identified by his letterhead, giving me five "impossibilities." Two of these simply didn't apply because the poor fellow apparently did not really know the problem, the most notable being the old saw about the "impossibility" of "squaring a circle." This, of course, is a pure example of a lack of semantic exactitude, because what is meant is that the *area* of a circle cannot be computed precisely by mathematical procedure—although it can, of course, be so with a piece of string and four pins. At the other extreme of his examples was the equally old saw about being unable to checkmate a Queen at chess, as now played in the West. (The answer to this one is, of course, "Change the rules.") Point is, in not one case did he give any *reasons* for stating that the problem was unsolvable and therefore impossible. But back to this business of K.

The man I mentioned above who has tried to do something about this is a very old friend, a brilliant editor of technical and scientific texts, and a profound fortean, by the name of Peter Kamitchis. He has been collecting Ks for some twenty years and subjecting them to statistical analysis. Quite early in his searches and researches he demonstrated just how complex this matter is. He also showed that there do, nonetheless, seem to be some "rules" of a mathematical nature, and possibly of a purely physical one as well, applicable to it. The first of these is that there are various "powers" of coincidence. The simplest, or K^1, is of everyday occurrence, like two people with exactly the same rather rare names meeting at a cocktail party; or your picking up the telephone and getting a wrong number, only to find out that it is one of your oldest friends whom you have not heard of for years. This random, junior-grade K happens to practically everybody at least once a day in one form or another, even if the average person concerned seldom recognizes the fact. The next thing that emerged was that you can have Ks up to the power of at least 20 (that's as far as Peter had got the last time I talked to him). This means that the same "thing" happens over and over again. However, this is where the complexity begins, because the circumstances (factors) themselves begin to vary, and these too may display a K series of their own. Nevertheless—and for all this complexity, and even if there is a perfectly pragmatic set of natural laws governing coincidence—nobody has any right whatsoever to invoke it as an explanation of anything until we have defined those laws and tested them. And this should apply most stringently to the subject now at issue; so that I refuse to waste your time by quoting anybody who puts coincidence forward as an *explanation* of the upcoming subjects.

Claims that rain can be artifically induced to fall are among the most persistent reports in both the written annals and the traditions of just about all peoples. There would now be, it seems, at least an identifiable reason for this *belief,* regardless of whether any such accomplishment was ever valid or not. This has only just now been brought to light by one Dr. John M. Allegro, Lecturer in Old Testament and Inter-Testamental Studies at the University of Manchester in England, in his most remarkable book

The Sacred Mushroom and the Cross.[140] Dr. Allegro is the British representative on the international editing team preparing the famous Dead Sea Scrolls for publication and is primarily a philologist. The subtitle of his rather terrifyingly scholarly work is "A Study of the Nature and Origins of Christianity within the Fertility Cults of the ancient Near East"; and its central theme is simply that all religions (at least from the borders of India to the Atlantic, and from the forested area of Africa to the subarctic) stem from the original fertility cult of Sumeria—the basis of which was simply that the sky was the Omni-god and the earth the Omni-mother, and that rain represented God's sperm (semen) with which *He* inseminated (annointed) *Her.* The first temples with their outer courts, folding doors, outer sanctum, and finally inner sanctum were but representations of the female external genitalia and internal reproductive paraphernalia, while pylons, obelisks, and other such erections were glorified penes, so that all the mystical rigmaroles of religion are nothing more than either practical or symbolic manifestations of copulation and impregnation. Naturally, therefore, one of the priest's first duties was to "make rain" as proof of *his* power, and God's munificence, in fertilizing the earth. (Please understand this is in no way to be equated with "making water" or micturition.)

Although Allegro does not say so, I have a shrewd suspicion that he might believe it possible that *all* religions, throughout the world, had a similar origin, if not *a single place of origin.* Further, the wider and more carefully we look into both the past history and the present manifestations of religious beliefs and their practical organization and implementation, the more often we stumble upon this (as Allegro designates it) "U-Cult," * based on certain fungi of a mushroom shape, and notably the famous *Amanita muscaria* with its flaming red canopy and pristine white stem, which, when consumed or otherwise applied to the human body in various ways, produces wild psychedelic hal-

---

* "U" in Sumerian meant "copulate" and thus "create."

lucinatory mental transports. This plant came to symbolize the male penis supporting and penetrating the female vulva, and this symbolism turns up all over the world, and most notably among the Amerinds of North, Central, and South America. No wonder the rain-making bit is so widespread and persistent and pervades even Islam and the Christian world. (I would sorely like to discuss the matter relative to the Buddhist religion, but I must refrain at this time.)

Up until now, it has apparently been more or less assumed that the profession of rain-making was a sort of generative myth of the peoples of the deserts and other drier areas of the earth's surface where rain was either virtually unknown, unreliable in its incidence, or totally unpredictable. Naturally, any fall of rain— coincidental or otherwise—would be more noticeable in such areas, but it is now clear that the whole idea of "rain-making" is just as prevalent, and has been going on just as long, in the moist and even in the *very wet* areas of the world, such as the periphery of the Amazon Basin, the Congo Basin, and throughout the whole Indo-Malayan area. Nor is the concept any rarer in the damp western and northern tier of Eurasia. In these wet areas, however, there is a complimentary claim made that is of particular interest to us. This is an insistence that rain can, conversely, be prevented or stopped. And this leads to another piece of business, namely, "cloud-busting."

I have always had a sneaking feeling that the Amerinds, and notably those of North America who have suffered most from the unasked-for intrusion of us Europeans and Africans, have always been ploying us with this whole business of rain-making. In support of this contention let me cite the following little ditties:

(1) Anadarko, Okla.—Apache Indians from New Mexico yesterday showed this drought-stricken area the power of their medicine dancing. They performed their ancient "rainbow dance," a ceremonial for rain, at the American Indian Exposition Monday night. The clear skies clouded over and a steady

rain soaked the exposition grounds yesterday morning. Four years ago Kiowa tribal dancers performed their "forbidden" sun dance over the protests of Indian officials of the exposition. Their plea for rain worked just as rapidly as did that of the Apaches this year. A deluge started the next morning and continued for six days, with disastrous results on the exposition's attendance.[142]

(2) Las Vegas, Nev.—This desert resort will think twice about inviting the Jemez Indians again for Helldorado [sic] Week. In the parade last Thursday the New Mexico tribe did a rain dance. It has rained every day since in this arid city, whose slogan is: "Fun in the Sun." [143]

(3) Durango, Colo.—Results; that's what the Navajo Indians get when they go after a good rain. Tribesmen sent here to fight a forest fire raging through the Mesa Verde national forest gave "a rain dance" for "the God's pleasure." Two days and nights of the primitive rites resulted in a downpour that greatly facilitated the work of fighting fires.[144]

(4) [I do not know whether this act was pro or con.] Three Pueblos did a brief ceremonial rain dance at the Gianini Food Fair at 1145 Market Street [San Francisco] at 10:00 a.m. this morning [the 12th December, 1960] and two hours later rain fell all over San Francisco for the first time in 85 days.[145]

Events like this make me feel much better. I have always felt complimented when I have been called an "Indian-lover," since I have, over the years, learned truly to love and respect these peoples. (I have, incidentally, sixteen Mayan Indian godchildren.) They carry the wisdom of the ages, and although terribly fatalistic to our way of thinking, their sense of humour is delicious. They are gentlefolk, and I am not at all sure that they won't win out over us brash barbarians in the long run. Actually, a true and workable ability to "make rain" or "make it go away" is just the sort of gimmick that they might hold unto themselves, even after we have taken away all their land and destroyed their material culture. But I pontificate.

It is an odd but notable fact that rain-making seems almost always to be accompanied and induced by dancing, and not only among our Amerindian friends. The same crops up in West and Central Africa, in southern India, in Indonesia, and among the Aborigines of Australia. The Yakuts of northeastern Siberia go through similar dreary and prolonged routines to get their autumn snows going on time. Nor are these the only chaps who seem to be able to put on a good act. Some of the popular accounts—and most of them seem to come from the normally rather stuffy news services—are often exquisite. For instance: "Tribesmen (the Bundekung) in South Africa, plagued by a long drought, asked German Missionary O. Brummerhoff to pray for rain. Nothing happened, so the tribesmen went off into the mountains and prayed to their own gods. It poured. Then, they complained in the local district court that Missionary Brummerhoff criticized their action in a sermon. The tribesmen told the court they had asked the Hermansburg Mission to remove Brummerhoff, but the mission refused. So they asked the court to eject the entire mission from their territory, where it had operated for the past 82 years. The court agreed." [146] Meanwhile, in neighbouring Swaziland, they once reported that: "During the South African tour of 1947, the King [of England] had a chance to meet a real autocratic ruler —Paramount Chief Sobhuza Dlamini II, of Swaziland. With him was the [his] queen mother who 'commands the heavens.' Before the British royal party arrived, the queen mother called for rain to lay the dust. It rained. Then she called for sunshine, which burst forth as George VI and his family arrived. 'I must,' murmured the British King, 'tell Mother about this.' " [147]

Dancing and incantation is not, however, the only method employed as an adjunct to this business. One other is best exemplified by a large block of soapstone, weighing two tons, which was apparently shaped and then transported to what is now Siskiyou County in northern California many generations ago by the Huppa-Huroc tribal group that still inhabits the Klamath River valley and adjacent areas. [148] This is a massive flat-topped block, with some 48 roughly circular holes apparently somehow

217

ground into its upper surface. Its location was known to all the Amerinds in that area, although it had been buried since before the coming of the white man. And it had been buried not only because it was greatly revered, but because it was considered extremely dangerous if left uncovered.

Then, one day in 1959, a road-building crew inadvertently uncovered it. When the doyen of the Hurocs learned of this from a member of his "band," who was running a bulldozer for the road-building crew incidentally, he immediately issued a warning to the local authorities. This was, of course, totally ignored—and perhaps rather naturally, since said authorities were palefaces. The old Amerindian gentleman stated very simply that uncovering the stone would bring on excessive rain or even snow. It did: five inches of the latter in one go, which was unprecedented in that area of mild oceanic climate, at low altitude, at that time of year. By then, somewhat rattled, said authorities reluctantly permitted the rock to be covered over with a thick layer of mud and clay, and its position marked.

Then, in 1966, some amateur folklore addicts uncovered it to take photographs; and they apparently banged on it, because the next day the disastrous floods got started that washed out most of the new roads and cleaned out all the gulleys and creeks throughout that whole area. This time, the Amerinds took matters into their own hands and buried the damned thing really deep, and removed the marker. Their tradition had it that their ancestors, while bringing on rain when needed in dry spells simply by uncovering this rock, had had to be very careful because *banging* on it brought on excessive rain (or snow falls) that sometimes could not be stopped before they caused floods. But the real trouble was that the local deer used to climb aboard this rock and jump up and down on it; so allegedly producing the same results, and this was the principal reason why they kept it covered. (I rather like this ditty.)

Another sort of mechanical rain-maker who intrigues me is a fellow named Dr. William Payne. His little effort goes as follows, and I quote from a brief piece in a weekly entitled the *National Insider* for the 6th of February, 1966: [149]

> In the old song, "The rain falls mainly in the plain," but in Costa Mesa, California, the rain falls wherever William Payne places his little clay replicas of an old Indian rain god, Cocijo. When Payne, an art instructor at Orange Coast College, set the ugly little statues out in the fields last November, Southern California got the heaviest rainfall in its history. On nine other occasions when rain was needed, Payne put little Cocijoes in the fields, and precipitation, ranging from drizzles to downpours, resulted. "Sure, I believe Cocijo brings rain," Payne told me when I talked with him at the college. "My students believe it, too—at least until after the final grading time. If Cocijo was good enough for the Zapotec Indians of old Mexico, he's good enough for me." The Zapotecs believed that if they placed stone likenesses of the god face up in the fields, they'd get rain. But, according to their legends, the faces of Cocijo were good for only one downpour. So Payne, following the tribal custom, molds fresh images of Cocijo after every successful performance. "The Indians believed that Cocijo worked because he was so ugly," he said. "He was designed to scare the heavens into letting loose with the water." Doesn't Payne perhaps check with the Weather Bureau before making up a batch of Cocijo images and putting them outdoors? I asked. "No, I never check with the weatherman," he said. "Cocijo just works, that's all."

There was some intriguing aspects to this case, and first, of course, is the ancient worldwide belief, mentioned above, that rain was God's semen. However, these Cocijoes (actually *kosytl*), are said to represent the face of the great *Mother* Goddess. Secondly, they are by no means exclusive to Zapotecas, nor are they the only little clay faces that are found by the millions all over Central America. They crop up from Sinaloa all down the south

219

coast of Central America to Costa Rica, and they are very prevalent in the isthmus of Tehuantepec, where I once stumbled across literally thousands of them, lying about on a bare desert. Curiously, the locals stated that these had been exposed by an unusual and torrential downpour some years before, and that, for some reason, it had never rained in that area since! Surrounding areas had continued to have a fairly normal rainfall. The "desert" as such where the little faces lay (and there was lots of other pottery thereupon) was clearly a new development, since there were multiple signs of very recent cultivation and even of adobe buildings that could not have been more than a decade old. Did these little Cocijoes lose their power after their first effort on being exposed?

All in all, if the Amerinds seem to have it over all the rest of us when it comes to rain-making, they are, as we will see in a moment, clearly pretty hot on cloud-busting and rain-stopping as well. While Eurasians seem to show a pretty good record in both departments, reports stemming from the European end of this land mass would seem to indicate that its inhabitants lost the "art" in early mediaeval times, though a tradition has remained almost everywhere of the efficacy of *prayer* in achieving these ends. Unfortunately, however, such prayer to God (within the Christian frame of reference) does not seem to work too well, if at all. The disastrous results of such efforts prompted both the Catholic and Protestant churches to withdraw official sanction from such exercises long ago. But Europeans seem to have achieved some notable successes (or disasters) by purely materialistic approaches; and I am not speaking of modern rainmaking by the cloud-seeding method which has had rather dubious results in some respects.

The first practical method came about quite by accident and was not recognized for some centuries. This was a marked increase in rainfall due to gunfire, both over artillery ranges in peacetime and during bombardments in wartime. It had at first been thought that gunfire *cleared* the weather! These results would appear to be due to sonic jolts causing condensation of

220

water vapour; and today, sonic booms from planes breaking the sound barrier have been shown to be able to sort of shake loose rain, but only briefly. Of a more practical nature is the extraordinary story of a bloke named Charles Hatfield which has been so often told and which is fully documented. The fullest and best version of his story that I know of, and the one which we have checked out most fully, appeared in the *National Enquirer*.[150] It is too good to be paraphrased, especially since the facts have checked out. It goes as follows:

> In two blazing hot years only two inches of rain had fallen on the parched earth around San Diego, Calif. By January of 1916, the city was on the brink of disaster for want of water. It had been three months since the last feeble shower. The reservoirs were virtually dry. At the risk of being regarded as idiots, the city council voted to employ the services of a professional rain-maker. They had been bombarded with proposals from Charles Mallory Hatfield, a former sewing machine salesman who claimed he could induce rain, for a fee. He got the job.
>
> He had noticed, he said, that after great battles there were often great storms. He had also noticed that during great battles clouds of cannon smoke rose into the skies. And, to Hatfield, this constituted evidence that the burnt powder had, as he put it, upset the balance of nature in the air. Once upset, clouds formed and rain fell, said Hatfield. For several years he had experimented on his father's farm in Kansas, setting up huge wooden tubs on towers—tubs from which clouds of chemical vapors drifted aloft. Rains came, torrential rains sometimes, and Hatfield found there were those who would pay him extremely well for his services. For example, the farmers of California's San Joaquin Valley hired him year after year to provide them with bountiful rains. They paid him $10,000 [before inflation!] a year, and were happy with the results. The miners of Dawson City, Alaska, paid him $21,000 to provide water for their dry sluice-boxes. So, when San Diego finally turned to Hatfield in January of 1916, it was not dealing with an unknown.

San Diego's main source of supply was Lake Morena, a man-made reservoir which had never been more than one-third full in its 20 years' existence. When Hatfield arrived on the scene, the lake was a hot, stinking mudhole. He made the city two offers: $1,000 an inch for each inch of rain that followed his efforts; or $10,000, for which he would fill the lake that had never been filled. For several days the city council stalled, vainly hoping that nature would provide the water. But when the fourth day dawned hot and cloudless, they hired Hatfield. And he put the workmen to setting up his tall wooden towers. Within 24 hours after those towers began sending their evil-smelling vapors into the skies, rain began to fall. Crowds stood in the streets to cheer Hatfield.

But the rejoicing didn't last long. On the third consecutive day of rain, the San Diego Exposition was washed out, and the Tia Juana [sic] race track was flooded. Telegraph and telephone lines were knocked down. Railroad bridges were swept away. And still the rains came. Otay and Sweetwater reservoirs filled—overflowed—and finally burst their earthen dams and thundered down the valley. A 50-foot wall of water carried 50 persons to their deaths. Troops were called in for emergency duty. Lake Morena filled and overflowed for the first time in its history. Then Hatfield turned off his towers and went to collect his money. The city, busy digging out of the flood, refused to pay him. And years later his lawsuit was finally dismissed. *Scientists declared that Hatfield was a fraud and that his method was worthless! {Italics ours.}* But before Hatfield died in 1958 he lived to see scientists making rain by sending chemical vapors into the air—just as he had done 42 years before.

Somehow this gives me a rather fiendish delight because it has so many facets that distress the stuffed-shirts. First, it sort of backs up my beloved Amerinds with their smoke signals; second, it apparently worked, so denigrating the pontifications of that fraternity; third, it was purely mechanical and pragmatic; and fourth, it *overworked*, which evokes still another repetition of good old Charlie Fort's expression, "Don't wish for anything too

much, you just might get it." By the same token, but in an entirely different frame of reference, I delight almost equally in
the following:

> UPI: London, England, 28th March, 1970: A housewife
> said this week she is making it rain 3,000 miles away in
> Canada so that seal hunts will be washed out. Doris Munday
> said she conjured up Canada's rains just sitting in her Brook
> Green parlor and "thinking very hard." That way, said Mrs.
> Munday, she has caused the torrential rains reported there
> to have cancelled out many seal-hunting operations, just as she
> had earlier ended droughts in India, China, and the United
> States, and caused hail to fall on an English cricket ground.
> "Nobody ever believes me," Mrs. Munday said. "There's no
> mumbo-jumbo, no incantations, no witchcraft—I just think
> very hard, concentrate on what I want the weather to do, and it
> works. At least, it works 90 per cent of the time. I love
> animals, and when I read about these poor little creatures
> being clubbed to death [in Canada], I got angry," she said.
> "So I made it rain."

Please understand that I am not even suggesting that this is
true, but it does nonetheless delight me. Just suppose for a moment that a similar claim should be made repeatedly and actually turn out to show the results predicted, what would the sceptics
say then? For your information, it *has*—but they haven't said a word!

I will now turn the coin and discuss the obverse of the above.
This is the matter of stopping rain and dissolving clouds. Here,
once again, we find our old friends the Amerinds in the forefront
of the expertise. The reports are enchanting, but repetitious, so I
will plunk for this one to illustrate their alleged competence in
this respect. This bit went as follows:

> In the summer of 1878 the Oglala Sioux were visiting
> their cousins, the Brule Sioux. A period of feasting and

223

dancing was planned. It was a bright sunny day. Everybody
was dressed up, the men in beaded shirts, colorful blankets,
fringed leggings, the women in bright buckskins or calico
dresses. Just as the dancing and games were about to begin
sudden clouds formed in the sky. A strong wind blew and
big drops of rain began to fall. It was evident a severe storm
was about to burst over the heads of the merry-makers. The
people began to run for the tipis. But Last Horse came
forward, carrying his sacred rattle. This was the rattle he had
made according to the instructions given him in a dream.
When he reached the middle of the clearing, Last Horse
looked up at the sky. A hush fell over the people. In silent
awe they watched while Last Horse shook his rattle and began
to sing. He sang the song that the Thunder Spirits had
taught him. The people believed Last Horse was contacting
the Thunder Spirits. Then Last Horse moved his hands the
way one might if he were trying to part water. As he
motioned, the clouds began slowly to separate. Last Horse
continued to motion the clouds apart and they kept moving
farther away. Soon the sky was entirely clear. Again the
sun shone brilliantly. Happily, the Indians resumed their
festivities.[151]

There are cases after cases of a similar nature in the records,
and they come from all over the world. One strange one which
would seem to imply both cloud-making and rain-making I take
from Curt Fuller's column in his magazine *Fate*, for September
of 1959,[152] with his kind permission, and in which he quotes
from the London *Times*. It goes as follows:

When the Dalai Lama escaped from Lhasa, a thick, un-
seasonable wall of cloud hung over the eastern Himalayas. The
very next morning the clouds lifted and the lofty snow peaks
"were again gleaming against a brilliant blue sky." How
did this happen? According to the Tibetian correspondent of
the *Times* of London, Divine power may have made the Dalai

Lama's escape possible. We quote the *Times* because it is
probably the most cautious and conservative newspaper in
the world. "Lamas are frequently called in to conjure rain and,
conversely, in the event of [over-]heavy storms or hail they
are not infrequently taken to task, or even beaten," the
correspondent cabled. The *Times* man reported that he had
one firsthand experience with "controlled weather." He watched
a cloudburst being held off during New Year dances.

But here again, we palefaces seem to have produced pretty
good results, too, at least if the reports are to be believed; though
in this sphere I do not have any example of purely mechanical
expertise like Mr. Hatfield's and his rain-*making* with smog. It
seems to be of an even more esoteric nature than the methods of
the Amerinds and Thibetans. The classic example is a certain Dr.
Rolf Alexander who claimed to be able to dissolve clouds by
looking at them and taking thought upon the matter. His is a long
and weird story so I have asked a very old friend, Walter J. Mc-
Graw, for permission to reproduce the account he gave of one of
Dr. Alexander's demonstrations in his book *The World of the
Paranormal*.[153] Walter is a reporter who has specialized in the
use of taped interviews for radio, and his series has been broadcast over the Westinghouse network for many years. He writes of
this demonstration:

> We, along with about a dozen other people, went to the
> roof of a large three-story building [in Florida]. It was a
> magnificent spring day as we looked at the long stream of
> cumulus clouds that moved lazily over the ocean in the very
> blue Miami sky. Of the hundreds of clouds we could see
> from our vantage point, Alexander told me to pick one. I
> did. I pointed it out, described it, and there was general
> agreement among the other onlookers as to which cloud I
> meant. Alexander then stepped forward, thrust his hands in
> his pockets and I stood behind him telling a tape recorder

225

what was happening. In a little over five minutes that cloud
. . . and *only* that cloud . . . had all but disappeared. All
the clouds had drifted with the wind, but none of the shapes
of the clouds around the target cloud had changed perceptibly.
Only that cloud had dissolved into a wisp which was surrounded by a hole of blue sky.

Once means nothing. I picked another cloud. This was a
bigger one that looked something like a dragon standing on
his hind legs. There was even a puff of smoke coming out of
his mouth. Alexander seemed to warm up to his job; and
(Saint) Alexander slew the dragon cloud in less than five
minutes just by looking at it intently. This time, warned by
my first experience, I watched the surrounding clouds even
more intently than I did the target. They did not change.

There is photographic evidence of this. No pictures were
taken that day in Miami but previous tests in both Canada*
and England had been photographed and published. According
to Alexander, *Life* had taken a series of photos but none
were ever published. Independent TV in England broadcast
motion picture film they had made of a demonstration on
the "This Week" program.

This all sounds absolutely balmy and certainly more in the field
of the so-called "mental," like the chanting and dancing of the
Amerinds, or the less noisy things like the "evil-eye," hexing,
and so forth, which are alleged to be produced without any
audible or visual mumbo-jumbo. But not at all. In answer to
Walter's simple question: "How do you do it?" the somewhat
ebullient Dr. Alexander stated flatly, "Very simply. When I look
at a cloud, I shut my eyes quickly and photograph that cloud. I
get the negative image in my mind and then I recreate the positive
image in my mind. Then I progressively imagine what I want
to happen to that cloud; the stages that it passes through as it dis-

* Photographs taken in Canada are reproduced in the June 1955 issue of *Fate*
magazine, pp. 42–45.

integrates. I visualize it disintegrating. Then I open my eyes, stare straight at the cloud and project that image. I believe the energy I use is biophysical." So there it is, laid out in over-simple—but in fact, totally incomprehensible—terms.

Another old friend of mine, Charles H. Hapgood, author of two remarkable books [154] and until recently Professor of the History of Science at Keene State Teachers College in New Hampshire, became greatly intrigued by the above account and so tried out the method himself—sceptical as he was. Somewhat stunned by the results, and being rather rudely kidded by all of us, he offered jokingly to put on a demonstration, and I must admit that he gave a rather worthy one in Charleston, West Virginia.

He, in company with twelve others including the writer, and Kent Wilcoxson, a geologist and a profound sceptic of all matters such as this, were in that state on an archaeological mission. It had rained torrentially for three days before our arrival and continued to do so all night. Next morning, we asked Hapgood kiddingly to *do* something about it. He went out onto a verandah alone for a time, and lo and indeed behold, a large break appeared in the dense, dark overcast precisely over Charleston. It stopped raining and the hole continued enlarging until the sun shone through from a perfectly clear blue sky. The weather remained almost perfect over about a hundred square miles of the Kanawha Valley for the two days while we conducted our operations, though *it continued to rain all around*. Within an hour of completing our field work, the sky clouded over and it began to rain again! I am quite prepared to admit that this was a straight case of K^1.

And so, you may think, endeth the First Lesson: but No! On returning home to New Jersey, I reported on our trip to my gang. We were lounging in deck chairs on the lawn behind the house. It was a perfect day, with lots of little fluffy cumulus clouds sailing majestically by, high overhead. One of my loyal assistants, the pragmatist and Navy electronics chap, Mike Freedman, became incensed when I came to this cloud-busting bit and asked us all, please to shut up. He then picked a cloud, lay back, and "did something." He *said* the cloud dissolved just like Dr. Alexander's. Unconvinced, but considerably impressed in view of the fact that this was Mike the sceptic talking, we started a sort of game, picking a particular cloud that we all agreed upon, and then asking Mike to "do it again." I'm sorry, sceptics, but I have—though very regretfully, I must admit—to state that it worked time and time again and, what was worse, that several other individuals *appeared* to be able to do the same thing!

At this point I frankly give up. As with the problem that I presented in the last chapter—to wit, the one-way stretch—I have absolutely no commonsense suggestions to make by way of explanation of all of this. Since there must *be* an explanation, and I refuse to accept "K" for this, one can but assume that there are manipulative forces of which we as yet have no knowledge. How far these should be sought "over the border," in the world of the mental and the mystical, I also do not know. *But,* until we have exhausted the possibilities on this, the materialistic side, I will go no further on that score.

CHAPTER FIFTEEN

HELL'S FIRE

O NE IS NOT just diffident, but duly humble and even somewhat tentative about bringing up this matter—and this for several reasons. First, it is alarming and frankly terrifying. Second, despite its seeming inexplicability, it not only seems to be, but most definitely *is* a fact, whatever anybody may say to the contrary. It has greatly alarmed everybody, from the wildest kooks to coroners, police officers, medical specialists, insurance people, and just about everybody else—and throughout history at that. Further, it has been written about by all manner of people and almost *ad nauseam,* but until recently, nothing intelligent was suggested even by way of possible explanation. I speak of the spontaneous combustion and consumption by fire of living things, and notably of human beings.

Like all the other "things" that we have discussed in this book, I started out on this one—and despite some decades of collecting facts and alleged facts about it—with the somewhat vague notion that it was (is) just another "unexplained," and one supported or brought to the fore by only a few famous cases. Oh, dear me! Just as in every other fortean matter, an overall survey turns out to lead into all sorts of by-ways and parallel throughways. Human beings bursting into flames and being burned to a crisp— and I mean crisp, such as it takes a professional incinerator hours to achieve at about 3000° Fahrenheit—while their surroundings, and even the chairs they are sitting in, are either hardly or sometimes not at all affected, turns out to be only a starter. Naturally, people are most interested in such "accidents" occurring to or being inflicted upon their own species, so that similar occurrences involving other animals and plants do not impress them to anything like the same extent, and such reports tend to get lost.

There are, however, a whole slew of further occurrences of like ilk that have somehow got shunted into another category, at least in popular estimation. These are the burnings of houses and ships and cars and what-have-you that so plague insurance companies, and which cause so much trouble and hard work for fire departments. Oh sure: naughty little boys love to start fires; and gasoline fumes accumulate in closed buildings, and then static electricity sets off an explosion; and birds peck through high-tension cables, and rats gnaw through power-line insulation; and so on and on. But still, well over half the so-called "spontaneous" conflagrations are never pinned down to any of these causes, nor can they be definitely attributed to *any* known specific cause. Only in the case of the two most commonly known types of what is recognized as "spontaneous combustion" do we get some conclusions. One of these is the widely accepted fact that old newspapers and other such trash that has accumulated in buildings and got damp may start to smoulder and eventually to burst into flames. The other is that *damp* straw, hay, or other organic vegetable matter may likewise start to "burn." And this brings us to the "country fires."

These constitute a most extraordinary business that also appears to have been going on since ever, and all over the place. It is mentioned by good old Pliny; and *local* literature, such as small-town newspapers, and the journals of historical societies, the records of monasteries, seminaries, churches, and even of scout camps and such modernities, are loaded with reports and accounts of these spontaneous outbreaks. Nobody seems to know what to do about this sort of thing. Confronted by a completely incinerated cow barn, local firemen, police, and insurance adjusters can but conjecture, and then go look for evidence of faulty wiring, smouldering hay, or for confirmation by neighbours of an electrical storm. The police must, of course, add the possibility of arson. I have been on dozens of cases of this nature and on three continents, but apart from some burned-out electrical boxes and many piles of damp hay—*not* burned, I should add—I have yet to be shown any one single piece of concrete evidence that any of these incidents were *definitely* caused by such means. However, all we can do, for now at least, is assume that one or other of these suggestions *was* the cause. But what of the absolutely endless "little fires" that take place all over every countryside in the world, away from and having nothing to do with man's habitations or any other of his works?

As everybody who has ever really lived in or spent much time in the country knows, if he or she will think back a bit, strange little burned patches keep turning up, month after month and year after year, all over said countryside. I am not talking of railroad or motor roadsides where engine sparks or cigarette butts so often start grass or brush fires. To the contrary, I am referring to those strange little areas of usually modest extent that one stumbles across at the back of fields far away from roads and buildings in cultivated areas, or in woods, forests, or the bush in tropical countries, or way out in the pine forests of the sub-polar and arctic regions, that are burned to a crisp, while all around is untouched. A fine case where the process was actually observed, was reported as follows:

Clifton, Tenn. (UPI)—Flames flick up out of the ground on Perry Davis's farm near here, drawing crowds from miles around to stare and wonder. "I've never seen anything like it," said Davis. "There are burned leaves all over the place. Blazes will jump out of the ground for four or five inches. It looks like the earth has been scorched from the ground up." Two persons have been injured by the mysterious fires. W. J.

231

Baker, 40, of Clifton, suffered burns when the earth collapsed from underneath him, and another man, unidentified, was reported slightly burned. Davis said despite warning signs posted in the area, "Persons have come from miles around to see. Forestry officials tell me that it could be very dangerous. There may be gas trapped under here and it could cause an explosion," Davis said. "I know there is a danger of these 40-foot oak and hickory trees toppling with the wind since their roots have been burnt," he said. Davis said the fire is burning about three feet under the ground over a two-acre area. "There have been several explanations given over the cause of the fire," he said. "Some think lightning caused the fire but I've seen no trace of trees being struck by lightning. I don't know the cause but it may have been spontaneous combustion." [155]

This is one of those puzzlers with which our ordinary, everyday life is filled, but which we ignore. Almost from birth we are conditioned to handle such enigmas in an entirely pragmatic manner and, in this case, by such consoling expressions as given above. These are all perfectly splendid and possibly quite true, but are they the real answers? Frankly, there are just too many of these little fires, month after month, year in and year out, and apparently all over the world, and even in areas of very high precipitation. What is more, the vast majority of them occur nowhere near a road; none ever seems to cause enough rumpus to prompt a call to the local fire department; almost none is ever seen burning; and there is very seldom any record of lightning at the time. But there they are nevertheless; just small, burned-out patches of ashes.

Now, this brings up a whole series of extremely nasty questions. First, just what is "fire," and just where does it start and end? Smouldering on the one hand, and flames on the other, are related questions. Rather than go into a long folderol and try to explain, I have obtained the kind permission of the *Encyclopae-*

dia Britannica to quote on these two knotty points. Their definitions go as follows:

> COMBUSTION. This term implies the process of burning and
> in the popular mind is generally associated with the
> production of flame (*q.v.*). So far as terrestrial conditions are
> concerned, it is due to the combination of a combustible
> substance with oxygen and the consequent evolution of heat.
> The condition of flame is due to the oxidation of gases or
> vapours at very rapid rate so that high temperatures are
> attained, the molecules concerned thereby become highly
> radiant.
> SPONTANEOUS COMBUSTION. *In certain circumstances*
> [*italics ours*] ignition may occur without the application of
> any external source of heat. Thus, when heaps of finely divided
> coal or of cotton waste soaked in oil are kept in badly
> ventilated places, oxidation, proceeding slowly at first, may
> cause heat to accumulate until ultimately the temperature is
> raised to the "ignition point," when inflammation occurs.
> The spontaneous firing of hay-ricks is the result of similar
> causes." [156]

Note first the highly necessary qualifying phrase that we have
italicized. Were it not so noted, every bit of hay and straw and
even dead grass and other vegetable products would—one would
have to presume—burst into flames and we would be living, if
at all, in a sort of perpetual *Götterdämmerung*. Other points
to note are, first, that the whole business of combustion is attributed solely to oxygenation and the (alleged) accompanying rise
in temperature. This is, of course, the classical (and classic)
explanation and interpretation. But we would point out that
these definitions lack the essential qualifying phrase "in certain
circumstances." Stuff will burn in gases other than oxygen and
wholly without its presence; and the basic questions as to just what
both smouldering and flaming *are* and just *why* they take place in

233

these "certain circumstances" and at just *what* temperatures, are neatly sidestepped.

Chemists, I find, tend either to shrug or to become a bit difficult if one presses these points, and in the case of spontaneous combustion sometimes even fall back on the layman's old standby of "electricity." Well, it is quite true that static electricity can produce a spark that can act as the trigger, just as a match does for gas released from a cooking range and which pushes the oxygenation over a critical point, and it is obvious that dynamic (i.e., generated or flowing) electricity can do likewise. It would seem, moreover, that the latter just might be the triggering force that sets off the phenomena that we are now going to discuss.

Let us never for a moment forget that we and all animals are basically electrical machines, and this goes for the functioning of both our corporeal bodies and our non-corporeal aspects such as nerve function and brain activity. However, we as thinking creatures have also another "entity," which we call the mind, and still another for which we have various names such as the Id, Soul, Personality, Spirit, and so forth, that apparently does *not* run on electromagnetism but on some other power- or force-spectrum that we have not yet identified. That this latter can impinge upon or influence our purely material chemical processes we have not yet proved, but in view of massive and highly technical work done in this field in Russia, Bulgaria, and Czechoslovakia,[157] it would seem that it might well do so, either directly or *via* the electromagnetic field.

I have quite a roster of reports of animals (other than of our species) being killed or afflicted by sudden inexplicable combustion; but these are, perhaps rather naturally, nearly all domestic animals. (Who keeps up with wild animals?) Personally, I have found only one wild animal that appeared to have been the victim of this plight. This was a large opossum that I stumbled across in the woods, far away from any human habitation or even trail, in West Virginia. The body was lying in a little clear patch among some weeds on the forest floor. Its front half, down to just in front of its hips, was perfectly normal and quite fresh; its back half was

234

literally burned to a crisp, so that all that remained of the flesh was a black cinder through which the bones showed, for the most part white but with all their extremities singed and charred.

Of domestic animals so afflicted, older cats that had lived wholly inside human habitations far exceed all the others, and horses in barns form a clear second. I have not heard of one single case of a dog going up in flames; and sheep, while some have obviously been "burned" *internally,* do not appear to "burst into flames." (This latter is *most* odd if one hopes to pin the business down to outside influences and especially because the wool of sheep is soaked with lanolin!) The few birds that I know of as having been alleged to catch fire are all members of the crow family (*Coracidae*) such as magpies, jackdaws, and jays.* Due not only to lack of space, but because I want to deal with this whole animal bit as a unit in another place and after I have had more time to conclude a whole batch of further enquiries, I am therefore going to jump right into the human aspects of this gruesome business.

In this matter it is quite useless starting a general discussion until it has been made quite clear that we are not talking about just one or two bizarre, unexplained incidents. Credibility depends basically on sheer volume, and any understanding of anything is greatly enhanced by quantitative analysis. However, there are so many cases on record that I once again resort to an annotated listing, and refer you to it now (see Appendix A).

The most interesting of these cases is that of Mrs. Reeser of St. Petersburg, Florida, but simply because it is the best documented one that we have. It contains almost all features reported in all other cases and it was most thoroughly investigated by all the appropriate, competent, and official authorities as well as by a most prominent physical anthropologist and anatomist specializing in death by fire. The facts are so pertinent that they must be given precisely, and among the dozens of accounts published there

* It is of interest to note that it is members of this group of birds that indulge in what is called "anting," one form of which is deliberately singeing the underside of the body, wings, and tail in flames.[158]

is only one, that I know of, which does just this. So, rather than paraphrase, I have sought and obtained the very kind permission of *True* magazine to reproduce verbatim the essential passages of a very fine article published by them in May 1964, entitled "The Baffling Burning Death" by Allan W. Eckert. This goes as follows:

On July 2, 1951, Mrs. P. M. Carpenter, owner of a four-apartment building at 1200 Cherry Street Northeast, St. Petersburg, Florida, had spent a pleasant hour or so the evening before in the one-room apartment of her favorite tenant, Mrs. Mary Hardy Reeser, a rather stout, kindly, 67-year-old widow. Mrs. Reeser had chatted amiably about her beloved Pennsylvania Dutch background with her physician son, his wife, and Mrs. Carpenter. She told her son she had taken a couple of seconal tablets at 8 P.M., as usual, and would probably take two more before going to bed. When the trio left at 9 P.M., she was seated in her armchair facing one of the two open windows, a small wooden end table beside her. She was wearing a rayon nightgown, a cotton housecoat and a pair of comfortable black satin slippers. She was smoking a cigarette.

The next morning, shortly before 8, a Western Union boy knocked at Mrs. Carpenter's door. "Got a telegram here for Mrs. Mary Reeser," he told her. "I knocked on her door but don't get any answer. You take it?"

Mrs. Carpenter said she'd deliver the message, but she was concerned. It wasn't like Mary Reeser, a light sleeper, to miss the sound of a knock. Mrs. Carpenter went to the woman's door and tapped lightly, then harder when there was no answer. Alarmed, she reached to open the door, but jerked her hand back in pain. The brass doorknob was so hot it burned her. She screamed, and two painters working nearby rushed to her aid.

They forced the door and found a macabre scene. Although both windows were open, the room was intolerably hot. In front of one open window was a pile of ashes—the remains of the big armchair, the end table . . . and Mrs. Reeser.

Firemen arrived at 8:07 A.M., followed by the police

[see Plate XX]. It was instantly apparent that this was no
ordinary accident. Only the severely heat-eroded coil springs
were left of the chair. There was no trace of the end table. Of
Mrs. Reeser, all that remained were a few small pieces of
charred backbone, a skull which, strangely, had shrunk uniformly
to the size of an orange, and her wholly untouched left foot
still wearing its slipper.

The heat necessary for such damage had to be incredible, yet
the room was little affected. The ceiling, draperies and
walls, from a point exactly four feet above the floor, were
coated with smelly, oily soot. Below this four-foot mark there
was none. The wall paint adjacent to the chair was faintly
browned, but the carpet where the chair had rested was not
even burned through. A wall mirror 10 feet away had cracked,
probably from heat. On a dressing table 12 feet away, two
pink wax candles had puddled, but their wicks lay undamaged
in the holders. Plastic wall outlets above the four-foot mark
were melted, but the fuses were not blown and the current
was on. The baseboard electrical outlets were undamaged.
An electric clock plugged into one of the fused fixtures had
stopped at precisely 4:20—less than three hours before—but
the same clock ran perfectly when plugged into one of
the baseboard outlets.

Newspapers nearby on a table and draperies and linens on
the daybed close at hand—all flammable—were not damaged.
And though the painters and Mrs. Carpenter had felt a wave
of heat when they opened the door, no one had noted
smoke or burning odor and there were no embers or flames
in the ashes.

Faced with a complete mystery, Police Chief J. R. Reichert
quickly asked for FBI assistance. Scrapings from the carpet,
metal from the chair, and the ashes and mortal remains of
Mrs. Reeser were sent to the FBI laboratory for microanalysis.
The first report had clarified nothing, but it contained a
blockbuster: Mrs. Reeser had weighed 175 pounds, yet all
that remained of her after the fire—including the shriveled
head, the whole foot, the bits of spine and a minute section of
tissue tentatively identified as liver—weighed *less than 10
pounds!*

237

Edward Davies, a top-notch arson specialist of the National Board of Underwriters, came in on the case. Hard to fool and quick to detect evidence of deliberate burning, he was stumped. "I can only say," he admitted glumly, "the victim died from fire, with no idea of what caused it."

Then came a lucky break. [The famous] Dr. [Wilton Marion] Krogman* was visiting his family just across Tampa Bay at Bradenton, and his presence became known. Told of the pathologist's reputation, Reichert promptly asked for his help. Dr. Krogman agreed to look in on the case.

The doctor quickly checked the findings of the other authorities who had been consulted and began eliminating possibilities. Had lightning struck her? No. No storms, no lightning, no thunder the night of July 1. Having swallowed sedatives, could she have fallen asleep in her chair, dropped her cigarette, ignited the nightgown and chair and burned? Hardly likely, since such a fire couldn't possibly have caused the heat—over 3000°F.—necessary to consume her. Even if an ordinary fire had reached that temperature, the room—or the whole building—would have been heavily damaged. Anyway, though the windows were open, no one saw smoke or smelled any burning odor. Was Mrs. Reeser burned elsewhere and then placed in the room? Residue in the room and other evidence ruled this concept out. Could an electrical induction current have gone through her from faulty wiring? Virtually impossible without blowing a fuse. And no short circuit could have caused such massive destruction.

Eventually, even Dr. Krogman admitted defeat. He told Chief Reichert, "I have posed the problem to myself again

---

* Dr. Krogman was incorrectly identified in the original article. He is a physical anthropologist and an anatomist, not a physician (or a member of the AMA) and is not "an outstanding authority on the nature and cause of disease." He states, in a letter to *True*, dated May 1, 1964, "I reject fully and unreservedly the concept of SHC/PC. Any statement direct or implied, that I do accept it is unwarranted and incorrect . . ." and further, "I have never, by stated or implied word, accepted or even considered as a possibility spontaneous combustion in or of the human body." He states quite simply that he has no explanation for such deaths (see his article in *The General Magazine and Historical Chronicle*, 1964; or, abridged, in *Pageant*, October, 1952).

and again of why Mrs. Reeser could have been so thoroughly destroyed, even to the bones, and yet leave nearby objects materially unaffected. I always end up rejecting it in theory but facing it in apparent fact."

He was unable to understand how the widow's body could have burned so completely without someone's detecting smoke or, especially, ". . . the acrid, evil-smelling odor of burning human flesh." Another major point he was unable to comprehend was the shrinking of the head. "In my experience," Dr. Krogman asserted, "the head is not left complete in ordinary burning cases. Certainly it does *not* shrivel or symmetrically reduce to a much smaller size. In presence of heat sufficient to destroy soft tissues, the skull would literally explode in many pieces. I have experimented on this, using cadaver heads, and have never known an exception to this rule. "Never," he concluded, "have I seen a skull so shrunken or a body so completely consumed by heat. This is contrary to normal experience and I regard it as the most amazing thing I've ever seen."

As many who have written on this distressing subject—and the professional medical men included—have pointed out time and time again, the preponderance of cases seem to occur among older women of sedentary or lethargic habits, or among bedridden men or persons in wheelchairs. There are also cases of infants not old enough to get about on their own outside their cribs. While obesity figures rather prominently, especially among women victims, it does not seem to do so among men or children. An astonishingly high percentage of the victims were known *not* to smoke or to carry matches or lighter fluids. In early times, and in fact right up to the end of the last century, alcoholism—and more notably excessively heavy drinking which is quite different in that such indulgers usually never get drunk or show any symptoms of disorientation that alcoholics (in the clinical sense) do—was almost invariably given as the cause of such "spontaneous" combustion. Further analysis of the recorded facts available, and of even some of the early cases, however, fails to support this view, while the number of cases in the more recent period is somewhat astonishingly contrary in this respect. Time after time the police blotter or the coroner's report states "did not drink or smoke," or "never known to have used alcohol in any form." In fact, it almost looks as if the *absence* of the intake of alcohol might be one predisposing factor in the incidence of these "fires." And this brings up a *very* interesting matter.

Some most illuminating discoveries have been made with regard to the vitamin designated B.10 (known to pharmacists as inositol). It is one of a group of phosphates, known as phosphagens. This has a molecular structure very close to that of the natural blood sugar, glucose—*not,* be it noted, to the synthetically produced substitutes such as corn sugars and syrups, dextrose, etc. Inositol is, or should be, formed naturally in mammalian bodies. It does not supply energy directly as does glucose but is a sort of stand-by which takes over temporarily for the sugars when they are oxidized to produce energy, and when their oxygenating potency becomes temporarily reduced. In cases of inositol deficiency, the liver converts sugar excessively into fat. In other words, phosphates, and particularly this one, are absolutely essential to our normal metabolism.

Trouble is, ever since man started cooking his food, he has tended to destroy certain essential ingredients his body requires. And since the invention of pasteurization of milk and the deplorable over-processing of wheat and other grains, resulting in such worthless horrors as "white" bread, he may be born to, grow up with, and finally end up with, not just a deficiency, but a virtual absence of this substance. If, on the other hand, a contrary imbalance sets in, phosphagen may begin to accumulate progressively; and then, since this substance is "a compound like nitroglycerine, of endothermic formation, it [can] no doubt [be] so highly developed in certain sedentary persons as to make their body actually combustible, subject to ignition, [and which will] burn like wet gunpowder in some circumstances." [159]

We therefore wonder—though mildly—whether this phosphagen, and its related complex compounds of phosphorus and potassium, might not be the primary cause of these spontaneous combustions both in soils and composts, and in living plants and animals. Even oil-soaked rags and damp newspapers could contain such substances; the first deriving them from the oils, and the second from bacterial action or fungoid growth, since these manufacture such phosphates. I have been unable to ascertain the smouldering point and the flash-point of these substances, relative to given concentrations, moisture content of the matrix, and other factors. These points must vary over a wide range; otherwise, what are these "special circumstances"? And anent this, we should note some cases in which a certain human factor would seem to have acted as the trigger.

This is *sweat*, soaking into fabrics closely adpressed to the human skin. In fact, sweat would seem to be the "trigger" in the majority of cases, as we may possibly infer from the number of victims who were invalids, either in bed or in wheelchairs and perhaps too warmly wrapped up, or people sitting for long periods in front of a fire, like the British author Temple Thurston who was recuperating from influenza at the time, *and* the heavy drinkers of old, who wore excessive amounts of clothing in order to keep warm in their frigid and uninsulated houses.

A most pertinent case in this respect is that of Paul V. Weekly of Sioux City, Iowa, who was awakened by an itching foot at 3:30 A.M., only to find, on throwing back the covers, that his bed was aflame. Having put out said flames, this phlegmatic character solemnly went back to sleep, only to have the same thing happen again an hour later! Incidently, he reported that the sheets, blankets, and bedspread were all new.[160] If his feet were sweating, and he had accumulated an excess of such compounds as phosphagen which were exuded in his sweat, they might, on coming in contact with the cellulose (i.e., nitroglycerin) of the sheets at the temperature engendered by the blankets and quilt, have reached a dangerous flash point.

Another very pertinent case is that of the Professor H. mentioned in Appendix A. This displays a very close similarity. It comes from a report by a medical man, Dr. John Overton, of

Nashville, Tennessee, and was published in the *Transactions of the Medical Society of Tennessee* for 1835. It makes delicious reading but is a very long and detailed report so that I will quote only some relevant passages. It transpires that "H" was professor of mathematics at the University of Nashville. He seems to have been a man of mathematical precision in all things, since Dr. Overton reports that:

> He was engaged as usual in his recitation room, in attendance upon the morning exercises of his class, till 11 o'clock in the forenoon. He then buttoned his surtout coat close around him, and walked briskly thus clothed to his residence, a distance of about three-fourths of a mile, taking exercise enough to produce a glow of warmth on the surface of the body, without inducing fatigue, but feeling at the same time his usual acidity of the stomach, for which *he resolved to take some soda as a remedy within a short time* [*italics ours*]. Having arrived at his lodging, he pulled off his over coat and kindled a fire, by placing a few pieces of dry wood on three burning coals which he found in the fireplace, of the magnitude of two cubes each; and immediately left the fire, and retired to a remote part of the room and made his observations on the weight and temperature of the atmosphere as indicated by the barometer and thermometer, which were suspended in that situation. He then took the dewpoint by the thermometer. These operations, together with the registration of the results, occupied about thirty minutes. This having been accomplished, he went immediately into the open air, made observations on the hydrometer, and was beginning his observations upon the velocity and direction of the winds. He had been engaged in this latter process about ten minutes, his body all the while sheltered from the direct impression of the wind, when he felt a pain as if produced by the pulling of a hair, on the left leg, and which amounted in degree to a strong sensation. Upon applying his hand to the spot pained, the sensation suddenly increased, till it amounted in intensity to a feeling resembling the continued sting of a wasp or hornet. He then began to slap the part by repeated

242

strokes with the open hand, during which time the pain continued to increase in intensity, so that he was forced to cry
out from the severity of his suffering. Directing his eyes at
this moment to the suffering part, he distinctly saw a light
flame of the extent at its base of a ten cent piece of coin,
with a surface approaching to convexity, somewhat flattened at
the top, and having a complexion which nearest resembles that
of pure quicksilver. As soon as he perceived the flame, he
applied over it both his hands open, united at their edges,
and closely impacted upon and around the burning surface.
These means were employed by Mr. H. for the purpose of
extinguishing the flame by the exclusion of the contact of
the atmosphere [i.e., oxygen] which he knew was necessary
to the continuance of every combustion. The result was in
conformity with the design, for the flame immediately went
out.

Then comes some information that is even more highly pertinent to our "theory", to wit:

Believing the combustion to have been extinguished by the
means just noticed, and the pain having greatly subsided,
leaving only the feeling usually the effect of a slight burn, he
untied and pulled up his pantaloons and drawers, for the
purpose of ascertaining the condition of the part which had
been the seat of his suffering. . . . The condition of the
pantaloons and drawers was next carefully inspected. The
left leg of the drawers, at a point exactly corresponding with
the part of the leg which had suffered injury, and at a point
accurately correspondent to the abraded surface, were burnt
entirely through their substance. They were not in the
slightest degree scorched beyond this limit, the combustion
appearing to have stopped abruptly without the least
injury to any portion of the drawers which had not been
totally consumed by its action. The pantaloons were not burnt
at all. But their inner surface opposite to and in contact with
the burnt portion of the drawers, was slightly tinged by a
thin frostwork of a dark yellow hue. The material of this

color, however, did not penetrate the texture of the pantaloons,
which were made of broadcloth, but seemed to rest exclusively
upon the extremities of the fibres of wool which were the
materials of its fabric. The drawers, which were composed of
a mixture of silk and wool, were made tight and close
at the ankle, and tied with tape over a pair of thick woollen
socks, in such a manner as to prevent even the admission
of air to the leg through their inferior opening.

It would be somewhat ridiculous to suggest that this case did
not occur, or did not occur as it did. Admittedly, it is now somewhat old, historically, but mathematicians and medical men were
just as cautious and precise in those days as they are today, and in
some respects more so. Moreover, this case with its pretty obvious evidence of over-clothing, over-heating, and more than probably excessive sweating, fits precisely into the pattern suggested
by those who did the research on phosphagen.[161] Thus, another
still older case may legitimately be placed on record, although it
is not from the pen of a medical man but a politician. It reads in
part as follows and was published in the *Philosophical Magazine*
in 1803: [162]

On the night of March 19, 1802, during the session of
congress at Washington, Jonathan Dayton, one of the senators
then attending from the state of New Jersey, sustained a loss
of a pair of black silk stockings in an uncommon manner.
On undressing himself at bed-time, his stockings were the
last of his garments which he took off. The weather being
cold, he wore two pair, the inner of wool and the outer of
silk. When he stripped off the silk stockings, he let them
drop on a woollen carpet lying by the bed-side; and one of
his garters, which was of white woollen ferretin, fell down
with the stockings. The understockings, on being pulled off,
were thrown at some distance, near the foot of the bed.
He observed static electricity on separating and removing the
silk stockings from the woollen ones.

He fell asleep, and remained undisturbed until morning, when the servant entered to kindle the fire. The man observed that one of the leather slippers lying on the carpet, and partly covered by one of the stockings, was very much burnt. Mr. Dayton then rose, and found that the leather over which the stockings had lain was converted to a coal. The stockings were changed to a brown, or what is commonly called a butternut colour. And although, to the eye, the stitches of the legs, and even the threads of their clocks, appeared to be firm and entire; yet, as soon as an attempt was made to touch and handle them, they were found to be wholly destitute of cohesion, their texture and structure being altogether destroyed. Nothing but a remnant of carbonic matter was left, except that a part of the heel of one of the stockings was not decomposed [sic].

Though this destruction of the stockings took place during the night, when nobody saw the manner and circumstances of the process, yet there was evidence enough of the evolution of much caloric while it was going on; for every thing in contact with the stockings was turned to coal or cinder. Beside the slipper before mentioned, the garter was burned. It was fallen partly on the carpet, and partly on and between the stockings. As far as it touched the stockings it was perfectly disorganized and carbonated, and immediately beyond that limit was as sound as ever. The part of the carpet, with its fringe, which lay between the stockings and the floor, was in like manner totally destroyed, just as far as it was covered by the stockings, and no further. The wooden plank, which was of pitch-pine, was also considerably scorched; and beneath the place where the thickest folds of the stockings had lain was converted to charcoal or lamp-black to a considerable depth. In throwing down the stockings when they were pulled off, it happened that about a third part of the length of one of them fell not upon the carpet, but upon the bare floor. This part of the stocking was decomposed like the rest, and the floor very much scorched where it had lain. [There was a very small fire in the hearth, 8 or 9 feet away; and the candle had been "carefully extinguished".]

The substances chiefly consumed were leather, wool, silk, and resinous wood. The linen lining of the slipper was indeed destroyed as far as the leather it touched was destroyed. But where it did not come in contact, it escaped, and the fire showed no disposition to burn even the linen beyond the boundaries prescribed to it on the leather.

While this business is all rather horrible and has got everybody who has ever heard of it in an uproar, it should be made quite clear that there is no reason as of now to think there is anything "out of this world" about it. Even if an imbalance of phosphate-potassium compounds, such as this phosphagen, in the bodies of animals is *not* the cause—or not the *only* cause—it is still more than just probable that the cause(s) *is/are* chemical, and that they are thus open to investigation and explanation without appeal to "witchcraft" or the supernatural.

At the same time, we are still confronted with a real enigma. This is—as any thinking person will ask—why do not such "fires," however induced, result in *normal* conflagrations? Why, and how come, the shrinking of Mrs. Reeser's skull? And why were not Billy Peterson's hairs singed when the flesh they grew from was reduced to a cinder? (See Appendix A.) Why, above all, do these "internal fires" stop so abruptly in surrounding flammable materials and not set off general conflagrations? How do they create the intense heat needed to demolish what they do, and yet not affect surrounding matter? But, the open-ended questions go on and on. Are these "blue flames" really flames or gaseous matter in the form of what we now call plasmas? Or are they of still another nature, having properties that we have not yet spotted or investigated?

Personally, I plunk for this last suggestion; and, when contemplating this, I think back to a day when a man threw a hunk of pure potassium into the sea off a ship. Ask any chemist what happened then. In any case these burnings are not what we could call "ordinary" fires. They seem to display more the properties of what we call atomic "heat."

246

CHAPTER SIXTEEN

FAFROTSKIES AND
SOME OOPTHS

IF OFFICIALDOM, science-
dom, commercedom, and just about every other dominion can
foist a seemingly endless flood of acronyms upon us, there can
be no possible reason for censuring us for doing the same. Besides,
it saves us even more verbiage than it does those offenders,
because some of our requirements are necessarily somewhat more
exaggerated to say the least. Such are the subjects of the coming
discussion, being (simply) "Things that are alleged to FAll FROm
The SKIES" and "Out Of Place THingS." This really *is* the world
of the unexplained, and on two quite separate and diametrically
opposed counts—first, the things themselves; second, the attitude
of the average person to them. In fact, the history of man's approach
to both—and of all kinds—displays a positively inexplicable and
almost incomprehensible sort of see-saw between belief and disbelief,
and between the crassest stupidity and the most blatant chicanery.

Fafrotskies first crop up in the earliest written records of which
we know—namely, those of Sumeria—and for the very simple
reason that *rain* was considered to be the Omni-God's semen
that fertilized the Omni-Mother-Earth-Goddess, as explained in
Chapter 14 (see also [163]). Rain, being little lumps of water,
and water being "heavy," it, falling from the sky, naturally constituted a considerable mystery to man as soon as he reached the
point of being able to put the simplest "twos" and "twos" to-

gether. To him, it apparently seemed dashed odd, to say the least, that this stuff should come down from on high when everything else, like apples falling off trees, and stones falling over cliffs, and people falling down stairs, sort of started at the bottom, or at least from where they could be seen. The very idea of enough water to cause a gentle rain, let alone a cloudburst, being able to be suspended up above *in the air*—which, incidentally, was then regarded as being "nothing," or just as we, until recently, regarded space—was incomprehensible. Ergo, by the then current logic, it must have fallen *out* of something else, as if a faucet had been opened on the bottom of some firmament that domed over the sky, or heaven. And, because this firmament was manifestly so enormous and all-encompassing (since rain fell everywhere all over the known world, which was then regarded as a flat surface), the only thing anybody could think of by way of explanation was that it was "an Act of God."

That other things fell from the sky was nonetheless just as readily accepted from the first. These, in the form of stones and hunks of metal (meteorites), were thus perfectly acceptable, as were other things supposedly dropped or thrown down by "God"; and, as a result, they were usually regarded as frightfully holy. The earliest records we have of such "other things" cascading down, are of rains of fishes, frogs, and other aquatic animals. This also initially seemed perfectly logical because, if God lived *in* water, or *was* water, either *He* himself or His home ground might well contain just such creatures as do our ponds, lakes, rivers, and seas. In fact, all our aquatic creatures might just as well have initially come down from on high, just as we ourselves were then alleged to have done. Other things, such as blood and "manna" are also mentioned as having fallen from the sky; but, as you may see by reading the Bible, nobody thought there was anything particularly strange about this. All that the ancients did was to "Thank Heaven" that items such as manna *did* arrive when they did—as, especially, in the case of the hungry Israelites who were suffering from a surfeit of desert quail at the time! And this is the way it went, from circa 4000 B.C. at the latest, until

248

the rise of what we call "science" at the end of the Renaissance in western Eurasia.

In what we now call the West, there was then initiated an entirely new and contrary outlook regarding this matter. The average citizen, and even the Churches continued, as always, to accept falls of all kinds of "stuff" and "things" as being almost as normal as the fall of rain, hail, and snow. But the new "philosophers," calling themselves "scientists," denied that anything other than these three undeniable "falls" ever happened, and asserted that all others were nothing but "old wives tales," "fairy tales," "hallucinations," or just pure lies. These wise men, however, predicated their pontifications upon almost the same premises that the most primitive peoples had used for their explanation of rain, hail, and snow—namely, that since there obviously was no water in the air (sky) but since it kept on coming from above, it must come from *heaven*. However, since the new science had discovered that there was no material heaven above, but that the air is a gas which contains water vapour, they contended that they had explained the whole business. But then, by that marvellous process so beloved of human beings—namely, arguing backwards—they solemnly tried to convince everyone that nothing else *but* rain, hail, and snow *could* fall from the sky!

The classic culmination of this non-reasoning is the oft-quoted rumpus that raged in the Academie Française for years about the validity of meteorites. These were declared fraudulent and completely unacceptable because, as one great savant put it: "Since there are manifestly no stones in the sky, stones cannot fall therefrom." This was logic carried *ad extremis;* but, as Charles Fort so succinctly observed: "Stones continued to fall from the sky." Reality can play havoc with logic, and facts can play hob with beliefs, but it apparently takes more than a shower of heavy fish landing on an ichthyologist to shake the "faith" of western scientists. Even then, as we shall see, they simply can't grasp what is really going on.

When meteorites were finally accepted officially as actually falling from the sky, still another strange phase set in. There began a positive rush by learned societies to list such things, going back to earliest times; and the damnedest—in both the colloquial sense, and that expressed by Charles Fort as being things "of the damned"—of all these lists must surely be that prepared by one R. P. Greg for the British Association for the Advancement of Science. The British Association had been publishing lists of "luminous meteors" for a number of years, and Greg had previously published "A Catalog of Meteorites" in the *Philosophical Magazine* and in the *Journal of Science*. His 56-page list in the *Report of the British Association* for 1860 [164] contained almost two thousand dated items, starting in A.D. 2. The most curious aspect of this is, however, that quite a number of scientific societies had been regularly reporting such items *before* the damned things were officially recognized! If you merely glance at Greg's listings, let alone analyze them in detail, you will find that an astonishingly high proportion of them could not possibly be meteors or meteorites—at least as we have been given to understand those things by astronomers or meteorologists. Half of these "oddities" appear to have behaved more like intelligently controlled machines, such as we today call "UFOs," since they either bounced along, stopped, hovered and started again, made instant angular turns, or just cruised about. In one case, one wandered about for ten hours over southern Italy, and then returned to the point of the compass from which it had originally come. But it is the other obvious "*non*-meteors" in this list that interest us most.

These are straight *fafrotskies,* or items said to have *come down with* "meteorites," or to have been left on the ground by them. Commonest among these are items described as "gelatinous substances." [165] However, one lot is said to have been "shot" out of what appeared to be a straightforward meteor, and to have resembled blood.[166] There were also some extremely off-items that seemed to resemble artefacts, such as pieces of iron chain welded together by heat.[167]

Greg worked in that marvellous period spanning the middle of the last century when science was still astonishingly open-minded and a bit starry-eyed. Seemingly having discovered that most of the *ancient* beliefs had deteriorated to nonsense by the seventeenth century and that, conversely, we really knew very little of reality, the new materialism started off wide-eyed and willing to "believe" just about anything, provided it was tangible and material. This attitude gained momentum until the middle of the nineteenth century; but about 1865 a reaction set in. "Science" had by then perfected—at least in its opinion—a set of rules, but in doing so, it had run into a lot of unexplaineds that these rules did not cover. As a result, said items were "damned," and even reports of and on them were progressively excluded from so-called "scientific" literature. They reverted to the category of "old wives' tales." Among these obnoxious items were "fafrotskies."

Then, around the turn of the century, there came another about-face in the whole field of the unexplained, in that scientists and laymen split into two camps, forming an increasingly clear-cut dichotomy of orthodoxy and unorthodoxy. Almost all scientists entered the first camp, followed by a vast majority of educated laymen; only a very few scientists took the unorthodox course, and these mostly into the fields of the strictly *in*tangible—such as spiritualism, spiritism, mysticism, myth, legend, folklore, and the occult generally. With them went the vast mass of humanity, who had never in any case changed their age-old beliefs on the one hand, or been "contaminated" by the new, rigid, scientific materialism on the other. And there matters rested until something cropped up. This was as follows:

The *tangible* unexplaineds had got completely lost in this shuffle, being classed by the orthodox along with the intangibles, and also being totally ignored and increasingly scoffed at by just about everybody—*except* the mass of ordinary folk, whose opinions were by this time denigrated to the point of censure, and who were scathingly referred to not just as "amateurs" but as uneducated and stupid bumpkins. But again with one exception.

This was an extraordinary man named Charles Hoy Fort, who not only rescued the tangible unexplaineds from limbo, but set wheels in motion that have now brought all of us, from scientists to bumpkins, back to *reality*. Fort did this single-handedly by the use of two weapons—a spear and a shield. The spear was nothing less than the amazing truth itself with which he jabbed and stabbed at orthodoxy and unorthodoxy alike whenever he spotted a chink in their armour; and there were not only chinks but gaping holes displayed by that of the former. His shield was a rather fiendish sense of humour, which he also used as an offensive weapon—and there is nothing more deadly than satire for puncturing stuffed-shirts. However, contrary to popular opinion, Fort never denigrated *true* science. He went after every type of pontificator or other idiot claiming superiority, and in doing so, he always chose first to quote from the pontificator himself before inserting his spear. Meanwhile, he spent his life collecting every type of "left-over" that he could find in the tangible world of reality. Most prominent among these were *fafrotskies* and *oopths.*

It has taken just half a century for the *unorthodox* to accept these things. Latterly, moreover, an increasing number of the *orthodox* have been forced every year to at least note the occurrence of the former (i.e., fafrotskies), but even since some of them have been literally hit by such—*vide,* this Dr. A. D. Bajkov, a professional ichthyologist, who was bombarded with fair-sized fish just after breakfast in Biloxi in 1949 [168]—there is still by no means even a preliminary acceptance of these things by them. Meantime, we neo-forteans have been doing a lot of legwork in order to get at the facts and to present them to all interested parties because, until the extent of the incidence of these items is appreciated we will never gain the attention or the cooperation of the fence-sitters. And among the latter are now a really astonishing number of orthodox scientists.

The above sort of historical review is essential before I can present the facts. Furthermore, having myself been trained in rigid scientific methodology, I know from now rather long experience that bombarding people with facts that they either don't want to believe, or which they have been led to regard as utterly ridiculous, is a pure waste of time unless the background of the whole business has been laid on the line. Truly, as I said in Chapter 15, credibility is founded on quantity, but piling Pelion on Ossa is a worthless procedure if nobody has ever heard of Ossa. The worst way to present a case such as this is, moreover, to present it by what we call in the publishing business, the "seed catalog approach." Even persons willing to believe in anything that they have not seen for themselves (and sometimes even if they have) become plain bored with page after page of repetitious items. In order to avoid this hazard, but still with a view to complying with the basic requirement for credibility, I asked my loyal assistant, Marion Fawcett, before I came to write this chapter, to please get me up a list of fafrotskies to put in as an appendix.

Now, on the typewriters in our joint we use an invention of mine which obviates the necessity for changing paper, since it employs continuous rolls with one or more subsidiary sheets that are the equivalent of carbons. This is the greatest boon to writers of all kinds because it saves—we found by running a prolonged series of tests—exactly one quarter of typing time, while corrections can be made on all copies simply by using a hard pencil on the top original. (Also, one can sell material by the yard!) Editors love this because pages cannot get lost in mailrooms or elsewhere; while linotype operators positively adore it because they simply put it, rolled up, on a piece of broom-handle to their left, and go right through the job!

So Marion pounded away on one of these machines: but when I got back from a trip and saw her effort snaking right across the office floor (see Plate XXI), I called a halt. Enough is enough, even for a seed catalog or an appendix, so I present what she did for then as Appendix B. Please understand, though, that this represents only a starter, and was gleaned *only from a part of our library* alone. I feel this ought to be enough to convince even the veriest sceptic that there *has* been something going on in this department.

So, armed with this list, and having thus got it out of the way, I shall now proceed to the much more worthwhile business of analyzing it, and then move on to the most essential requirement of all—which is to offer some suggestions in the general field of "How come?" Since I simply have not got the energy to write a second volume on this matter, I resort to the subpended and abbreviated classification of the items listed in this Appendix B. I would stress that I am *not* being, or trying to be, facetious. What is more, ridiculous as this list may appear, there *is* a distinct cogency and matter-of-factness to it, as we shall see on due analysis. It goes as follows:

A. INORGANIC
  (1) Artificial (i.e., "manufactured")
      (a) Brick, coke, slag, etc.
      (b) Foil and tinsel
      (c) Stone axes and wedges
      (d) Carbonate of soda, etc.
      (e) Buckshot
      (f) Nails
      (g) Money
      (h) Plastic balls, etc.
  (2) Natural (i.e., non-manufactured)
      (a) Ashes
      (b) Mixed "sand"
      (c) Ice (and peculiar hail)
      (d) Stones (alabaster, sandstone, asbestos, etc.)
  (3) Ambiguous
      (a) "Angel hair"

B. ORGANIC
  (1) Whole Animals
      (a) Terrestrial
          (i) Vertebrates
              (1) Mammals
              (2) Birds
              (3) Reptiles
              (4) Amphibians
              (5) Fish

254

(ii) Invertebrates
    (1) Organisms, small
    (2) Ants
    (3) Worms
    (4) Insects, exotic
    (5) Larvae, insect
    (6) Waterbugs
    (7) Snails
  (b) Marine
    (i) Jellyfish
    (ii) Mussels
    (iii) Periwinkles
    (iv) Prawns
    (v) Crabs
(2) Animal Parts
  (a) Flesh and blood
  (b) "Plain" blood
  (c) Hairs
  (d) "Butter" (manufactured)
(3) Plant Products
  (a) Marsh "paper"
  (b) Grains and seeds
  (c) Hay
  (d) Leaves
(4) Ambiguous
  (a) "Substances" (resinous, etc.)
  (b) Fibers (silky, etc.)
  (c) Plastic- or jelly-like masses
  (d) "Manna"

The first thing to do with such a list is to separate those items in it which could have been heisted aloft by such known natural forces as whirlwinds, tornadoes, and huracans, from those that could seemingly—at least on first thought—*not* be so lifted up. This exercise is, however, rather like the old game of "separating the sheep from the goats." * At first sight, it would seem to be readily divisible into two clear-cut categories; but watch out for the Chief!

If you have ever witnessed even a modest whirlwind (or wish-willy) in action, you will perceive that, while it indeed displays great lifting power, it behaves in a most "logical" manner, in that it picks up every loose item, within specific size and weight limits, up to its lifting capacity. As this stuff goes *up,* the lifting power diminishes, so that heavier (and smaller) items start to fall back to earth first, while others may sail on for miles. (The same presumably happens in tornadoes, though there are no valid observations on this on record.) Nonetheless, the items come down by size and density; *not* by "species."

Thus, a wishwilly passing over an open area in a wood picks up all manner of leaves and twigs and insects, and then drops them on purely random mechanical (physical) principles; but it does *not* sort out the leaves or the insects or anything else on botanical or zoological taxonomic principles! Yet, the vast majority of mass fafrotskies *are* of precisely and exclusively one "species" of animal, vegetable, or inanimate type. So, O.K., you may say, all the oak leaves were about the same size and weight, or all the frogs of *that* species were from the same "litter," so they were all the same size, and so all came down together. How then, may we ask, do massive falls of only one species of fish or frog or what-have-you, *but of all sizes and weights,* come down at the same time, and to the exclusion of all other species?

---

* Few of us Westerners seem to realize that, in making such a distinction in the hot, dry countries from Morocco to India, and from the southern shores of the Mediterranean, Black, and Caspian Seas to forested Africa and India, you often can't tell " 'tother from which," and you have to be frightfully careful. I once presented what I thought was a sheep to a frightfully important Chief in West Africa, as a gift and a gesture of goodwill, only to find out from third parties that I had mortally offended him because my damned-fool head-chap had picked a goat (instead of a sheep) for the offering, not knowing that this constituted a supreme insult! Did *that* take time and diplomacy! It also cost me my only remaining bathrobe to appease the dignitary.

I can personally attest to this seemingly inexplicable phenomenon, having witnessed such a "rain" of a certain rare species of frog in West Africa, of all sizes from tiny ones still losing their pollywog tails to full-grown ones, a hundred times more massive. And, incidentally, this "rain" took place up in the mountains and about four hundred miles from any region where this typically *lowland* species of frog had ever been reported. The locals had never seen anything like them up there. They landed by the millions and from a *clear midday sky*, and they covered the roofs of our tents and bush-houses.

The same thing goes for most of the vegetable items, and presumably for the inanimate ones such as are called "substances," at least when they are widespread. The matter of single items constitutes almost a separate subject; and with this I shall now endeavour to deal.

With these one-of-a-kind, the orthodox, the sceptics, and the plain scared are on much safer ground, because, given the requisite lifting power, certain types of winds *could* pluck a single item from a mass, or drop but one item of a specific weight and size at a time. However, these self-styled pragmatists find themselves confronted with another set of problems with this kind of fafrotsky: namely, how come things that are so rare as to be virtually unfindable by us, are suddenly hurled at us, and time and time again? I refer to such things as neolithic-type flint axes, old and rare coins, and bits of marble statuary of a completely unknown origin. It's a bit much to assign such super-selectivity to tornadoes, for it amounts to their doing a sort of "collecting" job for us.

But then comes the worst part of all: namely, that *hardly ever* has either a mass (or an individual) "fall" been recorded as having been associated with any whirlwind or tornado, or even with a huracan! These things do indeed very often come down in torrential rains—and notably the live or fresh animals—but a very high percentage land from perfectly clear skies, and (perhaps naturally) most of them in daylight. (Who knows what may come down at night, unless it bashes a hole through your roof?)

Then there are all manner of other problems to beset the sceptics. Where, for instance, could any discerning wind find a mass of buckshot, or of three-penny nails, or of British pennies, just lying about, already neatly selected, on the surface of the earth, waiting to be picked up? And how could such masses be transported to way beyond the storm that allegedly did so pick them up? Further, are we to suppose that, once so picked up, these objects are sort of shot selectively out of the top, like water out of the central spout of a huracan, and that they then go sailing away for miles (or hundreds of miles) in a high trajectory, before curving back to earth due to gravity pull, and then land all together? Aren't we getting a bit exaggerated? Yet there are other types of fafrotskies that defy even any such wild explanation.

The commonest and most puzzling to the pragmatists is *ice*. Now, as I have said, meteorologists have given us a perfectly adequate and logical explanation of this, provided it is in the form of hail, though even they become rather quiet when hailstones as big as golfballs, baseballs, or even footballs come thundering down, bashing in car roofs and killing cattle. But when other "things" such as moribund frogs and bits of statuary come down *in* hailstones, this fraternity becomes quite hysterical and usually states flatly and for the record that the report is a lie or a hoax, or some other form of fake. But ice fafrotskies have displayed some other tricks that have caught these atmospheric "experts" in a real bind.

Angular blocks of ice, and in some cases up to several hundred pounds in weight, have been landing all over the place, and since long before airplanes were invented. Moreover, some have made "near-misses" on such solid souls as police officers and even scientists. Nor is this all. This so-called sky-ice is of several varieties, sometimes being pure crystalline, other times apparently ancient or "blue" ice (known as palaeocrystic); stratified, or composed of "skins," like a golfball or an onion; and even—as in a number of repeat cases in northeastern Pennsylvania in the early 1950s—

in that most remarkable of all forms known as "cigar-ice" (see Plate XXII). This is a tabular form of ice such as is found at the edge of the arctic winter ice-blanket as it melts back during the summer, in which the ice itself forms sort of columns, vertical to the ground below, but all shaped like cigars and packed closely together. But worst of all, there are several cases of huge slabs of ice with one surface perfectly smooth and the other *festooned with icicles!* Now, what the hell do you make of that one?

It's all very well to have enormous hailstones from frightfully on high somehow forming on their way down while passing through supersaturated air; but, I ask, by what process can *rafts of tabular* ice, two feet thick, form aloft and then break up with *angular* edges that are not even rounded off by friction on their way down? And how can cigar-ice form aloft? That takes a very long time. And by what on earth (or off it) process can great slabs of ice stay aloft long enough for icicles to form on them? Surely this *is* a bit too much to ask of what we currently call "natural processes."

But we are not done with fafrotskies yet because we still have to deal with the really nasty items, like blood, flesh, "butter," *manna,* and this damned "angel hair." These cannot be explained by any of the good old saws like tornadoes with uncanny selective capabilities, or even the bottoms falling out of the kitchens on superjet airplanes. How do you get the blood or pure flesh (*only*) out of the animals you have hoisted aloft; and how do you get these to fall, when the bones and scrag-and-tail from any such butchering operations do not—either alone, or with those substances, or *anywhere?* Why never a rain of bones and offal; and why always *fresh* blood? And don't point a finger at those reports which say "a red substance resembling blood." Several lots have now been analyzed in modernly equipped laboratories; and the samples were clearly shown to be *fresh* mammalian blood, and specifically of ungulates, such as sheep, goats, and cattle!

The so-called "butter" presents us with still another problem. You have to "make" butter, and it is comparatively valuable, rather heavy, and not normally transported by air in bulk. But, if it is, then it is invariably in large solid containers. If the falls of flesh and blood are the dejecta of butchering operations on high by "ufonauts," as many people have suggested, who up there goes to the trouble of "making" 'butter and then tossing it overboard? Why not just toss out the milk and cream?

No! the whole idea is plainly nonsense—at least along any such lines of reasoning—so that one questions the identification of this substance. And, anent this, it is interesting to note that great blobs of this stuff have been found in Irish peatbogs since ever, and nobody has ever known what to make of them, and nobody has analyzed the substance.

The matter of so-called "manna" is something else again. Nobody has really defined just what is meant by this term either. It seems to cover quite a variety of substances, and the best and most frequent guesses that have been put forward as to its nature are to the effect that it is a kind of fungus that pops up out of certain desert soils after infrequent rains. In other words, there seems to be a general impression that it is not a *fafrotsky* at all but an *oopth,* since it was "there all the time," and only *appeared* to have come down from on high. There has been endless debate over this stuff, especially as mentioned in the Bible, and it once seemed that this fungus explanation had settled the matter. However, a Christian priest, of the Chaldean Rite of the Catholic Church, resident in Egypt, by the name of the Rt. Rev. Msgr. Ephem Bede, recently threw a real spanner (read "manna") into the works by publishing a long statement to the effect that this phenomenon has been known throughout the ages and is still of common occurrence in his country.

Apparently the pastor receives regular packages of manna from his home in Iraq, and hands it out to his flock and to personal friends. This manna is said to look like dirty dough but has a coarser consistency, and one account says that it tasted somewhat like almond icing. Monseigneur Bede states that this substance falls in small flakes, at night, over the desert, and that it is an age-old custom to gather it at dawn, clean it and knead it, and then bake it in a certain way. It apparently comes down most plentifully in autumn and late spring. In answer to the usual question as to what this priest thinks it is, we learn that, rather strangely, he considers it to be a perfectly natural phenomenon caused by a "chain of atmospheric reactions." He says he tried to have some analyzed in France, but the chemists remained baffled.[169]

The real stickler among fafrotskies is, however, so-called angel hair. There is no doubt that at least some of it (and there are several different kinds) *does* come down out of the sky, since it has been observed doing so by whole groups of witnesses and on many occasions. However, it also has been turning up *on the ground*, year after year, and in great piles, littered all over wide areas, and usually in uninhabited parts of the country. Within twenty miles one way, and ten the other, from where I sit writing this, I know of and have inspected two areas where such piles of it can be found in the woods at almost any time, and which arrive year after year, and then just lie there until they get overgrown. The published literature on so-called angel hair is massive. It crops up in heavy scientific journals, and from way back in the nineteenth century. Even modern meteorological publications mention it from time to time; and ufological books and periodicals are stuffed full of accounts of it.

Angel hair displays a rather wide variety of aspects, and the stuff it is composed of is most certainly of a very widely divergent nature. At one end of this spectrum is a very light, filamentous stuff that just drifts down from the sky when the air is still, settling on the ground, and on bushes, trees, telephone lines, and everything else, over wide areas, but which *vapourizes* very rapidly, and especially on being touched. In some cases it is said that it feels frightfully cold to the touch and that it either leaves no trace at all on your hand or, at other times, that it leaves a sticky "feeling," though nothing is to be seen. This type is usually described as being white and gossamer fine.

Another type is more substantial; lasts longer, and even through rain storms; disintegrates only gradually; does not dissolve or vapourize; and in every way looks like spider-web. This type possibly, and quite probably, *is* spider web, since many species of spiders, when fresh out of their brood capsules, spin a line of web that drifts out into the air and when long enough hauls them aloft. When millions of such tiny spiders hatch all about the same time, great clouds of them, suspended on their little strands, may be blown for miles on a light breeze and then slowly sink to earth as the wind drops. Such spider migratory habits are well known; but, curiously and rather maddeningly, the vast majority of accounts of this type of angel hair state categorically that *no* baby spiders could be found on or among the threads!

Still a third type of angel hair, and that which is most often found, and again year after year in the same places in woods and fields, is ribbon-formed and definitely of metallic constitution. (It has also been reported as being observed falling from UFOs.) Many samples of this have now been analyzed in competent laboratories, and their basic constitution has been identified as either very pure magnesium, lead, tin, nickel, aluminum, or a few other rarer metals. The ready explanation for this lot is, of course, that it is the sort of "tinsel" used (since World War II) by military craft to jam radar, and that it was tossed out of planes. Unfortunately, however, this stuff was reported long before the discovery of radar and even of airplanes. Also, no case that I know of that has been properly examined and tested, has matched this "tinsel" that *we* use. Further, we do not toss our stuff out in great blobs, and year after year over just the same areas! Of course, the UFO buffs insist that this is some form of dejecta from visiting space craft. I suppose that this *could* be so—given such craft— since it does definitely come down out of the sky, and there certainly is an almost overwhelming percentage of reports of it in connection with alleged "sightings" of UFOs.

But, there still remains one glaring problem that must be touched on, if only lightly. This is the other old standby of the sceptics, to wit: "All this stuff and all these things was/were on the ground in the first place."

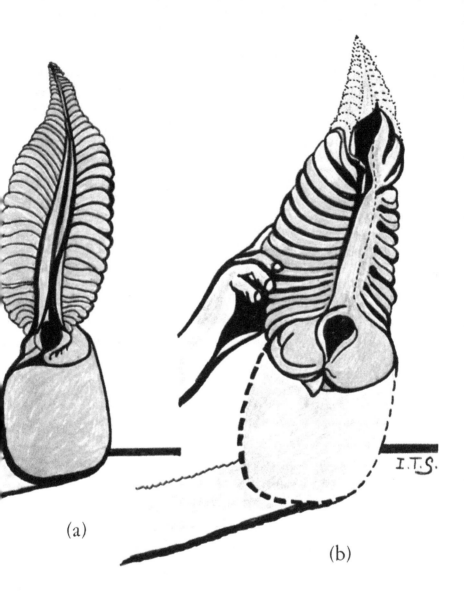

(a)

(b)

I.T.S.

Fig. 39. *The alleged fafrotsky from Venezuela:* (a) *large Caribbean Pennatulid or sea pen, a Coelenterate distantly related to the corals;* (b) *the Venezuelan object, held by the finder, reconstructed as if it were a Pennatulid*

Now this we would at first presume to be reasonable; but, if this is your contention, you still can't have ichthyologists being clobbered by fish from on high in broad daylight, or live periwinkles landing all over rooftops a hundred miles from the sea. Also, advocates of this theory are hard put to it to explain a very high percentage of oopths which *are* found on the ground!

Indeed, many such items do seemingly appear suddenly where they most definitely were *not* the day—or even a few hours or minutes—before. Further, the majority of these are so "odd" and "out of place" where they *are* found, that they readily draw the attention of their finders. Nonetheless, there can sometimes be possible explanations for their appearance. The most outstanding that I have heard of recently is the "thing" found in Venezuela (see Plate XXIII and Fig. 39).

The original story accompanying this photo read:

> A strange object shaped like a human kidney fell from
> the sky on July 22, 1969, in the Los Llanos area, near Zaraza,
> Guarico State, producing panic and excitement in the farm
> neighborhood. The object was composed of a very solid
> gray material. Its interior is completely empty, giving the
> impression of being a protective harness or armor-plate of
> an unknown instrument. Farmer Hilario Aponte carried the
> object to the nearest village, where it was turned over to
> government officials who indicated they would turn it over to
> the American Embassy! The paper added that the object
> showed little damage and could hardly have been a part of
> a satellite or other space shot. Ironically [sic], farmer Aponte
> died *from unknown causes* the day after he gave the story
> to the newspaper.[170]

There is a group of marine creatures called popularly sea-pens, and more scientifically the Pennatulaceans, that give rise to just such odd-looking structures. The remains of these are sometimes found on beaches after storms. They are a kind of coelenterate, holding a status somewhere between the sea anemones and the corals. They are gelatinous but become rubbery when dead and exposed to the air. The top part (see Fig. 39) readily breaks off, and the lower tentacles then curl inwards on drying—i.e., away from the viewer in this picture—until they go into their interiors, which are hollow.

Zaraza in Guarico State is about 50 miles from the sea. Trash-fish and other inedible animals that are brought up in trawls and dredge-nets off that coast, instead of being tossed overboard, are often harvested by the frugal Venezuelan fishermen and sold— and at a handsome price, we might add—as fertilizer for inland cornfields; and Zaraza is on the Ipiri River not far from the sea. There is no evidence that this thing actually "fell from the sky," and so we have it in mind that it turned up one day after rain, on the surface of a milpa (corn field), having arrived initially concealed in a load of fish manure.

It has been pointed out to me repeatedly that, as an avowed fortean, my primary function is or should be to search for *possible* explanations of the unexplained. To this I humbly submit, but I refuse to push this objective beyond a certain point. *As* a fortean, I demand facts, and tangible, measurable ones at that— however abstruse the subject. On looking back over this manuscript, I perceive that, unlike Alfred Hitchcock, I have been able to offer at least something by way of a *possible* solution of the mystery within the framework of our logic and of materialism, in all except two cases. These were the "cockeyed house" and rain-making and cloud-busting. I shall continue to leave these open, despite the fact that I have at last discovered a possible integrating explanation for just about everything else.

In this case—of fafrotskies and oopths—my suggestion is admittedly a bit abstruse and somewhat radical, but I would like to make it quite plain that, while I have arrived at it entirely on my own, it is *not* original, in that several others have recently come to the same conclusion. I have appended a brief epilogue to this opus in which I state briefly and boldly just what this conclusion is. For now, and to conclude this chapter and the main body of this text, I just want to say this about fafrotskies.

That these things exist (or "happen," as it were) simply can *not* be denied. Their "happening" is, however, in the vast majority of cases, unexplained and seemingly inexplicable to us at our present level of understanding of reality. However, they are tangibles, and therefore, to bring them into our understanding, we must revamp or extend our logic to conceive of a wider reality and of a greatly expanded universe. But even this is still not enough. Much more essential is that we try to comprehend at least the possibility of *other universes;* not, be it noted, of just another "dimension," but of an infinity of other space-time continua; for, if we do so, we will be able to accept a perfectly logical explanation of these fafrotskies. This is that they don't really *fall out of the sky* (like rain or airplanes) but that they "come through" from one or more other "universes." They have been appearing since ever; *and they must come from somewhere.* As to where that might be, and how they come, I ask you to read on to the epilogue.

EPILOGUE

WRITING THIS BOOK has completed at least one phase of my education. I approached it with a combination of great exuberance and pleasant anticipation, but without the slightest expectation of its leading me where it has. Starting as a bug-hunter when a youngster, I graduated to professional field collecting, and finally to "professional" scientific research. However, once you have indulged in *search,* you will find that *research* is a sterile cul-de-sac; so back to the field I went.

Now, nature—which is to say, reality—is not the simple thing we have been taught to believe that it is. Nor is it the cut-and-dried, one-way highroad built by our modern, western, mechanistic science, as I learned very early when searching for rare animals. This fact was best exemplified (for me) by an answer given by a tribal African chief whom I had asked about a certain excessively rare animal, specimens of which had been obtained only twice. After regarding my sketches, he nodded and turned to my interpreter with a simple statement. This came back to me, very simply, as "Which one does the 'master' want? The black one or the white one?" And, by jingo, there *were* two quite different species.

Another thing: The extent of what we *don't* know about nature is matched only by our inherent misconception of reality as a whole: and, to make matters worse, we have not yet graduated from the mental stone age—stone being a synonym for the rocks in our heads. Indeed, we may have come a long way in appreciating and understanding our environment; at least we like to so presume, but we've only just very recently run head on into the realities of existence. Irrespective of our current logic, which is likewise rather primitive, we simply have no pigeonholes set up as yet to receive the increasing number of "unexplaineds" and seeming "inexplicables" that our methodical searches are bringing to light. Such unexplaineds are, moreover, of two kinds.

The most troublesome are the *intangibles,* but the most aggravating are the *tangibles.* The former can be—or at least have been up till now—just swept under the proverbial rug; but the latter can not be so nimbly or conveniently disposed of. Even if you can not prove their nonexistence, you can no longer go on denying that there are sea monsters, and you can't just ignore them—because, being tangibles, one might just pop up to get you at any time. And one has, in the form of Tim Dinsdale's film of such a bogey in Loch Ness; a film which has made "monkeys" out of everybody who ever said that such animals *could not* exist. But now something else has happened. Let me introduce it this way.

Being born a pragmatist and a profound sceptic of anything nonmaterial, I just refused to have anything to do with any *in*tangible. This is not to say that I discounted them. They just were not, and still are not for the most part, of any interest to me. The unexplained *tangibles,* on the other hand, came to occupy an ever increasingly important place in my life; and mostly because, as time went on, I ran across ever more and more of them—ranging all the way from previously unknown animals to enormous enigmas and paradoxes of all kinds. Some of these, moreover, were intangibles, but *were* susceptible to measurement and could be reproduced, so being amenable to investigation and analysis by entirely pragmatic and *tangible* technologies.

Now at last, philosophers, if not scientists, and the thinking public, if not the nonthinking, have finally woken up to the fact that an ever increasing number of *in*tangibles have *tangible* aspects. (Please understand, I am not talking about purely spirit-ual, mental, ethical, or aesthetic concepts, but of those depart-ments that we have been taught to call psychic, occult, mystical, and so forth.) I am talking of, for instance, matters like telepa-thy, hypnotism, auras, biorhythms, and so forth—and most notably what is called *teleportation.* And this last would seem to be the key to just about all of them.

Work has been proceeding on these themes for almost half a century in Russia, going on right through the Stalinist period, but the findings are only now becoming known to our western world. What we so erroneously call ESP is of the same ilk, and so is a considerable amount of so-called "psychic" research. Both these expertises are misnamed, and both have been scoffed at by western science. Admittedly, a very great deal of both is unutter-able rubbish or, literally, "figments of imagination," but there is in both a hard core of reality. Trouble is, that we of the West have tried to tackle them from the *intangible* angle. The Russians have tackled them from the *tangible,* which is to say by way of a purely technological approach. The result is that they have what is called "proved" that a lot of these things and concepts have a very real basis in fact and reality. Hardly anybody any longer denies that there is something in hypnosis; but how many realize that auras have been photographed and analyzed for four decades?

So what has come out of all of this? Simply that, in addition to the electromagnetic spectrum on which we thought our whole universe ran, there is another spectrum of "forces," or whatever you want to call them, that may affect the EM band, but which does not seem to be affected *by* it. Moreover, it is on this other band that things like mental processes run. The catch-phrase of the uneducated to account for this, is that there is "another dimension." This is pure blather, as has now been demonstrated by such mathematicians as Drs. Büchel and Freeman; see Chapter 13, pp. 197 and 198.

What these people are trying to say is that not only could there be, but most probably is/are, another *whole set(s) of dimensions,* separated from us in various ways in both time and space, but that some may be so close to ours in either respect that bits and pieces "fall through" from one to the other, and then possibly back again. At the same time, there may be an infinity of other sets of dimensions, or universes, or space-time continua, more widely separated from us in either of these, or an infinity of other respects, from which things come, or to which things go, more occasionally, or only by *deliberate intent.* And here is another rub.

We cannot define intelligence, yet we babble about it all the time. While we are stuck with what *we* call this quality, as we see it on this earth and in *this* space-time continuum (i.e., universe), there are those who have always yakked about either a single other, or a multitude of other "superior intelligencies." This is the department of the religionists and other mystics; but, dealing only with the intangible as they have always been doing, they have not come up with any pragmatic evidence for their contentions. (As a pragmatic example, it is quite useless to get down on your knees and pray for light if the power has failed while you were out to dinner. Better you should ring up Con Edison.) But now we are being forced to accept the fact—and the "forcing" is coming ever more often, and from all manner of diverse angles—that there are tangible, measurable, and reproducible evidences of other "universes" in contact with ours. And inhabiting these there would appear to be intelligencies, ranging all the way from abyssmal idiots to godlike entities. The evidence for these contentions, moreover, lies primarily in our field of the *tangible unexplaineds.*

Despite the fact that not one of them has as yet been captured physically, things like large, as yet uncaught animals in lakes and seas, and hairy ultraprimitive hominids, are, one feels, perfectly natural, normal, and possible. But I am not speaking of such things at this point. To the contrary, I am referring to such items as these little gold airplanes and bulldozers, and Ancient Egyptian TV tubes, on the one hand, and to the much more abstruse items like fafrotskies, on the other. Here are solid, valid, and "concrete" objects all right, but ones which defy explanation by our current

270

standards of belief (scientific), understanding, and logic. Things like little gold models of delta-wing airplanes, dated one thousand years ago, present one problem; the fafrotskies quite another. Put simply, the former either indicate that there were some "people" building airplanes that long ago or that we have failed completely to allow for some "outside" interference. The latter can mean only that we have failed altogether to understand reality. These fafrotskies may therefore offer us a real clue.

Armed with the list in Appendix B, I defy anybody to deny that *ALL of this* is makebelieve. So then, at least *some* of it must be true. (This is the old saw about the white crow. Crows are black, so somebody declares that *all* crows are black. But then a white crow turns up. Where are you then? Next thing you know we will be having green, pink, and violet crows—possibly? Yes?) So, if there are *any* fafrotskies, there could be lots of them; but whether there *are* lots or not, the endless reports of them cannot just be swept under the rug. Therefore, it is incumbent upon us to at least start looking around for some concrete explanation that *is* logical (by some logic), practical, pragmatic, realistic, and at least halfway understandable. And here we run into the ultimate —which is why I stated that the writing of this book has completed one phase of my education, as of the moment, at least! The truth of the matter is that until very recently nobody had come up with a "logical" explanation of such things, within the framework of our currently accepted logic and scientific ideas. Therefore, we have to expand our logic and ideas.

A considerable number of real thinkers—philosophical, scientific, technological, and popular—have now done just this. Examples are people like Aimé Michel, the French engineer; Dr. Jacques Vallée, a physicist and computer specialist who worked for our NASA; Dr. John M. Allegro, philologist of Liverpool, England; John A. Keel, journalist; Dr. Luis Schonherr, mathematician; Dr. Edward Uhler Condon, of the "famed" Colorado Project; and both official and unofficial spokesmen for a dozen governments. All of them have, after long search, research, and apparently profound cogitation come up with exactly the same answer: (1) that there are other "universes" interrelated with ours, both timewise and/or spacewise, (2) that these may be infinite in number, (3) that some, if not all of them have, as intrinsic items of their makeup, "intelligencies," (4) that some of them at least learned long ago how to "come through" to us and go back where they came from, (5) that some of these—the intelligencies—are millions of years ahead of us in material technology and also by way of the understanding of reality, and finally (6) that some of them have controlled us, and our whole evolution, since ever. It all sounds very much like the novelization of Clarke and Kubrick's *2001*.

After going through all this exercise, I have to state definitely and without chagrin that I now subscribe wholeheartedly to this opinion; and I do not care one jot what anybody may think of my so stating. After all, men of the stature of Albert Einstein said just the same thing; and truly august bodies like the Roman Catholic Church and the orthodox Buddhists have done so also, and for centuries. The mystics, as I have said, could never "prove" their point because they were dealing with intangibles, but now, at last, our nit-picking western technology has been forced into providing some proof.

So, all I want to say in taking leave of you, is that I am willing to put it on the line now: first, that there is a hell of a lot going on of which we are not aware and of which we are usually not informed; and, second, the explanation for just what *is* going on in these more abstruse fields can *only* be interpreted by accepting the fact that ours is not the only Universe.

APPENDIX A

Cases of Spontaneous Human Combustion

DATE	PLACE	NAME AND CIRCUMSTANCES
17th century	Courland, Germany	Two noblemen, after a drinking bout, "died in consequence of suffocation by the flames which issued with great violence from their stomachs." 171
17th century	Germany(?)	"A soldier" drank "two glasses of spirits, [and] died after an eruption of flames from his mouth"; and another case "of the same kind after a drinking-match." 172
1692	Copenhagen	"A woman of the lower class"; no details given.*173
20 Feb. 1725	France	Mme Millet, no details given.*174
9 Apr. 1744	England(?)	Grace Pitt, no details given.*175
7 Feb. 1749	France	Mme de Boiseon, aged 80, no details given.*176
1763	Italy(?)	Countess Cornelia Bandi, aged 62, no details given.*177
2 March 1773	Coventry, England	Mary Clues, aged 50, found reduced to whitish ash except for a leg and thigh, between the bed and the fireplace; nothing else in the room damaged.178
Feb. 1779	France	Mary Jauffret, no details given.*179

273

1780	Limerick, Ireland	An almshouse keeper named O'Neil was wakened by a lodger who showed him the body of Mrs. Peacock who roomed on the floor above, lying "flaming and red as copper" in his room. A hole burned through the ceiling and shaped like a woman's body, showed where she had fallen through.[180]
3 June 1782	France	Mlle Thuars, no details given.*[181]
1788	England	"A young English chambermaid" was sweeping the kitchen floor when her back burst into flame, unnoticed by her until her master came in and shouted at her; he was unable to put out the fire.[182]
16 March 1802	Massachusetts	"The body of an elderly woman evaporated and disappeared from some internal and unknown cause, in the duration of about one hour and a half . . . [on the floor near the hearth] there was a sort of greasy soot and ashes, with remains of a human body, and an unusual smell in the room. All the clothes were consumed; and the grandmother was missing. . . ." [!] [183]
1813	England	An elderly gentleman, while drunk [on tincture of valerian and tincture of gum guaiacum!], rolled out of his bed "which was approximate to a fire, the flames of which extended to his saturated body, and reduced it to a cinder, without materially injuring the bed furniture." [184]
5 Jan. 1835	Nashville, Tenn.	Mr. H., Professor of Mathematics (see text, p. 241).[185]
1836	Cesena, Italy	Countess Cornelia Zangari, aged 62, was found on the floor of her room, reduced to a heap of ashes, except for her arms and legs and part of her head. The floor and furniture were undamaged, but there was fine soot throughout the room and a disagreeable odour.[186]
25 Feb. 1851	Paris, France	A house-painter, while drinking, bet that he could eat a lighted candle. "Scarcely had he placed it in his mouth, when he uttered a slight cry, and a bluish flame† was seen upon his lips. . . . In half an hour the head and upper portion of the chest were entirely carbonized. The fire did not cease till bones, skin, and muscles were all consumed, and nothing remained but a small heap of ashes. . . ." [187]
27 Dec. 1885	Ottawa, Illinois	The remains of Mrs. Patrick Rooney—a burned piece of skull, two charred vertebrae, a few foot bones, and a pile of ashes—were found on the

* The article from which these were taken lists a large number of cases, but primarily by source rather than by name of victim or date. At the time of writing, work on tracing all of these has just begun, and the above table should not—in any case—be looked upon as an attempt at a complete listing of all such cases.
† Note hereafter the persistent references to *blue* flames.

		ground beneath a 3 x 4 foot hole in the kitchen floor; there was soot throughout the house but no other damage.[188]
31 March 1908	Blythe, England	Mary Hart, an invalid, was found burning in a chair. Her sister smothered the flames, carried her up to her bed, and then ran for help. When they returned, they found Mary reduced to ashes except for the head and several fingers. The sheets were undamaged though there was soot on the walls.[189]
1933	England	The author Temple Thurston, recuperating from influenza, was found nearly consumed in his chair.[190]
30 July 1938	Norfolk Broads, England	A young woman, paddling in a boat with her husband and children, suddenly burst into flame and was quickly reduced to a pile of ashes; her family were uninjured and the boat undamaged.[191]
20 Sept. 1938	Chelmsford, England	A young woman was in the middle of a dance floor when blue flames burst from her body; the flames could not be extinguished and "in minutes she was ashes, unrecognizable as a human being."[192]
1942	Bloomington, Illinois	Aura Troyer, 59, was found in the basement of the bank where he worked as a janitor, almost all his clothing burned off. "It happened all of a sudden" was all he said before he died.[193]
1942	Orpington, Fulham, and Brighton, England	Ellen K. Kelly, 83; Mrs. Annie Coleshill, 66; and Mrs. Mary Forge, 94, all died by spontaneous conflagration. No details available.[194]
1942	Pittsburgh, Pa.	Carl Brandt, 33, was found on the sidewalk, "most of his clothing burned from his body."[195]
13 Jan. 1943	Deer Isle, Maine	Allen M. Small, 82, was found dead in his home. Fire "had burned the clothing from the upper part of the body." The carpet beneath the body was charred but, although the room was "in confusion," nothing else was burned.[196]
1 Feb. 1943	Lancaster, N.Y.	Arthur Baugard, 39, an invalid, was found burned beyond recognition in his home; there was no other fire damage.[197]
17 Oct. 1947	Liverpool, England	A 10-year-old boy was found in flames. There were no signs of fire in the shop after the incident.[198]
1 July 1951	St. Petersburg, Fla.	Mrs. Mary Reeser, age 67 (see text, p. 235).[199]
Apr. 1953	nr. Hanover, Md.	Bernard Hess died of a fractured skull and internal injuries in an auto accident; when examined he was found to have suffered second- and third-degree burns over two-thirds of his body. His clothes were undamaged and there was no trace of fire in the car.[200]
1 March 1953	Greensville, S.C.	Waymon Wood, aged 50, was found "crisped black" in the front seat of his closed car. "There was little left of Wood or the front seat. The heat

had made the windshield bubble and sag inward, yet the half-tank of gas in the car was unaffected." [201]

1956	Pleasantville, Ohio	Mrs. Cecil Rogers was "burned to a cinder." The bed was somewhat charred on top but nearby furniture was merely scorched.[202]
28 Apr. 1956	Benecia, California	Harold Hall, 59, was found on the kitchen floor, his chest, arms, and face charred; he was still alive but could not explain what had happened, and died shortly thereafter.[203]
Dec. 1956	Honolulu	Young Sik Kim, age 78, an invalid, was found "wrapped in blue flames too hot to approach. When firemen got there 15 minutes later, the victim and his overstuffed chair were ashes. All that remained were Kim's undamaged feet, still resting on his wheelchair where he'd propped them." There was no other damage to the room.[204]
31 Jan. 1959	San Francisco	Jack Larber, an elderly patient, was given a glass of milk by an orderly who then left for 5 minutes and returned to find the man "wrapped in blue flames." [205]
Spring 1959	Rockford, Illinois	Rickey Pruitt, aged 4 months, burst into flame and burned to death; the bedclothing and the crib were not even scorched.[206]
13 Dec. 1959	Pontiac, Michigan	Billy Peterson, aged 30, committed suicide by carbon monoxide poisoning in his car. When examined he was found to have third-degree burns of the back, arms, and legs; and *internal* burns. His clothing was not singed, and unsinged hairs stuck up through his charred flesh.[207]
24 Nov. 1960	Pikeville, Kentucky	The charred bodies of five men were found in a car; there was no evidence of any attempt to escape from the car. Death was attributed to "fire fracture," or internal heat—metal pellets first thought to be shotgun pellets proved to be melted metal from the car.[208]
3 Aug. 1962	Lockland, Ohio	Mrs. Mary Martin, aged 74, was heard to scream and was found seated in a kitchen chair, her clothing aflame; she died some hours later. The only sign of a fire was the burnt chair on which she was sitting.[209]
4 Dec. 1963	Glen Cove, Long Island	Thomas Sweizerski, aged 66, was found dead, his clothes burned off his body. There was no other evidence of fire.[210]
17 Dec. 1969	Toronto, Canada	John Komar, an elderly man, died from extensive untreated and badly infected burns of the arms and back. He was found unconscious in his room after the landlord became worried, not having seen him for several days. There was no sign of a fire in his room.[211]

APPENDIX B

A Partial List of *Fafrotskies*

"THING"	*PLACE*	*DATE*	*REFERENCES**

A. INORGANIC

(1) ARTIFICIAL (i.e., "manufactured")

"THING"	*PLACE*	*DATE*	*REFERENCES**
Bricks	Richland, S.C.	n.d.	*Am. J. Sci.* 2-34-298
	Padua, Italy	Aug. 1834	*Edin. New Phil. J.* 19-87
	London, England	5 July 1877	*Kilburn Times,* 7 July 1877
Coke, Coal,	Ornans, France	n.d.	*Eclectic Mag.* 89-71
Cinders, Slag,	Alais, France	15 March 1806	*Ibid.;* Greg, p. 63
etc.	Naples, Italy	14 March 1818	*Am. J. Sci.* 1-1-309
	Allport, England	Aug.? 1827	*Lit. & Phil. Soc. of Manchester Memoirs,* 2-9-146; Greg, p. 72

* Some of the references given are not as explicit as we should like, since magazines such as *Fate* and *Doubt* depend to a large extent on newspaper clippings, and these are often submitted by readers who fail to indicate the date or the source. This should not be taken to mean that the reference is any less reliable than those taken from scientific journals. Nor should an early date lead one to assume that the report was made by a "bunch of superstitious peasants": in fact, some of the early reports represent some of the most exhaustive and objective accounts in scientific literature.

Doubt is listed simply by the "whole number" of the issue, since its editors used an unusual style of dating—which they eventually abandoned since even they couldn't understand it. *FSR* is the standard abbreviation for *Flying Saucer Review.* "Greg" refers to that gentleman's "Catalog" discussed in Chapter 16. All other abbreviations should be readily understandable to librarians, should anyone wish to check these references.

There is, I believe, a small amount of "duplication" in this list, some of the falls having contained such a conglomeration of "stuff" that it was indexed several times. Too, some things landed as one kind of substance and then "metamorphosed" into something else.

Marion L. Fawcett

	Cape of Good Hope	13 Oct. 1838	*Scient. Amer.* 35-120
	Tennessee	1840	*Eclectic Mag.* 89-71
	Crieff, Scotland	18 Feb. 1841	*Am. J. Sci.* 2-28-275
	Darmstadt, Germany	7 June 1846	*Rept. Brit. Assoc.* 1867-416
	Ottawa, Illinois	17 Jan. 1857	*Am. J. Sci.* 2-24-449
	Hessle, Sweden	1 Jan. 1860	*Eclectic Mag.* 89-71
	Cranbourne, Australia	1861	*Eclectic Mag.* 89-71
	nr. Cape Cod	July 1861	*Edin. New Phil. J.* 26-86
	Montauban, France	14 May 1864	*Eclectic Mag.* 89-71
	Notting Hill, London	30 June 1866	*J. Roy. Met. Soc.* 14-207
	Goalpara, India	ca. 1867	*Eclectic Mag.* 89-71
	Deck of lightship [England?]	9 Jan. 1873	*Proc. Lond. Roy. Soc.* 19-122
	Victoria, Australia	14 April 1875	*Rept. Brit. Assoc.* 1875-242
	Chicago, Illinois	9 April 1879	*Am. J. Sci.* 3-18-78; *N.Y. Times*, 14 April 1879
	Argentina	30 June 1880	*Knowledge* 4-134; *Comptes Rendues* 96-1764
	Grazac, France	10 Aug. 1885	*Comptes Rendues* 104-1771
	Orne, France	24 April 1887	*Am. J. Sci.* 2-24-449
	Mortree, France	24 April 1887	*Trans. Roy. Soc. Edin.* 9-187
	Rajpunta, India	22 Jan. 1911	*Records Geol. Survey of India*, 44, pt. 1, p. 41
Foil & "Tinsel"	Sagetown, N.Y.	27 Aug. 1956 & 3 Oct. 1956	*Fate*, March 1957, p. 94-98
	Chosi City, Japan	7 Sept. 1956	*FSR*, Nov.-Dec. 1957, p. 3
	Little Falls, Minn.	1 Aug. 1957	*Fate*, Dec. 1957, p. 12
	Merion Township, Pa.	1957	Philadelphia *Inquirer*, 10 Sept. 1957
	Puerto Garibaldi, Argentina	c. 17 Jan. 1965	*La Gaceta*, 17 Jan. 1967; *FSR*, Nov.-Dec. 1965, p. 15
Stone axes, Wedges, etc.	Jamaica	periodic	*Jour. Inst. of Jamaica* 2-4; *Notes & Queries* 2-8-24
	Central Africa	periodic	Livingstone's *Last Journal*
	Prussia & Sweden	periodic	Blinkenberg, *Thunder Weapons*, pp. 71, 100
	Ghardia, Algeria	n.d.	*La Nature*, 1892-2-381
	India	n.d.	Dr. Bodding, see Fort, p. 121
	Japan and Java	n.d.	Dr. C. Leemans, *Archaeological J.* 11-118
	?Nachratschinsk, Tobolsk	16 July 1833	Greg, p. 74

278

Appendix B

	Kulsbjaergene, Sweden	n.d.	Blinkenberg, *op. cit.*, p. 71
Axes, bronze	Britain	n.d.	W. B. Tripp, F.R.M.S., see Fort, p. 116
Chemicals: Carbonate of Soda	Elizabeth, N.J. (in hail)	9 June 1874	*Scient. Amer.* 30-262
Nitric Acid	Nimes, France (in hail)	June 1842	*J. de Pharmacie* 1845-273
?	nr. Birmingham, England	24 May 1959	*Fate*, Sept. 1959, p. 8
Bullets, Buckshot, Metal pellets, generally	Walterboro, S.C.	1867	*Religio-philosophical J.*, 24 April 1880
	Lebanon, Ohio	1880	*Ibid.*
	Newton, N.J. (interior)	March 1929	San Francisco *Chronicle*, 3 March 1929
	Astoria, Oregon	17 April 1954	*Doubt* #45
	Woodside, Calif.	27 Aug. 1954	San Jose *Mercury-News* and Pasadena *Independent*, 29 August 1954
Nails	Algona, Calif.	n.d.	*Fate*, Nov. 1957, p. 124
	Brownsville, Texas	12 Oct. 1888	St. Louis *Globe-Democrat*, 16 Oct. 1888
	Raritan, N.J.	July 1955	Sacramento *Union*, 29 July 1955
Metal items, miscellaneous: Steel wire	off Java	n.d.	Zurcher, *Meteors*, p. 239
5-lb. Steel ball	Tacoma, Wash.	Aug. 1951	San Francisco *Chronicle*, 17 Aug. 1951
Solid cylinder	Bunkers Hill, Baxley, England	May 1954	*Star*, 24 May 1954; *Doubt* #46
Brasslike metal, pieces	England (Rye Lane, Peckham's Shopping Centre)	Dec. 1955	*Evening Standard*, 15 Dec. 1955
Hot aluminium	Little Oakley, Essex, England	Dec. 1956	*Daily Telegraph*, 14 Dec. 1956
Red-hot ¾-inch cube	Whitstone, nr. Oamaru, New Zealand	May 1961	New Zealand *Herald*, 9 May 1961; *FSR*, July-Aug. 1961, p. 31
Ball(?) larger than a football	Reading, England	Sept. 1961	Reading *Mercury*, Sept., 1961; *FSR*, Jan.-Feb., 1962, p. 27

Charred 12-lb. sphere	180 miles north of Broken Hill, New South Wales, Australia	April 1963	New Zealand *Herald*, 10 April 1963; *FSR*, July-Aug. 1963, p. 23
Oval object	Eagansville, Ontario, Canada	n.d.	Montreal *Star* (1964-5); *FSR*, March-April, 1965, p. 27
Iron chain 13 links, red-hot	Agram, Croatia St. Louis, Missouri	26 May 1751 14 May 1959	Greg, p. 58 *Fate*, Sept., 1959, p. 8; Sioux City [Iowa] *Journal*, 15 May 1959
Red-hot pieces of cast iron	Woodside, Calif.	Summer, 1954	*Fate*, April, 1955, p. 13
Nuts and bolts	Columbus, Ohio	23 Sept. 1936	Philadelphia *Evening Bulletin*, 23 Sept. 1963 (AP report)
Artillery shell, dated 1942, with cross and eagle design	Naples, Italy	7 Feb. 1958	Unident. newspaper clippings; and *Fate*, Aug., 1958, p. 10
"Machinery": "Strange and complicated piece of machinery"	Tabuleiro do Norte, Brazil	6 Feb. 1965	*O Jornal* (Rio de Janeiro), 7 Feb. 1965; *FSR*, May-June, 1965, p. 29
Small top-shaped object, hieroglyphics on outside; book of 17 thin copper sheets with 2000 "words" engraved on them	nr. Scarborough, Yorks.,	21 Nov. 1957	*FSR*, March-April & July-August 1958
Small flaming object with tiny lenses	Alexandria, Egypt	Nov. 1957	Chicago *American*, 6 Nov. 1957
Blue & white thread	Titchfield, Hampshire, Eng.	12 or 13 Mar. 1959	*Evening Standard; Evening News*, 13 March 1959

Money	Trafalgar Sq., London	n.d.	London papers, 1920's (see Fort)
British pennies	Ramsgate, England	Feb. 1969	Toronto *Star*, 17 Feb. 1969
"Mysterious object, size of baseball, with 4 points on it"	nr. Duncannon, Ireland	9 Sept. 1962	*Le Matin, Antwerp*, 9 Sept. 1962
Beads	Bijori, India	n.d.	*Fate, Jan.*, 1955, p. 9
Sheets of filmy, transparent plastic	Wilton, California	for two weeks, July-Aug., 1955	Sacramento *Union*, 29 July & 4 Aug. 1955
Little colored balls	England and France	Spring & Fall, 1966	*FSR*, Nov.-Dec., 1966

(2) NATURAL (i.e., nonmanufactured)

Ice	Tunis	n.d.	*Bull. Soc. Astro. de France* 20-245
	Hungary	8 May 1802	Flammarion, *The Atmosphere*, p. 34
	Derbyshire, England	12 May 1811	*Annual Register* 1811-54
	Birmingham, England	June, 1811	Thomson, *Introduction to Meteorology*, p. 179
	Candeish, India	1828	*Rept. Brit. Assoc.* 1851-32
	Cazorta, Spain	15 June 1829	Flammarion, *op. cit.*, p. 34
	Brussels, Belgium	18 June 1839	*Ibid.*
	Derby, England	30 June 1841	*Athenaeum* 1841-542
	Cette, France	Oct. 1844	Flammarion, *op. cit.*, p. 34
	Ord, Scotland	August 1849	*Edin. New Phil. Mag.* 47-371
	Balvullich, Ross-shire, Scotland	13 Aug. 1849	London *Times*, 14 Aug. 1849
	Bungalore, India	22 May 1851	*Rept. Brit. Assoc.* 1855-35
	New Hampshire	13 Aug. 1851	Lummis, *Meteorology*, p. 129
	Rouen, France	5 July 1853	*Cosmos* 3-116
	Poorhundur, India	11 Dec. 1854	*Rept. Brit. Assoc.* 1855-37
	Cricklewood, England	4 Aug. 1857	London *Times*, 4 Aug. 1857
	ship in South Atlantic	14 Jan. 1860	London *Roy. Soc. Proc.* 10-468

Upper Wasdale, England	16 March 1860	London *Times,* 7 Apr. 1860
Pontiac, Canada	11 July 1874	*Canadian Naturalist,* 2-1-308
Texas	3 May 1877	*Monthly Weather Rev.,* May, 1877
Colorado	24 May 1877	*Ibid.,* June, 1877
Richmond, England	2 Aug. 1879	*Symons' Met. Mag.* 14-100
Iowa	June 1881	*Monthly Weather Rev.,* June, 1881
Dubuque, Iowa	16 June 1882	*Monthly Weather Rev.,* June 1882
Salina, Kansas	Aug. 1882	*Scient. Amer.* 47-119
Davenport, Iowa	30 Aug. 1882	*Monthly Weather Rev.,* Aug. 1882
Chicago, Illinois	12 July 1883	*Ibid.,* July 1883
India	May 1888	*Nature* 37-42
Aitkin, Minn.	2 Apr. 1889	*Science,* 19 Apr. 1889
Texas	6 Dec. 1893	*Scient. Amer.* 68-58
Portland, Oregon	3 June 1894	*Monthly Weather Rev.,* July, 1894
Manassas, Virgina	10 Aug. 1897	*Symons' Met. Mag.* 32-172
Victoria, Australia	14 Nov. 1901	*Meteorology of Australia,* p. 34
Braemar, Scotland	2 July 1908	*Symons' Met. Mag.* 43-154
Oakland, California	8 Dec.1949	Oakland *Tribune,* 8 Dec. 1949
Braughing, Herts., England *(floated down)*	n.d. (1950?)	*Doubt #32*
Hampstead, Norris, Berks., England	Nov. 1950	*Doubt #32*
North Devon, England	8-10 Nov. 1950	*Doubt #32*
Wandsworth, London	24 Nov. 1950 & 3 Dec. 1950	Manchester *Guardian,* 24 Nov. 1950; *News Chronicle,* 27 Nov. 1950; *Doubt #32*
London	7 Dec. 1950	*Doubt #32;* Chicago *Tribune*
Helensburgh, Scotland	26 Dec. 1950	*Doubt #32; Evening Citizen*
Tooting, England	28 Dec. 1950	*Doubt #32*
Seattle, Washington	28 Dec. 1950	*Ibid.*
Pinner, England	24 March 1951	*Doubt #41; Sunday Express,* 25 March 1951

Brentford, Middlesex England	28 March 1951	*Doubt* #36
Putney, England	15 Apr. 1951	*Sunday Express,* 15 Apr. 1951
Slough, Bucks., England	1953	*Doubt* #41
Whittier, Calif.	15 Jan. 1953	*Ibid.*
Freeport, L.I., N.Y.	18 Feb. 1953	*Ibid.*
Ightham, Kent, England	15 May 1953	*Ibid.*
Long Beach, Calif.	4 June 1953	*Ibid.;* Long Beach *Tribune,* 17 June 1953
Heath Walk, Downend, England	8 June 1954	*Doubt* #46
Bristol, England	8 June 1954	*Doubt* # 47
Los Angeles, Calif.	Jan. 1955	*Fate,* June, 1955, p. 10
Kansas City, Missouri	Feb. 1955	Boston *Daily Record,* 22 Feb. 1955
Loughton, England	May-June 1955	*Evening Standard,* 1 June 1955
Seattle, Wash.	1-2 Dec. 1955	*Daily Times,* 2 Dec. 1955
Large, Pa.	Jan. 1956	*Fate,* June, 1956, p. 14
Jefferson, Pa. (honeycombed ice)	Jan. 1956	Pittsburgh *Sun* and *Post-Gazette,* 4 Jan. 1956
Los Angeles, Calif.	12 March 1956	*Doubt* # 53
Brampton, Ontario	6 July 1956	Hamilton *Spectator,* 6 July 1956
North Fresno, Calif.	6-7 Aug. 1956	Santa Monica *Evening Outlook,* 7 Aug. 1956
Bessinby Park, Ruislip, London	2 Oct. 1956	*Doubt* #53
Ojo de Agua, Nuevo Leon, Mexico	18 Oct. 1956	*Ibid.*
Valley Stream, L.I., N.Y. (couldn't be chipped)	2-3 March 1957	*Doubt* #57; *Fate,* July 1957, p. 14
Reading, Pa.	30 July 1957	Philadelphia *Inquirer,* 31 July 1957; *Fate,* Jan. 1958; p. 6
Philadelphia, Pa. area: Chester, Yeadon, Gowen City	30 July, 14 & 27 Aug., 8, 10, 12 & 25, Sept. 1957	Philadelphia *Evening Bulletin,* 25 Sept. 1957; *Fate,* Feb. 1958, p. 15; all Philadelphia papers, 9 Sept. 1957

	Shamokin, Pa.	13 Aug. 1957	*Doubt #55*
	San Rafael, Calif.	25 Jan. 1958	*Fate,* July 1958, p. 23
	Napa, Calif.	April 1958	*Fate,* August 1958, p. 8
	Barnes, England	21 Apr. 1958	*Evening Standard,* 21 Apr. 1958
	Richmond, Surrey, England	24 June 1958	*Daily Telegraph,* 24 June 1958
	Brownsville, Pa.	11 July 1958	*Doubt #59*
	Madison Township, N.J.	3 Sept. 1958	*Ibid.*
	Glendora, California	1959?	*Fate,* Aug., 1959, p. 7
	Atherton, Calif.	1959?	*Ibid.,* p. 8
	Arizona	March 1959	Arizona *Republic,* 29 Mar. 1959
	Los Angeles, Calif.	22 Apr. 1959	*Fate,* Aug. 1959, p. 8
	Amherst, N.Y.	11 Sept. 1959	*Fate,* Jan. 1960, p.24
	Acaia, Italy	25 Oct. 1959	*Fate,* Feb. 1960, p. 28
	Taccoa, Ga.	26 Oct. 1959	*Fate,* Apr. 1960, p. 21
	Cleveland, Ohio (three separate falls)	30 Oct. 1959	*Fate,* Feb. 1960, p. 28
	Toms River, N.J.	Dec. 1959	*Fate,* May, 1960, p. 14
	London, England	24 Dec. 1959	*Ibid.*
	Windsor, England	10 Apr. 1961	London *Daily Mail,* 10 April 1961; *FSR,* July-Aug., 1961, p. 27
	East Sheen, England	22 Jan. 1962	London *Times,* 22 Jan. 1962
	Hornsey, England	17 Sept. 1962	London *Daily Telegraph,* 17 Sept. 1962
	nr. Moscow	1964	*FSR,* July-Aug. 1964, p. 23; *Scottish Sunday Post*
Ashes	Ireland	1755	*Scient. Amer.* 5-168
	Fort Klamath, Oregon	8 Jan. 1867	*Smithsonian Misc. Coll.* 37, appen., p. 71
	Azores	ca. 1875	*Ann. Record Sci.* 1875, p. 241
	Western Australia	25 Aug. 1883	*Nature* 29-388
	Queenstown, S. Africa ("*pulpy* at first")	Nov. 1883	*Nature,* 10 Jan. 1884
	Summerville, S. C.	Oct. & Nov. 1886	*News and Courier,* 20 Nov. 1886
	Avellino, Italy	12 March 1901	*Bull. Soc. Astro. de France,* April 1901
	Northern Australia	12-13 Nov. 1902	*Sydney Daily Telegraph,* 18 Nov. 1902
	Annoy, France	27 March 1908	*Bull. Soc. Astro. de France,* 22-245
"Earthy matter"	Reading, England	3 July 1883	*J. Roy. Met. Soc.* 14-207

Mud (in enormous quantities)	Roseau, Dominica, B.W.I.	4 Jan. 1880	*Dominican & The People*, 4 Jan. 1880
	Jessore District, Bengal	29 June 1897	*Madras Mail*, 8 July 1897
	Thurgrain, Midapur, India	27 June 1897	*The Englishman* (Calcutta), 3 July 1897
	Pennsylvania, New Jersey, New York, Connecticut	12 April 1902	*Science*, n.s. 15-872; *Monthly Weather Rev.*, May 1902
	Tasmania; and Australia (red mud)	14 Nov. 1902	*Monthly Weather Rev.* 32-365;
	Lemburg and Cernowitz, Ukraine	27 Apr. 1928	N.Y. Sun, 27 Apr. 1928
	Danville, Va.	March 1929	*Doubt* #29
	Dijon, France	7 Nov. 1951	*Doubt* #37
	Beaver Valley, Pa.	n.d.	*Doubt* #41
	Long Island, N.Y.	25 Apr. 1953	*Doubt* #41
Salt Crystals	Switzerland	20 Aug. 1870	*Ann. Record Sci.*, 1872; *Amer. J. Sci.* 3-3-239
Sulphur	Pultusk, Poland	30 Jan. 1868	*Rept. Brit. Assoc.* 1874-272
	Allport, England	1827	*Lit. & Phil. Soc. of Manchester Memoirs* 2-9-146
Hot Water	Iverness, Scotland	30 June 1817	*Rept. Brit. Assoc.* 1954-112
Warm Water	Geneva, Switzerland	9 Aug. 1837	*Year Book of Facts* 1839-262
		31 May 1838	*Comptes Rendues* 5-549
		11 May 1842	*Comptes Rendues* 15-290
Stones (not meteoric) (innumerable reports; selected refs. only) Two dissimilar stones cemented together	Cumberland Falls, Ky.	9 Apr. 1919	*Nature* 105-759
Alabaster	Vicksburg, Mass.	11 May 1894	*Monthly Weather Rev.*, May 1894
Black pebbles	Birmingham, England	29 May, 12 June, 31 July, 1868	Birmingham *Daily Post*,

			14 June 1868; *Rept. Brit. Assoc.* 1864-37;*English Mechanic*, 31 July 1868, etc.
Black pebbles	Wolverhampton, England	19 June 1860 & 25 May 1869	*La Science pour Tous*, 19 June 1860; Wolverhampton *Advertiser*, ca. 25 May 1869
Brown stone	Mhow, India	27 Feb. 1828	*Arcana of Science* 1829-196
Limestone	Middleburg, Fla.	n.d.	*Science* 11-118
Quartz	Canada	n.d.	*Proc. Canadian Inst.* 3-7-8
	Schroon Lake, N.Y.	Fall 1880	*Scient. Amer.* 43-272
	Essex, England	23 Apr. 1884	*Knowledge* 5-336
	Vincennes, Indiana	May 1899	*Monthly Weather Rev.*, Apr. 1889
Sandstone	Sussex, England	n.d. (1885?)	*Knowledge*, 9 Oct. 1885
	Little Lever, England	n.d. (1887?)	*Science Gossip*, 1887, p. 70
"according to Arago, a common stone or fallen pillar"	Constantinople	416?	Greg, p. 50
"Friable sandstone . . . cold & moist"	Raphoe, Ireland	9 June 1860	Greg, p. 107
"Stone-fall; no meteor; . . . musical sounds in the air"	Killeter, Co. Tyrone, Ireland	29 Apr. 1844	Greg, p. 82
"Stone-fall . . . one . . . so intensely *cold* as to benumb the fingers and hands"	Northeast of Lahore, India	July 1860	Greg, p. 96
"Meteorite" landed 14 feet from witnesses; *cold*	Hoekmark, Sweden	24? Aug. 1954	London *Times*, 25 Aug. 1954
Boulder, 30x30"	Dundalk, Maryland	27 Jan. 1956	Baltimore *Sun*, same date

Pebbles and rocks	Pumphrey, West Australia	March 1957 (several days)	Dunedin [N.Z.] *Evening Star*, 19 March 1957; *Daily Express*, 22 March 1957
	West Australia, 150 mi. from Pumphrey	March 1957	Paris ed., *Herald Tribune*, 23 March 1957
Straw-caked mud, with tire tracks in it, came through roof	Topeka, Kansas	Dec.? 1959	Fate, Apr. 1960, pp. 21-22
Sand, usually mixed with organic and unidentified materials, and of various colours—a few examples only	Europe generally	repeated	e.g. *Nature* 68-54, 68-65, etc.; *Intellectual Observer* 3-468;
	Trier, Germany	7 Nov. 1951	*Doubt* #37
	Times Square, N.Y.C.	2 May 1953	N.Y. *Times*, 2 May 1953; *Doubt* #41
	Switzerland	1962 & 1968	*National Observer*, 13 May 1968
	London	1 July 1968	N. Y. *Daily News*, 1 July 1968

(3) AMBIGUOUS

"Angel Hair": Vapourizing type	Marysville, Ohio	1 Oct. 1954	*Fate*, April 1955, p. 12
	St. Louis, Missouri (Foamy "lumps")	20 Aug. 1956	*Fate*, Dec. 1956, pp. 20-21
	Washington, Sharon, and Crawfordsville, Ga.	Oct. 1959	*Fate*, April 1960, p. 22
	480 mi. NE of Perth, Australia	Aug. 1961	Melbourne *Sun*, 15 Aug. 1961; FSR, Nov.-Dec. 1961
	Montreal, Canada	10 Oct. 1962	FSR, May-June, 1964, p. 15
	Gadsby, Utah	18? Oct. 1962	Utah *Desert News and Telegram*, 19 Oct. 1962; FSR, Jan.-Feb. 1963, p. 24

Nonvapourizing type	Bradly, Selborne, & Alresford, England (in large "flakes")	21 Sept. 1741	*All the Year Round* 8-254
	Carlisle, Kendal, & Tiverton, England	12 & 15 Oct. 1869	Carlisle *Journal*, 5 Oct. 1869; *English Mechanic*, 19 Nov. 1869; Tiverton *Times*, 12 Oct. 1869
	Milwaukee, Wis.	Oct. 1881	*Scient. Amer.* 45-337
	Redpa, Tasmania	Oct. 1950	*Australian Post*, 5 Oct. 1950
	Horseheads, N.Y. (radioactive)	20 Feb. 1955	*Fate*, Aug. 1955, p. 10; and Sept. 1955, pp. 62-65
	Melbourne, Australia	June 1956	Bournemouth *Echo*, June 1956
	St. Louis, Missouri (fiberlike material containing no protein; "may not have been of biological origin . . .")	Oct. 1969	Personal communication, Terry W. Colvin, 1 July 1970 with letter from St. Louis County Health Department, 29 June 1970
Olive-gray power, identified as "alkali" & "hairs"	Shanghai	16 Mar. 1846	*J. Asiatic Soc. Bengal*, 1847, pt. 1, p. 193
Two objects about the size of soccer balls; ¼"-thick "skin"; holes in them; brown; soft, not rubber, leather or plastic; shrank and turned white	nr. Kimberly, S. Africa	15 June 1962	*Diamond Fields Advertiser*, 19 June 1962; *FSR*, Jan.-Feb. 1963, p. 5
Icelike substance; not ice, glass or plastic	Stebbing, Essex, England	26 Nov. 1950	*Doubt* #32

288

Bluish-green, phosphorescent snow, "nettled" the skin	Dana, Calif.	8 Apr. 1953	*Doubt* #41
Salty white "goo"	Salt Lake City, Utah	25 March 1955	AP report, same date
"Frozen bubbles," ⅛-¼" diam.	Rutherford, N.C.	n.d.	*Doubt* #53
"Hail," containing:			
Iron pyrites	Sterlitamak, Russia	20 Oct. 1824	Greg, p. 70
Metallic interior	Mayo, Ireland	21 June 1821	Greg, p. 68
White flint gravel & sand	Fayette Co., West Virginia	1892	*Fate*, Aug. 1958, p. 118
Frogs: see below Sticky dust, caused burns & ulcers	Lachaud, France	14? Oct. 1966	*Nice-Matin*, 15 Oct. 1966; *FSR* Mar.-Apr. 1967, p. 31
Asbestoslike, phosphorescent substance	Montgomery, Alabama	21 Nov. 1898	*Monthly Weather Rev.* 26-566
"Bits of polished china"	Portland, Oregon	21 July 1920	Los Angeles *Times*, ca. same date

B. ORGANIC

(I) WHOLE ANIMALS

(a) Terrestrial

(i) *VERTEBRATES*

(1) MAMMALS

Rats	(general reference)		*American Weekly*, 13 May 1951
	Lombok Island	1969	AP report, 18 Dec. 1969

(2) BIRDS

Puffin with fractured head	not stated	n.d.	*Zoologist*, 18 March 1821
Various, with fall of blood	Lyons & Grenoble, France	Summer 1896	*Comptes Rendues* 24-625, 812

Various (thousands) Baby chicks	La Grande, Oregon	3 May 1954	*Doubt* #45
(dead)	Venice, Calif.	ca. 1 May 1956	Santa Monica *Outlook*, 1 May 1956

(3) REPTILES

Snakes	South Granville, N.Y.	3 July 1860	*Scient. Amer.* 3-112
	Memphis, Tenn.	15 Jan. 1877	*Monthly Weather Rev.* 15 Jan. 1877; N.Y. *Times,* ca. 15 Jan. 1877; *Scient. Amer.* 36-86
Lizards	Montreal, Canada	28 Dec. 1857	*Notes and Queries* 8-6-104
Tortoises	nr. Vicksburg, Miss.	11 May 1894	*Monthly Weather Rev.,* May 1894
	(?)Decatur, Indiana	25 Sept. 1937	Indianapolis *Star,* same date

(4) AMPHIBIANS

Salamanders	Portal, N. Dakota	n.d.	*Outdoor Life,* Oct. 1949
Frogs & Toads	Toulouse, France	Aug. 1804	*Comptes Rendues* 3-54
	London, England	30 July 1838	*Notes and Queries* 8-7-437
	Kansas City, Mo.	1873?	*Scient. Amer.* 12 July 1873
	Pontiac, Canada (in hail stones)	11 July 1874	*Canadian Naturalist* 2-1-308
	Dubuque, Iowa (in hail stones)	16 June 1882	*Monthly Weather Rev.* June, 1882
	Kanawha Co., West Va.	ca. 1887	*Fate,* Aug. 1958, p. 116, 118
	Wilsonville, Ala.	ca. 1888	*Fate,* July 1958, p. 126
	Savoy, France	2 Aug. 1889	*L'Astronomie,* 1889-353
	Birmingham, England (white frogs)	30 June 1892	*Symons' Met. Mag.* 32-106
	Wigan, England	1894 *et seq.*	*Notes and Queries* 8-6-190
	(?)Somerville, N.J.	July, 1903	*Fate,* Nov., 1958, p. 118
	Lovelock, Nevada	n.d.	Pers. comm. to Fort
	Stirling, Conn.	31 July 1921	N.Y. *Evening World,* 1 Aug. 1921
	London, England	17 Aug. 1921	London newspapers 18-19 Aug. 1921
	Chalon-sur-Saone, France	3-4 Sept. 1922	London *Daily News,* 5 Sept. 1922
	Vryburg, Transvaal	n.d. (1925?)	*Northern News,* 21 March 1925
	Horsham, Victoria, Australia	19 Nov. 1925	*John O' London,* n.d.; *Doubt* #20

Providence, R. I.	pre-1930	*Fate*, Aug., 1955, p. 120
Groton, Conn.	ca. 1930	*Ibid.*
Canova, S. Dakota	Summer 1930	*Fate*, Nov., 1958, p. 118-119
Tarpa, Hungary	29 Aug. 1937	*Doubt #3* (Jan. 1940)
Decatur, Indiana	25 Sept. 1937	Indianapolis *Star*, 25 Sept. 1937
Trowbridge, England	1939?	*American Weekly*, 24 Sept. 1939
De Witt, Ark.	18 Oct. 1942	Buffalo *Evening News* 31 Oct. 1942
Towyn, Merionethshire, Wales	14 Aug. 1948	*Doubt #20*
Memphis, Tenn.	n.d. 1949?	*Doubt #27*
Kasalinsk, Kazakhstan	21 Sept. 1949	*Doubt #27*
West Memphis, Ark.	23 Sept. 1949	*Doubt #29*
Torrisholme, nr. Morecambe, England	18 June 1950	*Empire News*, same date
Buenos Aires, Argentina	19 July 1951	*Seattle Times*, same date
Leicester, Mass.	2 Sept. 1953?	*Doubt #43*
do.	7 Sept. 1953	*Fate*, Jan., 1954, p. 5
Verona, Italy	ca. 18 June 1956	*Daily Telegraph*, 18 June 1956
St. Julian-sur-Suran, (French-Swiss border), with hail)	8 Aug. 1958	*Doubt #59*

(5) FISH

Eels

Coalburg, Alabama	29 May 1892	N.Y. *Sun*, 29 May 1892
Piacenza, Italy	9 June 1957	*Doubt #55*

Fish, other

Paris	n.d.	*Living Age* 52-186
Cambridge, Md.	n.d.	*Am. J. Sci.* 16-41
Meerut, India	July, 1824	*Living Age* 52-186
Fifeshire, Scotland	Summer 1824	*Wernerian Nat. Hist. Soc. Trans.* 5-575
Moradabad, India	July, 1826	*Living Age* 52-186
Ross-shire, Scotland	1828	*Ibid.*
Perthshire, Scotland	n.d.	*Ibid.*
Feridpoor, India	19 Feb. 1930	*J. Asiatic Soc. Bengal* 2-650; *Am. J. Sci.* 1-32-199
Argyleshire, Scotland	9 March 1830	*Recreative Science* 3-339
Futtepoor, India	16 May 1833	*Living Age* 52-186
Calcutta, India	20 Sept. 1839	Ferrel, *A Popular Treatise*, p. 414

Boston, England	30 June 1841	*Living Age* 52-186
Derby, England	8 July 1841	*Ibid.; Timb's Year Book* 1842-275; *Athenaeum* 1841-542
Dunfermline, Scotland	7 Oct. 1841	London *Times*, 12 Oct. 1841
Rajkote, India	25 July 1850	*All the Year Round* 8-255
Norfolk, Va.	1853	*Cosmos* 13-120
Valley of Aberdare, Glamorganshire, Wales	11 Feb. 1859	*Zoologist* 2-677 & 1859-6493;*Ann. Register* 1859-14; London *Times*, 2 & 10 March 1859; *Rept. Brit. Assoc.* 1859-158
Benares, India	Summer 1860	*Canadian Inst. Proc.* 2-7-198
Singapore	16 Feb. 1861	*La Science pour Tous* 6-191
Chico, Calif.	20 Aug. 1878	N.Y. *Times*, 2 Sept. 1878
Holland	13 June 1889	*L'Astronomie* 1889-353
Montgomery Co., Calif.	6 Feb. 1890	*Public Ledger*, same date
Seymour, Indiana	8 Aug. 1891	Philadelphia *Public Ledger*, same date
Meerut, India	1896	*John O'London*, n.d.; *Doubt* #20
Tillers Ferry, S. C.	1901?	*Monthly Weather Rev.*, June 1901, p. 263
Sunderland, England	24 Aug. 1918	*Nature*, 19 Sept. 1918, p. 46
Wyndham, West Australia	12 May 1921	*John O'London*, n.d.; *Doubt* #20
Vryburg, Transvaal	n.d. (1925?)	*Northern News*, 21 March 1925
Tuscon, Arizona	21 Aug. 1933	*Doubt* #51
South Bend, Indiana	16 July 1937	Los Angeles *Times*, same date
Ontario, Canada	21 March 1939	Los Angeles *Herald-Express*, same date
Hillsdale, Michigan	24 June 1944	*Doubt* #12
Marksville, La.	25 Oct. 1947	*Sci. News Letter*, 14 May 1949; *Doubt* #20, etc.
Ballysaggart, Donegal, Ireland	15 Feb. 1949	London *Daily Express*, same date
Hawkes Bay, New Zealand	13 July 1949	*Doubt* #27

	Garrigcastle, Ireland	4 Dec. 1950	*Doubt* #32
	Wrangell Narrows, Alaska	13 Dec. 1950	*Ibid.*
	Long Beach, Calif.	2 Jan. 1951	*Ibid.*
	Washington, D. C.	27 Nov. 1951	Buffalo *Evening News,* same date
	Washington, D. C.	3 May 1952	N. Y. *Times,* same date
	nr. Bingham, New Mexico	3 May 1952	*Fate,* Aug. 1966, p. 62
	Oklahoma City, Okla.	5 Oct. 1953	*Doubt* #44
	Toronto, Canada	3 Apr. 1954	San Francisco *Chronicle,* same date
	Toronto, Canada	March 1954	*Fate,* March 1955, p. 56
	Washington, D. C.	16 June 1954	Washington D. C. *News,* same date
	Alexandria, Va. (frozen solid)	23 Dec. 1955	Pittsburgh *Press,* same date; *Fate,* May 1956, p. 8, etc.
	Port Elizabeth, South Africa	13 Jan. 1956	*Reveille,* same date
	Chula Vista, Calif.	14 Apr. 1956	*Doubt* #53
	Tortosa, Spain	7 Aug. 1956	*Ibid.*
	Dallas, Texas	18 June 1958	Dallas *News,* same date; *Fate,* Oct., 1958, p. 17
	Edmonton, Alberta	Dec., 1959	*Fate,* June, 1960, p. 20
Fish scales	Louisiana	1873	*Ann. Rec. of Sci.* 1873-350

(ii) *INVERTEBRATES*

Organisms, small	Peckloh, Germany	27 Feb. 1877	*Monthly Weather Rev.,* May 1877
Ants	Cambridge, England	Summer 1874	*Scient. Amer.* 30-193
	Nancy, France	21 July 1887	*Nature* 36-349
	Strasbourg, Germany	1 Aug. 1889	*L'Astronomie* 1889, p. 353
	Manitoba, Canada	June 1895	*Scient. Amer.* 72-385
Worms: Black	Bramford Speke, Devonshire, England	14 Apr. 1837	London *Times,* same date
Brown	Clifton, Indiana	Feb. 1892	New Orleans *Daily Picayune,* 4 Feb. 1892
Red	Halmstead, Sweden	Jan. 1924	London *Evening Standard,* 3 Jan. 1924
Scarlet	(?) Massachusetts	ca. 14 Feb. 1892	San Francisco *Chronicle,* 14 Feb. 1892
Unspecified	Bath, England	22 Apr. 1871	*Zoologist* 2-6-2686; *Trans. Entomol, Soc. London* 1871, proc. xxii

	Christiania, Norway	Winter 1876	*Timb's Year Book* 1877-26
	Randolph Co., Va.	Winter 1890	*Scient. Amer.* 21 Feb. 1891
	Utica, N. Y.	Winter 1890	*Scient. Amer.* 7 March 1891
	Lancaster, Pa.	Early 1892	*Insect Life* 1892, p. 335
	Kinomaeki, Finland	May 1955	Reuters Report 15 May 1955
Insects	Lithuania	24 Jan. 1849	*Trans. Entomol. Soc. London*, 1871-183
"Exotic"	Swiss Alps	March 1922	Boston *Transcript* 21 Mar. 1922
Chironomids (midges) encased in ice	Banff National Park	16 Feb. 1952	Pers. comm., Dr. W. R. Henson, Forest Insect Lab., Sault Ste Marie, Ontario, Canada
Larvae (insect)	Silesia, Germany	1806	*Trans. Entomol. Soc. London* 1871-183
	Eifel, Germany	30 Jan. 1847	*Ibid.*
	Lithuania	24 Jan. 1849	*Revue et Magasin de Zoologie* 1849-72
	Upper Savoy, France	30 Jan. 1869	Flammarion, *The Atmosphere*, p. 414
	Switzerland	Jan. 1890	*L'Astronomie*, 1890-313
Waterbugs	Moultrie, Ga.	20 Sept. 1952	*Doubt* #41
Snails	Redruth, Cornwall, England	13 Aug. 1886	*Science Gossip* 1886-238; *Redruth Independent*, same date
	Bristol, England	n.d.	*Philosophical Mag.* 58-310
	Algiers	19 May 1952	Reuters report, same date

Invertebrates, Marine

Jellyfish	Bath, England	Aug. 1894	*Notes and Queries* 8-6-190
Mussels	Paderborn, Germany	9 Aug. 1892	*Das Wetter*, Dec. 1892
Periwinkles	Worcester, England	28 May 1881	*Land and Water*, 4 June 1881; Worcester *Daily Times*, 30 May 1881
Prawns	India	Aug. 1949	*Current Science* [India], Aug. 1949
Clam (one only)	Yuma, Arizona	20 Aug. 1941	N. Y. *Post*, same date
Crabs	Oxford, England	n.d.	*Doubt* #27

(2) ANIMAL PARTS

"Animal matter," unspecified	France, Spain; Genoa, Italy	30 Apr. & 1-2 May 1870	*J. Franklin Inst.* 90-11; *Comptes Rendues* 56-972

Flakes of flesh ("lung tissue")	Olympian Spring, Ky.	3 March 1876	*Scient. Amer.* 34-197
Flesh and blood	Chatillon-sur-Seine, France	17 March 1669	Records of French Academy
	Wilson County, Tenn.	n.d.	*Am. J. Sci.* 1-41-404
	Santa Clara Co., Calif.	ca. June 1869	San Francisco *Evening Bulletin,* 9 Aug. 1869
	Los Nietos Twnship., Calif.	1 Aug. 1869	*Ibid.*
	nr. Sao Jose dos Campos, Brazil	27 Aug. 1968	Sao Paulo papers, 30 Aug. 1968; *FSR,* Nov.-Dec. 1968, p. iv.
Blood	Mansfeld, Thuringia, Germany (from a "meteor")	6 Nov. 1548	Greg, p. 52
	Ulm, Germany	1812	*Annales de chimie* 85-266
	Djebel-Sekra, Morocco	n.d. (ca. 1880)	*La Nature,* 25 Sept. 1880
	Cochin China	13 Dec. 1887	*L'Annee scient.* 1888-75
	Mediterranean region	6 March 1888	*L'Astronomie* 1888-205
	Messignadi, Calabria, Italy	15 May 1890	*Pop. Science News* 35-104
	Southwest China	17 Nov. 1920?	*Literary Digest,* 2 Sept. 1921
	Tolu Viejo, Colombia & Campinas, Sao Paulo, Brazil	Oct. 1952	*A Epoca,* 2 Oct. 1952
Hair	Charleston, S. C.	16 Nov. 1857	*Am. J. Sci.* 2-28-270
	Shanghai	16 March 1846	*J. Asiatic Soc. Bengal* 1847, pt. 1, p. 193
Skinlike substance	Kelso, Washington	n.d.	*Current Topics,* Amesbury, Mass., n.d.; *Doubt* #43
Eggs (hard-shelled)	nr. Cape Town, S. Africa	1954?	*Fate,* Oct. 1954, p. 14
	Orlando, Fla. (one, ice-cold)	19 May 1959	*Fate,* Sept. 1959, p. 8
"Butter"	Limerick and Tipperary	Nov. 1695	*Philosoph. Trans.* 19-224
	Munster and Leinster	Spring 1695	*Ibid.*
	Corsano, Italy (yellow fatty substance in rain)	11 March 1955	*Kolner Stadt Anzeiger,* same date

(3) PLANT PRODUCTS

"Marsh Paper" (coal-black leafy substance)	Memel, Germany	1686	*Proc. Roy. Irish Acad.* 1-379
	Carolath, Silesia	1839	*Edin. Rev.* 87-194
Cereals: Red meal	Along Mediterranean, esp. Perpignan, France	May 1863	*Intellectual Observer* 3-468
Wheat (in hail)	Wiltshire, England	1686	*Philos. Trans.* 16-281
Decomposed remains of cereals, est. *500 tons*	London, Ontario (area 50 x 10 miles)	24 Feb. 1868	*Chemical News* 35-183
Unknown to natives	Rajkit, India	24 March 1840	*Am. J. Sci.* 1841-40
Barley & corn	New York City	1951	*American Weekly,* 13 May 1951
Seeds, unspecified	Marienwerder, Germany	15 July 1822	*Bull. des sciences* 1-1-298
	Heinsberg, Erklenz & Juliers, Prussia	24-25 Mar. 1852	*La Belgique horticole* 2-319
	Macerata, Italy	Summer, 1897	*Notes and Queries* 8-12-228
Rice	Parts of Mandalay	Jan. 1952	*Daily Telegraph* 10 Jan. 1952
Navy beans	Van Nuys, Calif. (in hail)	6 Mar. 1958	Detroit *Free Press,* 11 March 1958
Beans	St. Louis, Mo.	22 Sept. 1945	*Doubt #14*
White beans (allegedly "magnetized")?	nr. Long Beach, Calif.	17 Apr. 1954	*Fate,* Nov., 1954, p. 116
Hay	Wrexham, England	25 July 1875	*Scient. Amer.* 33-197
	Monkstown, Ireland	27 July 1875	Dublin *Daily Express,* same date
Oak leaves	Autriche, France	10 Apr. 1869	*Cosmos* 3-4-574
	Clairvaux & Outre-Aube, France	7 Apr. 1894	*L'Astronomie* 1894-194
Perfumed matter— sandalwood	Khurdah & Nadia, India	July 1897	*Englishman* [Calcutta], 7 July 1897; *Madras Mail,* 8 July 1897

¯ree-limb, ⌐5-feet long	Meridian, Miss.	5 Sept. 1956	*Fate,* Jan. 1957, p. 9

4) AMBIGUOUS

"Resinous matter"	Gerace, Calabria	14 March 1813	*Blackwood's Mag.* 3-338; *Ann. Philos.* 11-466
	Neuhaus, Bohemia (after fireball)	17 Dec. 1824	*Rept. Brit. Assoc.* 1860-70
	Kourianof, Russia (combustible)	March 1832	*Ann. Register* 1832-447
	Genoa, Italy	17-19 Feb. 1841	Arago, *Oeuvres,* 12-469
	Wilna, Lithuania	4 Apr. 1846	*Comptes Rendues* 23-542
	France and Spain	30 Apr. & 1-2 May 1870	*Ibid.,* 56-972
	Kaba, Hungary (in a "meteorite")	15 Apr. 1887	*Rept. Brit. Assoc.* 1860-94
	Mighei, Russia	9 June 1889	*Scient. Amer.,* Supp. 29-11798
"Silky" substances	Naumberg, Germany	23 March 1665	*Ann. Phil.* n.s. 12-93; *Ann. de chimie* 2-31-264
	Pernambuco, Brazil	1 Nov. 1820	*Fate,* July 1957, p. 54
	Pernambuco, Brazil	Oct. 1821	*Ann. Register* 1821-681
Vesicular masses	Lobau, Germany	18 Jan. 1835	*Rept. Brit. Assoc.* 1860-85
Black capillary matter	Charleston, S. C.	15 Nov. 1857	*Am. J. Sci.* 2-31-459
Gluelike substance	Sart, Belgium	8 June 1901	*Ciel et Terre,* 22-198
Lavender substance	Blankenberge, Holland	2 Nov. 1819	*Ann. Phil.* 16-226
Pink substance	Lilleshall, Shropshire, England	28 Apr. 1884	*J. Roy. Met. Soc.* 11-7
	St. Louis, Mo.	29 May 1889	St. Louis *Globe-Democrat,* 30 May 1889
Purple-red substance	Llanelly, Wales	7 Sept. 1905	*Cambrian Observer* 1905-30
Yellow substance	Genoa, Italy	14 Feb. 1870	*J. Franklin Inst.* 90-11
	Pictou Harbour, Nova Scotia	June 1877	*Am. J. Sci.* 1-42-196
	Europe generally	27 Feb. 1903	*J. Roy. Met. Soc.* 30-56
	Invercargill, N.Z.	20 Oct. 1951	New Zealand *Echo,* same date
"Organic matter"	Giessen, Germany	1820	*Rept. Brit. Assoc.* 5-2, 1821

	London, England	1875	*Year Book of Facts* 1876-89; *Nature* 13-414
	Mediterranean region	1888?	*L'Astronomie* 1888-205
	England, Canary Islands, Ireland Etc., etc., *ad nauseam*	1903	*Nature* 68-54, 65, 109; *Rept. Roy. Chem. Soc.* 2 Apr. 1903
Yellow microcrystalline "wax"	Los Angeles, Calif.	24 Sept. 1954	Los Angeles *Daily News*, same date
"Manna"	Persia	1829	*Amer. Almanac* 1833-71
	Asia Minor	1841, 1846, May 1890	*Nature* 43-255; *La Nature* 36-82
	Kirkmanshah, Persia	13 Aug. 1913	London *Daily Mail*, 13 Aug. 1913
	Central Angola	March 1939	*Fate*, March 1956, p. 126, and May 1956, p. 48
15-foot square piece of thin, rubberlike, "silky," heavy, wet & stinking material	Lansdowne, Md.	26 Aug. 1957	Baltimore *Sun*, same date
"Glutinous drops"	Bath, England	22 Apr. 1871	London *Times*, 24 April 1871
Light, honey-coloured substance, appeared soft & jellylike or silky; covered area 900 miles long & ?? wide	At sea between Pitcairn Is. and Wellington, N.Z.	1960?	*FSR*, May-June 1960, p. 8
"Gelatinous matter"	Siena, Italy	May 1652	*Ann. Phil.* n.s. 12-94
"Viscid substances," etc.	Lethy Is., East Indies (jellylike mass, silvery & scaly, found after large fiery mass fell & exploded)	24 March 1718 [or 1728?]	Greg, p. 56; *Am. J. Sci.* 1-26-133

Lusatia, Italy	March 1796	*Ann. Phil.* n.s. 12-94; *Edin. Phil. J.* 1-234
Between Barsdorf & Freiburg, Germany (jellylike mass found where "shooting-star" landed)	21 Jan. 1803	Greg, p. 62
Skeninge, Sweden	16 May 1808	*Trans. Swed. Acad. Sci.* 1808-215
Heidelberg, Germany (fireball seen)	July 1811	Greg, p. 64; *Ann. Phil.* n.s. 12-94
Amherst, Mass.	13 Aug. 1819	Greg, p. 67; *Ann. Register,* 1821-687
Gotha, Germany (shooting-star fell, leaving jellylike mass)	6 Sept. 1835	Greg, p. 75; *Philos. Mag.* 4-8-463; *Rept. Brit. Assoc.* 1860-63 and 1855-94
Wilna, Lithuania	4 Apr. 1846	*Comptes Rendues* 23-542

REFERENCES

[1] Joint Air Reconnaissance Intelligence Centre (UK), Photographic Interpretation Report No. 66/1; "Report on a Film Taken by Tim Dinsdale, with an Introduction by David James," Loch Ness Phenomena Investigation Bureau Ltd., 1966.

[2] Oudemans, A. C., *The Great Sea Serpent,* Leiden: E. J. Brill, 1892.

[3] Ley, Willy, *The Lungfish and the Unicorn,* New York: Modern Age Books, 1941.

[4] Gould, Cmdr. Rupert T., *The Loch Ness Monster,* London: Geoffrey Bles, 1934.

5. Heuvelmans, Bernard, *In the Wake of the Sea Serpent,* New York: Hill & Wang, 1968.

6. Lee, Captain Stanley E., personal communication, 1 May 1969.

7. *Kodiak* [Alaska] *Mirror,* 30 April 1969.

8. *"POP" Technique: The Echo Sounder;* "Locating" Fish with Echo Sounder;" folders on Simrad Basdic, Skipper Sounder, Super-Sounder EH. All from Simonsen Radio A.S., Oslo, Norway.

9. Carlsen, Bjørn, personal communication, 2 July 1969.

10. One-page sheet entitled "Here's Proof Positive," Simonsen Radio A.S., Oslo, Norway.

11. Lee, Captain Stanley E., personal communication, 9 August 1969.

12. Joint Air Reconnaissance Intelligence Centre (UK), *op. cit.* (ref. 1).

13. Burton, Maurice, in "Letters," *New Scientist,* 23 January 1969, p. 191; and many articles in the *Illustrated London News,* e.g. 30 July 1960, 1 Oct. 1960, 26 November 1960, 27 May 1961, 24 February 1962.

14. Mackal, Dr. Roy P., " 'Sea Serpents' and the Loch Ness Monster," *Oceanology International,* Sept./Oct. 1967; Braithwaite, Hugh, and Tucker, Prof. D. Gordon, "Sonar Picks Up Stirrings in Loch Ness," *New Scientist,* 19 December 1968, p. 664.

15. Von Stein zu Lausnitz, Freiherr, quoted in Ley, Willy, *The Lungfish, the Dodo, and the Unicorn,* New York: Viking Press, 1948. James, C. E., letter to the editor, London *Daily Mail,* 26 December 1919. Hagenbeck, Carl, *Beasts and Men,* London, 1909.

16. *Orlando* [Florida] *Sentinel,* 18 October 1953 and 25 October 1953; UPI, 30 September 1963: "Moscow: Soviets Claim a Serpent, Too."

17. Sanderson, Ivan T., *More "Things,"* New York: Pyramid Books, 1969.

18. *Batracochoseps.*

19. AP (ex Tass News Agency), Moscow, 16 October 1966; *Piroda* [*Nature*], USSR Academy of Sciences, November 1966.

20. Spicer, F. T. G., letter to F. W. Holiday, 16 December 1936.

21. Lehner, Ernst and Johanna, *A Fantastic Bestiary,* New York: Tudor Publishing Co., 1969.

22. OE *wyrm* vs. Icelandic *ORMR.*

23. *Megascolides australis,* studied at Rothamstead Agricultural Station; Colombian specimens sent to Dr. Ralph Buchsbaum, University of Pittsburgh.

24. Ley, Willy, *The Lungfish and the Unicorn,* New York: Modern Age Books, 1941, p. 106. Heuvelmans, Bernard, *On the Track of Unknown Animals,* London: Rupert Hart-Davis, 1958, pp. 32–36.

25. Ley, Willy, *The Lungfish and the Unicorn,* New York: Modern Age Books, 1941.

26. Holiday, F. W., personal communication, undated; see also his *The Great Orm of Loch Ness,* New York: W. W. Norton, 1969.

27. Oudemans, A. C., *op. cit.* (ref. 2).

28. Sanderson, Ivan T., *Animal Treasure,* New York: Viking, 1937, p. 300.

29. Sanderson, Ivan T., *More "Things,"* New York: Pyramid Books, 1969, pp. 18–20.

30. Lane, Frank, quoted in Heuvelmans, Bernard, *On the Track of Unknown Animals,* New York: Hill & Wang, 1959, p. 494.

31. Bartels, Ernest, "The Aül," mss in files of the Society for the Investigation of the Unexplained, Columbia, N.J.

32. Bartels, Ernest, with Sanderson, Ivan T., "The One True Batman," *Fate,* July 1966.

33. Bartels, Ernest, in *Tong-Tong* [The Hague], 15 November 1962.

34. Romer, Alfred S., *Vertebrate Paleontology,* ed. 2, Chicago: University of Chicago Press, 1945, p. 228.

35. Sanderson, Ivan T., *Living Mammals of the World,* Hanover House-Doubleday, 1955, p. 60.

36. *Ibid.,* p. 59.

37. New York *Daily News,* 4 April 1961.

38. *Ibid.*

39. Colbert, Edwin H., "A Gliding Reptile from the Triassic of New Jersey," *American Museum Novitates,* No. 2246, 19 May 1966.

40. *Ibid.*

41. Cope, Edward Drinker, "Synopsis of the Extinct Batrachia, Reptilia and Aves of North America," *Trans. Am. Phil. Soc.* 1869–70, vol. 14, pp. i–viii & 1–252, pl. 1–14.

42. Robinson, Pamela Lamplugh, "Gliding Lizards from the Upper Keuper of Great Britain," *Proc. Geol. Soc. London,* No. 1601, pp. 137–146, 1962.

43. *Webster's Encyclopedic Dictionary,* Chicago: Columbia Educational Books, 1940.

44. Seyffert, Oskar, *Dictionary of Classical Antiquities,* New York: Meridian Books, 1956, p. 586.

45. *Webster's Encyclopedic Dictionary* (ref. 43).

46. White, John T., *A Complete Latin-English and English-Latin Dictionary for the Use of Junior Students,* London: Longmans, Green, and Co., n.d.

47. *The Concise Oxford Dictionary,* ed. 5, Oxford University Press, 1964.

48. Seyffert, Oskar, *op. cit.* (ref. 44).

49. Bakker, Robert T., *Discovery,* June 1968; *New York Times,* 2 June 1968; Priestly, Michael; "Pteranodon: First of the Hot-Blooded Flappers," *Science Digest,* Sept. 1970, p. 86.

50. Colbert, Edwin H., *op. cit.* (ref. 39).

51. National Geographic Society release, n.d.; also, an undated unidentified (?New York *Herald Tribune*) newspaper clipping states that a Frigate Bird was clocked, by a ship's chronometer, at 261 mph!

52. Lehner, Ernst and Johanna, *op. cit.* (ref. 21); Ley, Willy, *The Lungfish, the Dodo, and the Unicorn,* New York: Viking Press, 1948, chap. 4.

53. Seyffert, Oskar, *op. cit.* (ref. 44).

54. *Pursuit,* vol. 2, no. 1, p. 15 [journal of the Society for the Investigation of the

Unexplained]; Houseman, Mrs. Helen W., of the Merck Scientific Club, personal communication, 8 February 1962.

55. Undated, unidentified newspaper clipping.

56. AP Wirephoto, ex New York *Daily News,* 11 April 1969.

57. Owned by T. R. Reed, Kincardine, Ontario, Canada.

58. Palmer, L. S., *Man's Journey Through Time,* New York: Philosophical Library, 1959, pp. 66–67.

59. Romanoff, Alexis L. and Anastasia J., *The Avian Egg,* New York: J. Wiley, 1949.

60. Andrews, Roy Chapman, *Under a Lucky Star,* New York: Viking Press, 1943, pp. 210–234.

61. *The Travels of Marco Polo,* New York: Orion Press, 1958, p. 313.

62. Letters to the editor, *The Field,* undated clipping.

63. Butler, Harry, "Australia's Embarrassing Egg," *Science Digest,* March 1969.

64. *Pursuit,* vol. 2, no. 3, p. 47.

65. *Ibid.;* see also Chapter 8.

66. Butler, Harry, *op. cit.* (ref. 63).

67. Sanderson, Ivan T., *More "Things,"* New York: Pyramid Books, 1969, chapter 3.

68. See particularly: Glob, Peter Vilhelm, *The Bog People,* London: Faber & Faber, 1969; also Cohen, Daniel, "The Medieval Riddle of Bodies in the Bog," *Science Digest,* February 1969, p. 9.

69. Rudenko, S. I., *Frozen Tombs of Siberia,* Berkeley, Calif.: University of California Press, 1970; M. I. Artamonov, "Frozen Tombs of the Scythians," *Scientific American,* May 1965, p. 100.

70. Ley, Willy, *The Lungfish, the Dodo, and the Unicorn,* New York: Viking Press, 1948, chapter 13.

71. Ley, Willy, *Dragons in Amber,* New York: Viking Press, 1951, chapters 1 and 2.

72. Stach, Jan, *Summary Guide to the Natural History Museum of the Polish Academy of Science and Letters,* Cracou: Polish Academy of Sciences and Letters, 1948, pp. 17–24.

73. *Geological Survey of New Jersey: Cape May County,* 1857; Cunningham, John T., "Cape 'Miners' Hewed Sunken Logs" ["Tercentenary Tales"], undated clipping from unidentified New Jersey newspaper; private information from Mrs. Ray Dixon, Dennisville, N.J.

74. Ley, Willy, *Exotic Zoology,* New York: Viking Press, 1959, pp. 5–8.

75. Hapgood, Charles H., *The Path of the Pole,* Philadelphia: Chilton Books, 1970.

76. Dietz, Robert L., "Astroblemes," *Scientific American,* August 1961, p. 50.

77. Nininger, H. H., "A Résumé of Researches at the Arizona Meteorite Crater," *Scientific Monthly,* February 1951, pp. 75–86.

78. Dietz, Robert L., *op. cit.*

79. *Ibid.*

80. Struve, Otto, "The Great Meteor of 1947," *Scientific American,* June 1950.

81. Ley, Willy, "Meteorite Craters," *Astounding Science Fiction,* date unknown but

ca. September 1951; Dietz, Robert L., *op. cit.* (ref. 76).

[82.] Dietz, Robert L., *op. cit.* (ref. 76).

[83.] Lane, Frank W., *The Elements Rage,* Philadelphia: Chilton Books, 1965; Johnson, D. W., *Shore Processes and Development,* New York: John Wiley, 1919; Shepard, F. P., *Submarine Geology,* New York: Harper & Row, 1963; Carson, Rachel, *The Sea Around Us,* 1951.

[84.] However, see Hart, George, "The Mystery of Wild Bill Hickok's Remains," *Real West,* vol. XIII, no. 86, October 1970.

[85.] "Things Are Hard at the Petrifying Well," *Science Digest,* February 1970, p. 24.

[86.] Wyckoff, Ralph W. G., "Sur la composition de quelques protéines dinosauriennes," C. R. Acad. Sc. Paris, t. 269, pp. 1489–1491, 20 October 1969; "The Microstructure and Composition of Fossils," to appear in *Biological Mineralization,* ed. by I. Zipkin, John Wiley & Sons; "Trace Elements and Organic Constituents in Fossil Bones and Teeth," paper read at North American Paleontological convention, Chicago, 5 September 1969; and Miller, Mahlon F., and Wyckoff, Ralph W. G., "Proteins in Dinosaur Bones," *Proc. Nat. Acad. Sci.,* vol. 60, no. 1, pp. 176–178, May 1968.

[87.] Miller, Mahlon F., and Wyckoff, Ralph W. G., *op. cit.*

[88.] *The Concise Oxford Dictionary of Current English,* ed. 5, 1964.

[89.] Ashe, Thomas, *Travels in America . . . in 1806 . . .* London, 1808, p. 206.

[90.] "Account of Bituminization of Wood in the Human Era," in a letter to Prof. Silliman, from Prof. Wm. Carpenter, Jackson College, La. [Territory], Dec. 18, 1838, *Silliman's Am. J. Sci.,* vol. XXXVI (1839), pp. 118–124; see also letter dated 8 November 1838, *ibid.,* vol. XXV (1839), pp. 344–346.

[91.] *Electrical Engineering,* May 1952.

[92.] Bunning, Erwin, *Physiological Clock,* New York: Academic Press, 1964; Cloudsley-Thompson, J. L., *Rhythmic Activity in Animal Physiology and Behavior,* New York: Academic Press, 1961.

[93.] Silverberg, Robert, *Sunken History,* Philadelphia: Chilton Books, 1963, p. 18; AP report, 30 December 1958.

[94.] Drake, W. R., *Gods or Spacemen,* Amherst Press, 1964, pp. 17–18.

[95.] *Encyclopaedia Britannica,* 1948 edition, vol. 23, p. 959.

[96.] *Ibid.*

[97.] "Primitive Ox, Horse Created by Zoologists," by *Sunday Tribune* correspondent, undated clipping; Ahrens, Theodore G., "Breeding Back the Extinct Auerochs," *J. of Mammalogy,* August 1936, pp. 266–68.

[98.] Clark, Grahame, "Prehistoric Ancestors of the Weapons which brought England Victory at Crecy . . . ," *Illustrated London News,* 10 February 1962.

[99.] One gun which never quite made the grade was patented by Jones Wister on the 13th June 1916 (patent #1,187,218); it was designed to shoot around corners. See *Wildlife Review,* vol. V, no. 3, September 1969, p. 12.

[100.] Tingleaf, Mrs. Elfriede, personal communication, 5 March 1970.

[101.] Young, Arthur M., personal communication, 3 July 1969.

[102.] Young, Arthur M., personal communication, undated.

[103.] [Inventors Show Feature] "Fantastic Flying Sub," *Popular Mechanics,* September 1967, pp. 114–115.

[104.] *El Museo del Oro* Ediciones commemorativas de la fundacion del Banco de la Republica en su XXV aniversario, Bogota, Colombia: Banco de la Republica, 1948; Covarrubias, Michael, *The Eagle, the Jaguar, and the Serpent,* New York: Alfred A. Knopf, 1954, p. 126; Josephy, Alvin M. Jr. (Ed. in charge), *American Heritage Book of Indians,* 1961, p. 48.

[105.] Mason, J. Alden, *The Ancient Civilizations of Peru,* Baltimore: Penguin Books, 1957, pp. 79–84; Bushnell, G. H. S., *Peru,* London; Thames & Hudson, 1963.

[106.] Emmerich, André, "Master Goldsmiths of Sitio Conte," *Natural History,* October 1965, pp. 19–24.

[107.] Private communication.

[108.] Private communication.

[109.] Emmerich, André, *op. cit.*

[110.] *Ibid.,* p. 19.

[111.] *Ibid.,* p. 22.

[112.] *Ibid.*

[113.] *Encyclopaedia Britannica,* 1948 edition, vol. 17, pp. 344–345.

[114.] Cottrell, Leonard, *The Anvil of Civilization,* NAL-Mentor Books, 1957.

[115.] Allegro, John M., *The Sacred Mushroom and the Cross,* London: Hodder & Stoughton, 1970.

[116.] *Ibid.,* p. 2.

[117.] Cambel, Halet, and Braidwood, Robert J., "An Early Farming Village in Turkey," *Scientific American,* March 1970, p. 50.

[118.] *New York Times*—Chicago *Tribune* Service, date-lined Johannesburg, South Africa, 8 February 1970.

[119.] *Encyclopaedia Britannica,* 1948 edition, vol. 8, p. 182.

[120.] Leslie, Desmond, and Adamski, George, *Flying Saucers Have Landed,* 1953, pp. 90–94; Shahani, Ranjee, "Space Travel in Ancient India," J. Interplanetary Exploration Society, vol. 1, no. 3, Dec. 1961.

[121.] Mariette, A., *Denderah,* II.

[122.] Chassinat, E., *Le temple de Dendara,* II.

[123.] Troëng, Ivan, *Kulturer Före Istiden,* Uppsala, Sweden: Nybloms, 1964.

[124.] Allegro, John M., *op. cit.* (ref. 115).

[125.] Bielek, Alfred D., personal communication, 18 July 1969.

[126.] Finch, Dr. Bernard, "The Ark of the Israelites was an Electrical Machine," *Flying Saucer Review,* Vol. 11, No. 3, May-June, 1965, p. 18.

[127.] Neuman, Erich, *The Great Mother: An Analysis of the Archetype,* New York: Pantheon Books, 1963.

[128.] Quoted in Neuman, Erich, *op. cit.*

[129.] Neuman, Erich, *op. cit.*

[130.] Macdonald, Julie, *Almost Human: The Baboon: Wild and Tame—In Fact and in Legend,* Philadelphia: Chilton Books, 1965.

131. Gaddis, Vincent and Margaret, *The Strange World of Animals and Pets*, New York: Cowles, 1970, p. 35; Hix, Elsie, *Strange As It Seems*, New York: Doubleday, 1953.

132. Rose, Peter H., and Wittkower, Andrew B., "Tandem Van de Graaff Accelerators," *Scientific American*, August 1970, p. 24.

133. Black, Newton Henry, and Little, Elbert Payson, *Introductory Course in College Physics*, New York: Macmillan, 1956.

134. Keynes, R. D., "The Generation of Electricity by Fishes," *Endeavour*, October 1956, p. 215; *Science News Letter*, 5 May 1951.

135. Weigall, Arthur, *Laura Was My Camel*, New York: Frederick A. Stokes Co., 1933, pp. 107–108.

136. Heinlein, Robert A., "And He Built a Crooked House," in *6 x H*, New York: Pyramid Books, 1961 [originally published in 1940].

137. Buchel, W., "Warum hat der Raum drei Dimensionen?" *Am. J. Physics*, vol. 37, p. 1222.

138. *New Scientist*, 19 February 1970.

139. Sanderson, Ivan T., "Forteans of the World, Unite," *Fate*, September 1964.

140. Allegro, John M., *op. cit.* (ref. 115).

141. *Ibid.*, p .20.

142. UP, 20 August 1952.

143. AP, 20 May 1949.

144. AP, 2 August 1934.

145. Unidentified newspaper clipping dated 12 December 1960.

146. AP, 9 September 1954, date-lined Johannesburg, South Africa.

147. Reuters report, n.d.

148. *Fate*, July 1960, p. 43; private information.

149. Worker, Lois, "Rain God Bringum Heap Cloudburst," *National Insider*, 6 February 1966.

150. By arrangement with Lyle Stuart, Inc.

151. Goshe, Frederick J., "Could the Sioux Control Weather?," *Fate*, April 1957, pp. 59–60.

152. *Fate*, September 1959, pp. 20 & 22.

153. New York: Pyramid Books, 1969, pp. 170–173.

154. Hapgood, Charles H., *Maps of the Ancient Sea Kings*, Philadelphia: Chilton, 1966; and *The Path of the Pole*, Philadelphia: Chilton, 1970.

155. UPI, in Sacramento *Union*, 28 July 1969.

156. *Encyclopaedia Britannica*, 1948 edition, Vol. 6, p. 98.

157. Ostrander, Sheila, and Schroeder, Lynn, *Psychic Discoveries Behind the Iron Curtain*, Englewood Cliffs, N.J.: Prentice-Hall, 1970.

158. Burton, Maurice, "Phoenix Reborn," *Illustrated London News*, 6 July 1957, and "Phoenix Reborn: Unique Colour Photographs of 'Anting' with Fire," Supplement to *Illustrated London News*, p. iv, 1957. For general articles on anting, see Burton's articles in the *ILN* for 4 October 1952, 21 July 1956, 16 May 1958, 3 October 1959, 3 April 1965.

159. "Inositol, (vitamin B_{10}), Potassium, and Phosphoric Acid," *Applied Trophology,* vol. 1, no. 12, December 1957, pp. 1–4.

160. *Doubt: The Fortean Society Magazine,* June 1943, p. 5.

161. "Inositol . . ." (ref. 59), p. 3.

162. *Philosophical Magazine,* Vol. XVI (1803), pp. 92–93.

163. Allegro, John M., *op. cit.* (ref. 115).

164. Greg, R. P., "A Catalogue of Meteorites and Fireballs, from A.D. 2 to A.D. 1860", *Report of British Association,* 1860, pp. 48–107.

165. *Ibid.,* pp. 56, 57, 62, 63, 64, 67, etc.

166. *Ibid.,* pp. 52, 53.

167. *Ibid.,* p. 59.

168. *Science,* 22 April 1949; *Science News Letter,* 14 May 1949.

169. Balouny, Lisette, feature article for AP.

170. *Saucer News,* Spring 1970, vol. 17, no. 1, p. 27.

171. Lair, Pierre-Aimé, "On the Combustion of the Human Body, produced by the long and immoderate use of Spirituous Liquors," *Journal de Physique,* an. pluv. 8, reprinted in *The Emporium of Arts & Sciences,* vol. I (1812), pp. 161–178. (Lair's original source, hereafter given in brackets, was the German *Ephemerides,* Observation 77.)

172. *Ibid.* (German *Ephemerides*).

173. *Ibid.* (Jacobaeus, *Transactions of Copenhagen*).

174. *Ibid.* (Le Cat, memoir on spontaneous burning).

175. *Ibid.* (*Trans. Roy. Soc. London,* 1744).

176. *Ibid.* (Le Cat).

177. *Ibid.* (Memoir of Bianchini, *Annual Register,* 1763[?]).

178. *Ibid.* (Account by Mr. Wilmer, surgeon, *Annual Register,* p. 78, 1774); also *Phil. Trans.,* Vol. LXIV, 1774; and Moffitt, Jack, "Ladies in Combustion," Los Angeles *Herald-Express,* 14 March 1956.

179. *Ibid.* (*Jour. de medicine,* vol. 59, p. 440).

180. Moffitt, Jack, *op. cit.* (ref. 178).

181. Lair, Pierre-Aimé, *op. cit.* (ref. 171) (*Jour. de medicine,* vol. 59, p. 140).

182. Eckert, Allan W., "The Baffling Burning Death," *True,* May 1964, p. 112.

183. *Philosophical Magazine,* vol. XIV (1802–03), p. 96.

184. *Ibid.,* vol. XLI (1813), pp. 462–463.

185. Overton, John, *Transactions Med. Soc. Tennessee,* 1835.

186. Moffitt, Jack, *op. cit.* (ref. 178); Johnson, Walter, *A Familiar Introduction to the Principles of Physical Science,* Philadelphia, 1836.

187. *Annals of Scientific Discovery,* 1851, p. 358 (from Paris *Gazette des Tribunaux,* 25 February 1851).

188. Eckert, Allan W., *op. cit.* (ref. 182), p. 33.

189. *Ibid.,* p. 105.

190. Unidentified newspaper clipping.

191. Eckert, Allan W., *op. cit.,* p. 105.

192. *Ibid.*
193. *Doubt,* vol. II, no. 29, p. 26 (1942).
194. *Ibid.*
195. *Ibid.*
196. *Doubt,* June, 1943, p. 5 (ex Ellesworth, Maine, *American*).
197. *Ibid.*
198. *Ibid.,* #20 (1948), p. 302.
199. Eckert, Allan W., *op. cit.,* p. 106–107.
200. *Ibid.,* p. 112.
201. *Ibid.*
202. Moffitt, Jack, *op. cit.* (ref. 178).
203. Eckert, Allan W., *op. cit.,* p. 112 (ref. 182).
204. *Ibid.,* p. 33.
205. *Ibid.,* p. 112.
206. *Ibid.,* p. 112.
207. *Ibid.,* p. 104; and Lonergan, Tad, M.D., letters column, *True,* August 1964.
208. Springfield, Mass., *Union,* 24 November 1960.
209. Cincinnati *Enquirer,* 3 August 1962.
210. Long Island *Press,* 5 December 1963.
211. Toronto *Star,* 17 December 1969.

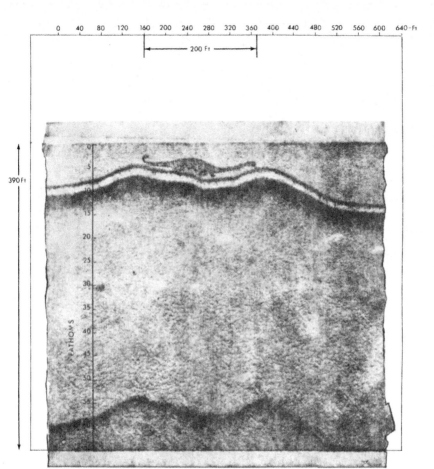

Plate I. From Simrad echo-sounder. Original strip. *This is built up from almost innumerable tiny dots, running vertically in lines, each due to a single "pulse" directed straight down, and by the automatic "pen."*

Plate II.   Mr. O'Connor's Beast. *Large animal caught by photo-flash immediately offshore (about 25 yards) by Mr. Peter O'Connor at 6:30 A.M. on the 27th May 1960.*

Plate III.   Skeleton of Icarosaurus *as found,* in lithium, *natural size.* (THE AMERICAN MUSEUM OF NATURAL HISTORY)

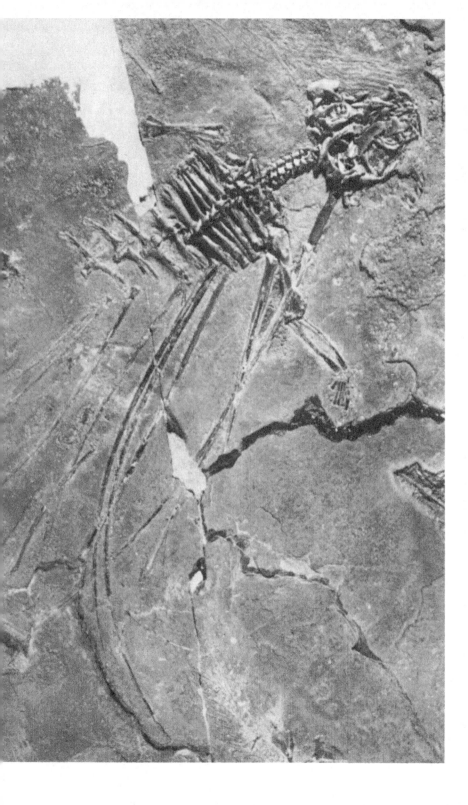

Plate IV. *Hen inspecting its best effort*: Salem, Oregon, 1969.
(WIDE WORLD PHOTOS)

Plate V. *Mynah (size of large starling) inspecting egg of an ostrich.* (IAN TYAS)

Plate VI. *Mr. Adolph Heuer, an honored member of our Society, holding the shell of an ostrich egg eaten as an omelette by our Board of Directors, in July 1968.*

Plate VII. A pickled Dane. *The famous Tolund Man, found in a peat bog in Jutland, Denmark, in 1950.*

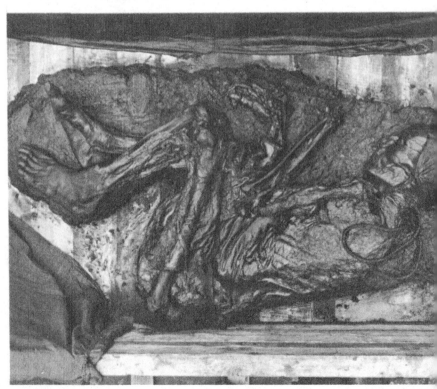

Plate VIII. *Southern New Jersey tree stumps broken by some unknown force.*

Plate IX. A cay lagoon, British Honduras. *A closed, freshwater lagoon on a small reef atoll. Trees probably killed due to flooding by salt water during a hurricane.* (ALMA SANDERSON)

Plate X. Giant robber crab (*Birgus*). These are hermit-crabs but do not use shells as protective covering. They climb cocoanut trees and feed on the nuts which they open with a trip-hammer action of the falces. (BRITISH MUSEUM)

Plate XI. *A "zoomorfic" gold artefact from the collection of the Government of Colombia, S. A.*

Plate XII. *Side view of the gold artefact.*

Plate XIII. *Front view of the object.*

Plate XIV. Another gold Colombian trinket. *A similar object owned by Chicago Natural History Museum. Also of Sinu workmanship and similar date.* Compare Flying Fish in Fig. 32.

Plate XV. (A) *Nine copies of model from the Colombian National Gold Collection, arranged in a flight pattern.* (B) *Official Swedish photograph of nine new "Sabre," delta-wing fighters, flying in a Xmas demonstration over Malmo, Sweden, on the 22nd December 1970.* (WIDE WORLD PHOTOS)

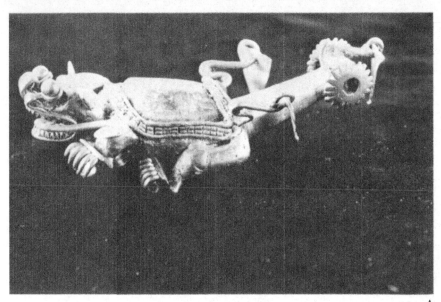

A

Plate XVI. (A) and (B) Panamanian gold and "emerald" pendant *unearthed from a grave at Coclé on the south coast of Panama. Said to represent a crocodile or a jaguar (!). The stone is now thought to be a nephrite jade* (See Fig. 33.) (UNIVERSITY MUSEUM, PHILADELPHIA)

Plate XVII. Panamanian pendant, front view. *Note the chisel-shaped "teeth," the central "grill" above, and the "skid-plate" below.* (UNIVERSITY MUSEUM, PHILADELPHIA)

Plate XVIII. Modern static generators: (A) *Van de Graaff*, (B) *Wimshurst*. (EDMUND SCIENTIFIC CO.)

A

B

Plate **XIX**. (A) *The author pointing to high book shelf* *could not be "fitted." (B) Michael R. Freedman sho* *"cat" that had previously fitted between roof bean* *SITU headquarters garage, but which would not fit* *where the next day.* (MARTIN DAIN)

Plate XX. Mrs. Reeser's room after fire. *Police and fire marshal inspecting the room in which Mrs. Reeser lost her life in a classic case of human spontaneous combustion.*

Plate **XXI.**   A list of some fafrotskies. *We started to list fafrotskies as found in scientific journals and elsewhere in our Society's library. By the time we were about a quarter of the way through, our librarian had this roll. It is single-line (per entry), double-spaced, and twenty-six feet long!*

Plate **XXII.**   *Dr. Malcolm J. Reider, of Reading, Pennsylvania, examining a hunk of "cigar-ice" that fell from the sky on Allbridge, New Jersey, on the 2nd September 1958.* (M. J. REIDER ASSOCI-ATES)

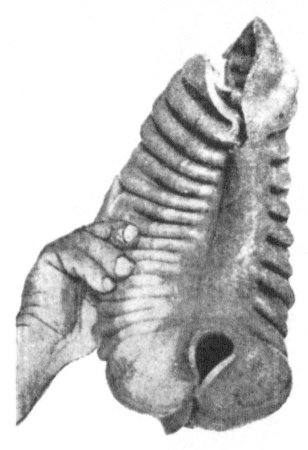

Plate XXIII. The alleged Venezuelan fafrotsky, *news-photo from a local paper.*

INDEX

Made in the USA
Monee, IL
28 February 2021